Central Station is a blog where the men and women
of the outback come together to share insights
into their lives. Find the blog at
www.centralstation.net.au and
www.facebook.com/centralstationlife

CENTRAL STATION

TRUE STORIES FROM AUSTRALIAN CATTLE STATIONS

CENTRAL STATION BLOG

EDITED BY JANE SALE & STEPHANIE COOMBES

ABC
Books

The ABC 'Wave' device is a trademark of the Australian Broadcasting Corporation and is used under licence by HarperCollins*Publishers* Australia.

First published in 2016
by HarperCollins*Publishers* Australia Pty Limited
ABN 36 009 913 517
harpercollins.com.au

HarperCollins*Publishers*
Level 13, 201 Elizabeth Street, Sydney, NSW 2000, Australia
Unit D1, 63 Apollo Drive, Rosedale, Auckland 0632, New Zealand
A 53, Sector 57, Noida, UP, India
1 London Bridge Street, London, SE1 9GF, United Kingdom
2 Bloor Street East, 20th floor, Toronto, Ontario M4W 1A8, Canada
195 Broadway, New York, NY 10007, USA

National Library of Australia Cataloguing-in-Publication data:

Central station : true stories from Australian cattle
stations / Central Station Blog, edited
by Jane Sale and Stephanie Coombes.
ISBN: 978 0 7333 3519 8 (paperback)
ISBN: 978 1 4607 0677 0 (ebook)
Subjects: Central Station Blog.
Blogs – Australia.
Country life – Australia, Central – Anecdotes
Ranches – Australia, Central – Anecdotes
Online social networks – Australia, Central – Anecdotes
Australia – Rural conditions – Anecdotes
Australia, Central – Social life and customs – Anecdotes
Other Creators/Contributors:
Sale, Jane, editor.
Coombes, Stephanie, editor.
307.720994

Cover design by Christa Moffitt, Christabella Designs
Front cover image: A cow gives James a run for his money on Birrindudu, NT, by Alexandra Rose
Back cover images (from left to right): by Pippa Bain, Gillian Sirl Photography, Jane Sale
Typeset in Bembo Std Regular by Kirby Jones
Printed and bound in Australia by Griffin Press
The papers used by HarperCollins in the manufacture of this book are a natural, recyclable product made from wood grown in sustainable plantation forests. The fibre source and manufacturing processes meet recognised international environmental standards, and carry certification.

Dedicated to the pioneering and resourceful people
of the North Australian cattle industry,
those who came before and who lead the way,
and to our families, near and far, who support us.

Contents

Foreword

Australians are passionate about their animals and the animals' welfare. And that includes those Australians who live on the land.

But most people know little of life outside the cities, particularly about life on the land in the northern beef industry. I started the Central Station website and blog to give the isolated, pioneering people up north a voice, and to spread the message that wherever we live, our values are the same: we all care for our families, our animals and the land.

Each week a different cattle station shares their world – the good, the bad and the dusty.

Here are some of their stories.

– Jane Sale

The regions covered in the book

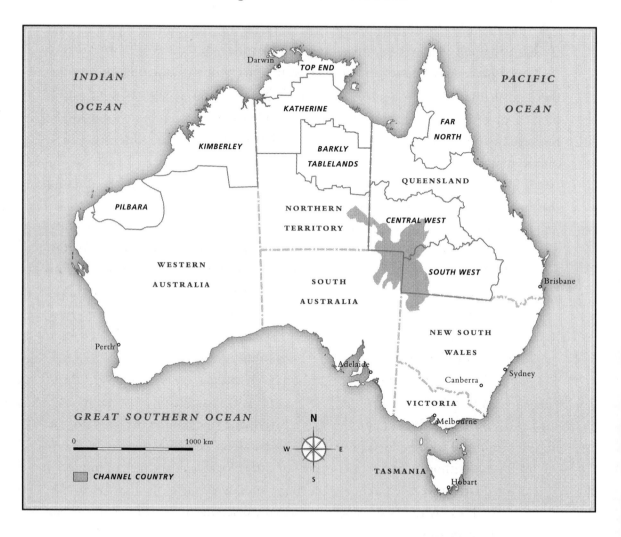

INDIAN OCEAN

PACIFIC OCEAN

Darwin

TOP END

KATHERINE

FAR NORTH

KIMBERLEY

BARKLY TABLELANDS

QUEENSLAND

PILBARA

NORTHERN TERRITORY

CENTRAL WEST

WESTERN AUSTRALIA

SOUTH WEST

SOUTH AUSTRALIA

Brisbane

NEW SOUTH WALES

Perth

Adelaide

Sydney

Canberra

VICTORIA

GREAT SOUTHERN OCEAN

Melbourne

0   1000 km

N

W   E

S

TASMANIA

CHANNEL COUNTRY

Hobart

Introduction

Jane Sale, Yougawalla Station

In 2001, I met my future farmer husband, Haydn, while on a girls' weekend on King Island. Haydn had just purchased his first property, a cropping business, with a partner, in Moulamein, New South Wales. I was far from living a rural life then, working for my father, Russell, in his business importing headwear for the promotional advertising industry, and having just bought an apartment in Melbourne's south-eastern suburbs.

Over the next two years, our long-distance relationship blossomed with fun and very enlightening farm stays at Haydn's property and some long weekends and holidays together. With a drought affecting Haydn's business, we decided to move together to the Northern Territory to run another cropping venture in Katherine.

Those who knew me well thought it was my destiny, as I had spent most of my childhood on my horse or on my best friend's farm. But many people questioned my commitment to the man and the lifestyle. Even Haydn was concerned about how I'd cope. I was a hard worker, but I knew nothing about life on the land – and horse riding wasn't particularly useful in agriculture anyway.

I was in for a huge adventure and an even steeper learning curve. Life up north was a wonderful eye-opener. I went with friends on cattle musters; swam in beautiful, freshwater billabongs; helped to load cattle trucks at an export yard; and in the evenings I'd come home to ride my horse along the Katherine River.

We went without a lot of luxuries on our little block, heat and lack of insulation in the old quarters we lived in being the main ones, which was not easy for me. But my love for this new lifestyle far outweighed any discomfort and helped prepare me for the next stage of our lives.

After four years in Katherine, we had the opportunity to buy and develop Yougawalla Station in the east Kimberley. By then we had an eighteen-month-old son, Angus, and I was pregnant with our daughter, Matilda (Tilly). We moved to a portable building on a sandy flat, chosen because it had drinkable water and was in the middle of the property's 340,000 hectares (840,000 acres). At the permanent homestead site, which was on a flat-top hill sixteen kilometres away from the portable building, we had to put in houses, sheds and water, and on the rest of the property we had to put in fencing and yards, and truck in cattle to add to the 800 head we started with. We had to work out how to access services such as electricity, television, telephone and the internet – things that are hard enough to line up in the city. Securing each of these services was its own victory and demanded much planning and perseverance. The responses I received on my Facebook posts from friends back in Melbourne when we finally got internet reminded me of how different my life now was.

We were four hours from the nearest town on a dirt road, so we had to bring in everything we needed, not least the food required to feed the fifteen or so staff needed to complete these tasks. Our lives were about logistics, logistics, logistics.

By early 2009, Tilly had officially joined the Yougawalla crew. We were finishing three houses, workers' quarters, a shed, and a hangar for our aeroplane. We were also installing solar electricity and still waiting on a permanent telephone line. We also managed to get weekly mail plane deliveries later that year.

Once we had developed the property and brought cattle to the new dams, daily life moved from building and planning to handling the cattle. This was a massive responsibility, but more enjoyable. Working with animals is a great learning experience. If you take the time to watch and listen, they tell you a lot about themselves – and a lot about yourself too. Handling people is harder! Living in a small community can test your social skills, self-management and self-control. We have been lucky with our staff. We all have tough times and can generally help each other through.

In 2011, we purchased the adjoining Bulka Station. About a month later, in June, the Live Export Ban happened. With two stations now to muster, sale cattle ready for market and nowhere to sell them and no more income for the year, this was the start of an incredibly stressful time.

A month later, I had a near-death accident in our yards.

We were loading some bulls into the race to truck off the property when one cleanskin bull smashed the draft gate off its hinges, right where I was standing. I had no way to escape and was badly mauled and thrown around by it. I was saved by our brave and capable staff, including one who put himself in harm's way to help me climb over a rail. Scalped and badly bleeding from my head, I was flown to hospital in Broome. Our world stood still for the second time.

My recovery was brief. Despite a smashed sternum and other aches and pains, after just four days in hospital and two weeks' recovery at home I had to get back to work. We couldn't afford to hire extra staff, but our cattle still had to be cared for and mustered.

In the months that followed, I found myself getting angry. I was angry with our situation, with the Australian government, and with our workload. Most of all, I was frustrated and angry with the lack of understanding from the general public, particularly those in urban areas. After the ban, many of us in the industry were shocked at the outrage towards our industry and pastoralists. I found myself arguing with unknown people on social media, trying to explain our industry's situation. The terrible footage and treatment of the animals in the media footage that led to the Live Export Ban (LEB) was unacceptable to everyone, none more than those of us who raise these cattle. But I could not understand why the majority of the Indonesian and Australian people involved in the industry, who do the right thing, had to suffer because of the actions of a few.

A year later I went to an Influential Women's forum in Broome, which focused on the divide between the urban and rural populations since, these days, most Australians have no family link to agriculture. There was a panel that explained food integrity and social media, and how well animal activist groups use it and the media to spread *their* message. Listening, I realised we had no one to blame but ourselves for the lack of information about our industry. We work hard, but because of our isolation, and being that we are stoic people and mostly private, the message about how our animals were raised and treated wasn't getting through. Talking about what we did would feel like boasting. The forum taught me that we needed to find common values with the urban population, and show that we care just as much for our families, animals and land.

Before the forum I thought that I wasn't qualified to talk about the industry because I hadn't grown up in it. But after these few days, I realised no one was more qualified to tell our story or talk about what our business does than me. I wanted to tell others about how we look after our animals and take great pride in the way they are treated, and how we invest money and time to ensure their proper treatment when they move off our property to transport and feedlots, then respectfully meet their end in Australia or overseas markets, such as Indonesia, where the majority go.

Armed with improved skills for handling controversial issues and a bit more knowledge of the minefield that is social media, a group of us who attended the forum decided that before we went into action, we would see for ourselves the treatment of our cattle in Indonesia. We organised a trip to see everything from export boats to eating an Australian beef rendang cooked in an Indonesian family home. For those of us who live in isolation in an environment that in the past has been male–dominated, travelling with a group of wonderful women was not only a learning experience, but a time to make new local and overseas friends. We came away with a huge respect for our beautiful cattle and each other. The Indonesians who care for the cattle have much less than us, and the cattle industry provides so much for their local communities. And waste is minimal as they use every part of the animal. It was an enlightening trip.

The idea for the Central Station blog began as we drove around Indonesia. As we are all busy women with families, staff and animals to care for, we knew we couldn't write regular individual blogs that engaged with the urban audience. So we came up with the idea of a station hosting each week. I volunteered to build the website with my fellow travellers, who promised to host when needed. The only problem was, I didn't know how to build a website.

Luckily, I had met Steph Coombes, the 2013 NAB Agribusiness Rising Champion Initiative winner, at the Broome forum. She's a Generation Y girl, passionate about the industry and IT savvy. She didn't start working with cattle until she was eighteen and in her second year of an agricultural science degree. Eight years later, she's worked on farms, stations, studs, feedlots, and in abattoirs, and been on three live export voyages to the Middle East, China and Malaysia. I couldn't pay her much, so it was passion that kept her going.

Steph built and managed the Central Station site in 2013 while living in Canada. She's since managed it from Canberra, Perth and cattle stations across northern Australia. Steph currently manages Central Station from the USA, where she moved in 2015 to do her Master of Science in Agricultural Education and Communication. Steph loves her job, and it shows in the way the site has grown; she has helped bring in sponsors, new hosts, develop competitions and promotions for our readers, and even redesigned our current website.

The support and involvement from our hosts and sponsors across northern Australia over the past three years has been beyond expectation. This book is the result of their honesty, their generosity and their talented writing. Stephanie and I warmly thank everyone who has contributed a blog or photo to this collection, the proceeds of which will go back into keeping the blog going and promoting our industry.

We might be isolated, but we are never alone.

Stories from the Pilbara region of Western Australia

Our Extreme Sea Change

Margareta Osborn, 'The Voice of the Bush', Glenforrie Station

Most people I know, when given the gift of four months' long-service leave, would pack a caravan and tour around Australia or at least head to the glorious beaches of sunny Queensland.

Not us. We chose to work a mustering season on a half-million-acre cattle station in the remote Pilbara region of WA.

Crazy? Perhaps.

Life-changing? Absolutely.

We run a beef property in the rolling foothills of Victoria's rugged high country. Both my husband and I work 'off-farm' to sustain our farming dreams and provide the rural life we want for our children. While my partner works a rolling shift in the energy industry, my own off-farm employment is a little more unusual. Working with one of the biggest publishing companies in the world, I write Australian women's fiction in the sub-genre popularly called 'rural lit' or 'chook lit', if you want to get a little more bogan. *Bella's Run* (a number 1 bestseller), *Hope's Road* (one of Better Reading's Top 100 Homegrown Reads), *Mountain Ash* and *Rose River* are some of my works and all required lots of research. Usually it's pretty good fun, but other times it's just plain hard work. I think our recent Pilbara experience seesawed on an hourly basis between the two.

Being a fifth-generation farmer who has lived and worked on the land all her life, it is never really possible for me to 'go on holiday' and my husband is much the same. So, when a good friend mentioned she needed a few months' help on her cattle station with mustering, bore running, truck driving, cooking and cattle work, hubby and I looked at each other and said, 'Why not?'

Cue deep breaths, some hurried organising and a lot of crossing of fingers. Thankfully, my husband's 'other' employers allowed him leave, our extended family were happy to look after our farm for a few months and everything fell into place surprisingly quickly. We pulled our two younger children – a boy aged twelve and a girl of ten – out of school for the term and travelled 8000 kilometres across Australia with a trailer loaded with two motorbikes, four swags and one kelpie, to experience a whole new way of life.

'The Wild West' is probably the closest I can come to describing our initial two weeks on the station. Within forty-eight hours of traversing the 100 kilometre-long driveway (three-and-a-half hours from the nearest settlement) we were heading even further east out into country that I suspect very few white men have seen before. The twelve-year-old got to drive his own bull wagon (mustering vehicle) more than 100 kilometres out to the satellite camp, which took a few hours. The ten-year-old, after spending hours in the cattle truck carting mickey bulls with her dad, scored a ride in the mustering helicopter. Within just a few days, the kids were already clocking up firsts.

They were long, hard days. We told time by the moon, waking when the generator cranked to life at 4.30 am. We went to sleep when that same motor shuddered to a stop, long after the moon had risen again. Meals were cooked over an open fire, beds – our swags – rolled out under a tarp.

'Pick a tree,' they said, 'that'll be home for a few days.'

We had two small bags of clothes, four water bottles, a roll of toilet paper and a bottle of hand disinfectant to make our personal little camp cosy. And a few days turned into a couple of weeks. It's amazing how quickly your tree becomes home sweet home.

I think we spent those first few weeks in a daze, wondering if we'd ever get the hang of things. Despite running our own property, we were southerners and thus needed to be taught the 'northern' ways of doing things. It was like running up Mount Kosciuszko. My friend Teesh told us that new chums like us usually sink or swim, reassuring us that we were swimming beautifully. I didn't dare tell her the other common saying running through our heads: 'fake it till you make it'.

The country we were working in hadn't been mustered for a number of years. The cattle were wild, the landscape untouched and beautiful. There were so many moments amongst the rough and tumble of those weeks out east that I'd loved to have caught on life's camera and rewound: my husband rolling his first bull, our daughter laughing uncontrollably as she disembarked from a four-wheel drive looking like a tree – leaves and sticks sprouting from her hair – after a wild ride through the scrub.

There were surreal moments too, such as droving cattle beside a debonair Parisian, a wwoofer on holiday who wanted to experience the 'real' Australian bush. He tried to resurrect my halting schoolgirl French with a new list of words each day. Or a lay preacher who gave our family a beautiful blessing while we waited for a replacement tyre for a truck. I guess any help counts even if it is totally left-of-field while you're waiting for spare parts.

Our return to the station after the first few weeks' baptism of fire was wrought with new challenges. A contract mustering crew took over the week-to-week mustering schedule, so it was now my husband and son's job to cart cattle from the temporary stock camps back to the station yards, where our daughter and I worked with an all-girl crew to process the thousands of cattle. The boys also did the windmill runs, travelling for hours to check and repair bores and solar pumps, water being the lifeblood of any Australian rural grazing property. Thankfully my husband is one of those incredibly talented blokes who can fix pretty much anything with whatever he has to hand. He can also ride a motorbike like a pro, a talent that came in handy for the long hours spent mustering with the contract crew.

Besides working in the homestead yards, drafting and processing cattle, my daughter and I ended up pretty much in charge of feeding everyone each day. While breakfast was a help-yourself affair, it was up to us (with input from the boss and from the other girls) to provide a savoury smoko, lunch, sweet baked treats for afternoon tea and a main meal at the end of the day. A reasonable cook, I still learnt so much, like 101 ways to cook with beef, revamp leftovers (garlic and fresh herbs became my new wonder ingredients) and making a perfect loaf of bread (it's the oil and bread improver, I tell you). Living so far from town with limited power and freezer space, most things had to be made from scratch. You also had to eat what was put in front of you or go hungry, a great lesson for the kids.

Despite the yard work and cooking commitments, mustering still featured, along with droving cattle to and from the homestead. Horses, motorbikes, bull wagons, trucks – you name it, we rode or drove it. Our daughter got so adept at cattle work she was as good as many of the grown-ups, and her work ethic astounded even us. Cattle work and cooking, looking after the chooks and the vegetable gardens, and poddying calves – that child did not stop.

And our son can now change buckets on a mill, pull a bore, or give you the rundown on the workings of a solar pump. His sense of direction and observation skills were honed to geographical weigh points, like a star picket sitting out of place, a change in gravel texture on the track, or a particular cleft in a rocky outcrop. On half a million acres with few signposts of note, these were the things that counted. You didn't want to get lost.

The other love of our family, our working dogs, were also well catered for. Teesh runs a team of kelpies as does another mutual friend, Courtney. Time spent with these two gorgeous and talented trainers gave our son and I – the keenest of the family – valuable skills. It also gave me my very first trained working dog, a beautiful five-year-old girl called Ange. Subsequently there were two dogs in our trailer on the way back (yes, thanks, hon, another dog cage please!).

When it came time to leave the station after three months, we were changed people.

We are even happier and more 'together' as a family unit. We are fitter and I know I, for one, am more willing to just take each day as it comes. To deal with whatever gets thrown at me without getting too stressed. If it can't be fixed today, there is always tomorrow.

We have made some beautiful friendships and our children have grown from the experience immeasurably. Our daughter is chock-full of confidence without being cocky. Our boy, as one relative said on our return, has matured into a man. And I have so much hands-on research and material for a new book – or perhaps books – that it's going to take a while to work out a plot. Authenticity is key when you write novels like mine and you can't get much more authentic than going out and doing it yourself.

But here's a bit of advice should you decide to uproot yourself in the spur of the moment and go mustering with your family in the Pilbara like we did.

Take comfortable boots, jeans and long-sleeved, lightweight cotton shirts.

Pack a good sleeping bag – it gets cold at night sleeping under the stars.

Buy a five-litre water bottle, fill it, drink from it often and guard it with your life.

Chapsticks – essential lipstick, even for boys.

If you're a girl, take LOTS of face moisturiser. Smoothing it on at the end of a long, hot day is heaven.

And chocolate. Take a box-full. You'll need it. Energy and comfort are a good mix, especially when you're swimming like hell.

The Ballad of Another Bloody Southerner

Jordan White, Glenflorrie Station

Two weeks into my time at Glenflorrie and the body clock was behaving itself, waking me in the dark a few minutes before the opening riff of The Beards' song 'You Should Consider Kissing a Bearded Man' burst through the pre-dawn quiet. Best alarm tone ever.

I'd begun to appreciate a great many luxuries that my last job in the cold of the central wheatbelt wouldn't allow, namely getting around in footy club shorts and a shearer's singlet, instead of rugged up in a jumper and beanie.

With brekky done and the day's plans discussed, we were dispersed to our duties, which ranged from yard work processing cattle from the muster a couple of days before, to determining the origins of leaky troughs, flat tyres on buggies, and a slack wire or two on the laneway fences. Pretty much all the general maintenance that happens, plus the extra that comes with mustering.

First things first – you may enter the homestead yard to the yipping of pups and ignore it in the pursuit of caffeine, but you can't walk back again without letting the dogs out for a gallop around the lawns.

It was funny to see just how distracted a handful of 'adults' could become in the presence of baby animals. You could watch the pups for hours, from the rough-and-tumble sibling fights, complete with tiny grunts and growls and wrestling moves that perhaps lacked the intended finesse and execution, to the cuddles from the smallest ones, who just wanted to curl up ever closer into your lap until they were half wrapped up in your shirt. You soon find yourself covered in puppies, hanging from shirt buttons, boot loops, fingers and, more painfully, beard hairs. You'd have to be a pretty sour soul to not laugh in the company of these characterful, clumsy weapons of mass distraction.

The pre-smoko task was to mark the calves that had come in with the muster. I was to keep the lead-up race to the crush full of calves whose brown noses could be seen poking out between the rails, trying to spot their mums in the next pen who, with bellies full of hay, were lying about in the warm morning sun, their sleek coats shining and stretched over well-conditioned bodies. The only cows that stirred were the ex-pets who would stand right next to thoroughfares and man gates, looking to nab the odd chin scratch from an idle hand.

The one-way communication from the calves was at times near deafening; I can only imagine how loud it would've been for one of the other calves with their huge ears that they hadn't quite grown into yet. For those unfamiliar with Brahman calves, they've got the ear-to-noggin ratio of a mouse that's successfully had banana leaves grafted to their skull.

The calves proved mostly easy to work, except one who was too busy inspecting a butterfly on the lower rails of the force pen to notice that all his mates had progressed into the race without him. He looked up, saw me, turned to his mates who were nowhere to be seen, panicked and decided there should be a gate somewhere in the left fence of the force pen. He came stopping and starting excitedly down the fence, head bobbing, searching for the invisible gate, snorting in frustration until he came to a dead end – me.

In the calf's mind, this tall predator with iridescent white legs, a brightly coloured body and barely a coat to speak of except on his face, was blocking his way out. Mustering all the adrenaline in his bovine body, he pinned back his banana-leaf ears and, using all the power in his fortnight-old spindly neck and legs, lunged forward, eyes tight shut as his tough, Elmer Fudd head connected with the legs of his enemy who cried out in … pain?

I tried not to laugh too hard lest I bruised the poor little chap's ego, as he stood at my feet spasmodically and unsurely rubbing his head furiously against my shin, exhaling with gusto and rage, falling well short of the knee-crushing cranial attack he envisaged. I picked him up with an arm under his brisket and one under his belly, but he would not surrender. Instead of struggling or kicking, he drove his now slobber-covered nose into my bare shoulder and began licking forcefully with his tongue, as rough as a rasp, his head flailing maniacally as he sought to make good this last-ditch effort at escape.

I struggled to walk and carry the calf, until the little terror came to accept his fate. He looked around incredulously with wide eyes, astonished that he'd been vanquished, despite his best brave efforts. Although when I placed him into the race, he bouncily trotted forward to his other mates, head held high and looking back over his shoulder as if to say, 'I've let you off lightly this time, human; next time I may not be so easy on you'.

Smoko at the yards is pleasant, though you do have to be on your guard not to lose pikelets, cakes and biscuits to the circling pack of canines. All were watched over during smoko by Stroppy the bull, who promptly presented himself to be counted on the first day of processing, then waited at the gate out of the yards, subtly hinting that he did not need to remain with the commoners till he was let out to roam. Since then he'd been hanging around the yards, waiting out the day in the shade near the crush, chewing his cud when someone stopped to scratch behind his ear or under his huge gullet. He was a pretty tolerant soul, letting us put a hat and sunglasses on his hump for a photo, and he wouldn't get too excited if you tried to jump on his back. He spent the next few weeks around the house and workshop, making a cosy home between a pallet of mineral lick and the fencing ute in the shed.

After smoko, the cows and calves were shifted to the laneway, ready to walk to a paddock where they were going to be living. We left the cows to wander up the lane for a couple of hours, allowing them to mother up and get a graze on, enjoying mouthfuls of sweet Buffel grass. We busied ourselves with other jobs, one of which was to handle the weaners, getting them used to being worked through the yards and then putting them out to feed. For this particular task the boss's dogs took the lead, having faithfully remained within a few metres of her quad bike all morning, aware that they were at the yards for a reason, and absolutely champing at the bit to do what they enjoy – playing the psychological game of mustering by eye.

This brilliant team of kelpies were a dream to watch even when things weren't going right. It was as graceful as a ballet at times, but more often resembled a fencing match where canine and bovine fleshed out their nerves, each trying to predict the other's next move, where a meandering beast intent on breaking the mob would be delivered a swift and measured riposte. I was completely enchanted by two of the dogs, Diddy and Chrissie, leading a group of weaners through the yard, both dogs lying flat in the churned-up earth, with ears and eyes the only visible breaks in the ground, looking up at the inquisitive cattle bearing down on them, holding to the last until told to 'get off'. Then the dogs would retreat several metres and flatten themselves motionless against the ground again, like two brown magic carpets, holding the lead animals and measuring the advance of the mob as a whole. They made the job of moving these unlearned youth through the yards so much neater and less stressful on the cattle, as they now had something to follow.

Mealtimes in the large homestead were very much a family affair, like most things here. I've been lucky to work for a number of genuine family units around the place in my time, and this was amongst the most loving. A reciprocal relationship between everyone existed, where you'd give freely and receive the sincerest thanks in return, all the while enjoying banter and laughs over the dining table, then over the dishes, which sometimes progressed into tea-towel whip fights.

I enjoyed having a family for a change; for a long time I'd been living on my own, away from my own blood. One thing was for sure – you could eat your fill and then some here, this was 'The Feedlot' and my return to reserves footy is still pending, as I try to shake what remains of the spare motorbike tyre I put on while I was at Glenflorrie. (That's one excuse anyway!)

After lunch we got behind the cows and calves we had left in the laneway, carefully keeping an eye out for those calves that had pegged out a little hollow or a patch of tall grass as their bed while their mums grazed. They'd wake with the bleary eyes of a napping teenager and blink a couple of times, before realising they were in the presence of a human, then they'd be up like a ninja and gallop towards the nearest cattle, bellowing for mum.

With a bike in the lead and three of us bringing up the tail, we made a lazy cloud of dust as the mob padded steadily, cows stopping every few strides to gobble hurried mouthfuls of Buffel, calves trying to suckle on the move, gaining little sustenance, but getting instead some pretty mean milk moustaches.

Once we got to the three-mile bore, one fence of the laneway stopped and our formation had to shift a little. I had the job of keeping the unfenced flank in order, which became slightly worrying when the mob began to stretch as the leaders started to pace out, now that they had some room to widen their front a bit, testing where they thought they could. After five kilometres of trotting along, some calves were slowing down, and one or two seemed convinced that their mothers had been left behind. After some shouting and wildly flailing arms, the calves didn't cause any more troubles.

We paused at the six-mile bore to water the cattle and have a quick cuppa, before heading to the water point. I love the rivers here – lined at the bottom with deep crunchy drifts of smooth stones of every colour and complexion. The amount of money people pay for rocks like these in landscaping beggars belief, and here I was standing in a million tonnes of it.

After crossing the river, I noticed one of the massive, white-barked gums that stood in the soft, silty loams of the riverbank had an interesting mark of the past. A spiralling hollow, almost big enough to stand in, half encircled the leviathan trunk, an injury that had grown with the tree and could have been a decades-old burnt branch or lightning strike scar. I love how the bush remembers the past. There's so much more to the landscape than just a few trees and rocks.

A pretty uneventful walk to the water point ensued, and once we were satisfied that the cattle would remain there, we headed home, the sun not far off going down. I hung back till the dust settled before following the others, stopping to look at a pair of wild-dog tracks that followed the road. They'd left their footprints in the tyre mark of a buggy that had come out earlier in the day to open gates ahead of our mob. The numbers of dogs around at the moment were a bit concerning, although we hadn't had many dog-bitten calves come through the yards.

Standing in the middle of a wide valley like this highlighted your isolation. Right at that very moment, I wasn't within earshot or line of sight of another human being. Anything could happen and the only animals that would notice would be crows, eagles and dingoes, for their own survival reasons.

With that thought, I got back on the track and took stock of what I'd learnt in a couple of short weeks. I'd had a lot of imagery in my head of what I thought the Pilbara would look like, but the reality was far wilder and more beautiful than I could have imagined. I couldn't remember what was on my mind before I left the wheatbelt and realised that my worries had left me. This holiday had been exactly what I needed. I'd connected with a completely different way of life, and become a new person. It made me want to be actively good and selfless just like this crew, family and country had been to me.

And I still had two weeks more to enjoy it!

The Barmy Army

Kristie de Pledge, Koordarrie Station

The alarm goes off. It is a nice, quiet sort of alarm; I detest the nerve-jangling, brain-rattling alarms that give you a heart attack. So at the early hour of 3.30 am, we rise out of bed to get the kids ready to head to Karratha, a four-hour drive away. Darcie has a doctor's appointment at 9.30 am for her all-over body rash that is itchy and not very nice.

Rory and I had made sandwiches, cut up fruit, packed those fantastic fruit jelly squeezies for the kids and filled water bottles the day before, so it was all ready and waiting for us to grab – or forget, as has sometimes happened!

We wake the kids, who are such troopers. Having done this so many times before, they get out of bed and start getting dressed into the 'town clothes' I'd laid out for them the night before. Once done, they each grab a water bottle and something small to carry to the car – and yes, we remember the chiller bag with the food in it this time.

It being so early, they go back to sleep fairly quickly. I grab a few Zs as well and leave Rory to battle on alone, poor fella. Halfway to Karratha, I remember something important … my hairy legs. Possibly hairy armpits as well – not so much of a worry, being hidden under my shirt, but perhaps I smell? No, quick check and they did get a burst with deodorant this morning.

Thankfully I also remembered to scrub the red dirt out of my heels the night before; it's unbelievable how much the red dirt stains and dries your feet, and cracks your heels. Often you don't realise how dirty you look, despite showering every day, till you go to town!

So now I am in full knowledge that I have cactus legs. Great. I know no one cares, but I like to get really clean sometimes – just sometimes! Occasionally it's nice to wear make-up too. Only started wearing it a few years ago; finally felt old enough.

At least my hair looks OK. There used to be a 'disciplinary' hairbrush in the car, but I have lost it unfortunately. A tap on the legs of screaming, squealing, fighting kids does wonders. Recently we bought them a DVD player – oh my, how the silence amazed us! Having resorted to wearing ear plugs and/or turning the music up to drown them out at times, the peace and quiet the DVD player created was quite incredible. Especially on those eight- to ten-hour trips, the silence was pure heaven.

Anyway, back to the trip. We get there with some time to spare, so we grab a bit of smoko for the hungry ratbags in the back. After that, it's appointment time – but when I speak to the receptionist, she tells me that Darcie is *not in the system*.

WHAT?!

We've just driven four hours to be told that either I stuffed up the times (it's happened once before) or the receptionist who took the booking stuffed it up. Please, please let it not be me, I prayed!

Luck is in – they can fit Darcie in, we are handed the paperwork and now we wait. I hide up the other end of the room, while the kids are down the other end with the toys. They are being very normal, playing and talking at the top of their lungs. Not everyone is amused. Rory reports on some downturned lips on other mothers sitting nearby. That is amusing.

Well, we finally get Darcie sorted, get our prescription and head back to the shops. It's starting to get tiring now! The kids are getting sick of hopping in and out of the car and the day is warming up. The bitumen and buildings make everything hotter, I think.

Time to wind up this trip and get home ...

* * *

Another day, another trip, this time to Carnarvon, about 400 kilometres away. Our youngest child was suffering from a hacking cough, which had been troubling her for some time. I had taken her to another doctor in another town a few weeks before, but after trying the treatment prescribed, there was still no improvement in my poor bub's cough. A cold that has appeared in the last week has not helped at all.

So we book the appointments – one with the doctor and one with the School of the Air for my oldest child, so she could do schoolwork with her teacher and attend the Air lesson on the other side for once.

With all the rainfall we've had, our main road is not accessible at the moment, which means trying to get out of the property via various station tracks. So with the car packed and ready to go, and the trailer attached, we set off from Koordarrie before dawn. I am very thankful Rory is driving as it's wet and muddy. We take it very slowly and make our way along the windmill tracks fairly easily at first. But as we get closer to the boundary gate, we had to stop some metres back from the gate to get a run-up through a potential bog hole, which very conveniently was all around the gate.

Quite stupidly, I'm wearing town clothes, which I don't want to get muddy. The smarter move would have been to put normal work clothes on and pack the town clothes away till we got through the station roads. Anyhow, we keep creeping along the roads, driving through what we call 'crab hole' country, which is sticky, muddy, soft ground; very, very rough when dry and very, very boggy when wet. It's rather hairy. The old four-wheel drive lives up to her reputation and we keep going – just!

Long story short … what normally takes forty minutes takes us nearly two hours.

Once we arrive at the next homestead, I make a call to the school to let them know of our delay and that student–teacher time might have to be tomorrow morning. The doctor's appointment is not till the afternoon, so we're going to make that.

Off we toodle down the highway. By the time we arrive it's lunchtime, so we have a bite to eat and I take the kids to the park for an hour or two while Pippa, my au pair, attends her own doctor's appointments. The park was great fun to begin with. We zoomed on the flying fox, climbed the nettings. Then my almost-four-year-old son informs me he needs to do a poo.

No worries, I take his hand and we head to the public toilets.

Uh oh – they are not open for use yet. Oh dear.

Stress levels start to rise and I very firmly tell him to not let his poo out just yet. I try to think of possible back-up plans. He looks at me sideways and heads for the sand around the playground: 'Mum, I'll do it on the sand.'

NO!

At home this would be acceptable – if there is no other option, they can just go do their business in the dirt somewhere. I would then bury it beyond the house in the surrounding bush. But it's not OK today!

I muster the other two and we all hold hands and head to the pub several hundred metres down the road. All the while I'm praising my son for his self control and reminding him we are not at home and it's not a good idea to go to the toilet on the pathway. We make it there, he does his business and it's a happy ending.

Youngest child attends her own doctor's appointment and is prescribed a different treatment. We complete our other town job of collecting items: motorbikes sent to town for fixing, oil, small mechanical parts, mail and more socks for little feet and trackies for fast-growing children. After settling into our room for the night, we treat ourselves to some Chinese takeaway for dinner. Yummy!

The next day, eldest daughter is dropped off at the school for her morning session with the teacher. I am so proud of her; it's kind of strange but nice to see her attending the same primary school I did.

We do more town jobs, which include buying some beautiful fresh produce from a plantation. Chocolate-covered strawberries and bananas complete our homeward-bound trip provisions and once again we hit the road.

A long day and everyone is tired, but my kids constantly amaze me with their acceptance – this is the way things are and we just get on with it. It's not easy for them to be strapped into their car seats for hours on end.

Yep, town trips are exhausting.

A Blessed Childhood on a Station

Kate Paull, Noreena Downs Station

'What did you get up to as a kid?' people sometimes ask.

Well, my siblings, Niffy, Chooky, Joe and I grew up on Noreena Downs Station, and we had a blast as kids. We were so lucky, we had the most divine time!

Those who haven't lived on a station are probably thinking, 'How could it have been divine?'

Well, I have compiled some memories of our fun play from our childhood to show you. You might think halfway through 'What strange children' (I think we were normal), but this is what happens when you're not well endowed in the money department and you have to create your own fun.

We all did Port Hedland School of the Air, which was lessons done at home and over the wireless. Once we finished our lessons for the day, usually before 11.30 am, we would conjure up our plan for the next few hours. You should have seen me on the first day of boarding school – come lunchtime I'd started heading back to the dorms only to have someone chase me to drag me back to school. Oh, the naivety of it! I was dumbstruck.

The Noreena Downs homestead is on a hill and we have a creek below us called … wait for it … House Creek! Quite often we would take off after we'd finished school and doing chores for Mum and go play down the creek. Niffy made a cubbyhouse there out of a busted spring bed in an old gumtree; it's still there today. We would walk up to seven kilometres easy one way just to go exploring up or down the creek, or get up in caves and happily stay out all day, being bush kids playing games, pretending to hunt and doing whatever else came into our imaginations.

There was a mulga thicket in the middle of the steer paddock, and we were pretty convinced there was a big, wild scrub bull living in it, so we used to follow the cattle pads (their tracks) through the thicket and see if we could get to the other side without getting done in by the mystery bull. Even the kangaroos' 'chi chi' noise used to scare the hell out of us. What imaginations, hey!

We also had to watch out for Mammasnoot the psycho cow who was sometimes in the steer paddock if Dad happened to have put her there. Mammasnoot was a cow we'd purchased from somewhere along with a few hundred other cows to increase breeding numbers.

'What was the deal with Mammasnoot?' you are probably wondering. Well, to say the cow was as mad as a cut snake would be an understatement. When she had a calf she was at her worst, but she was still nuts even without a calf. I mean, what sort of cow gets wound up and stroppy and turns her head around and cocks her rear leg and sucks milk from her own udder? A CRAZY COW!

One day, when I was still reasonably young, we were in a paddock yarding up. My dad's buggy broke down, so he commandeered Mum's buggy (which I was a passenger in) off her. One thing about my dad is he never liked to have passengers in the vehicle when he was working cattle that were playing up, so he told me and Mum to climb a tree. Up the old bloodwood tree we went – the biggest tree in the paddock – and we stood up on a branch. Well, almost all the cattle were in the yards except for one … Yeah, it was Mammasnoot, standing under the bloodwood tree, snorting up and down, ramming the trunk with her big horns, terrorising my mum and me. Then along came Dad with his newly acquired buggy! After a bit of a workout with this nutcase cow, and having her trying to climb into the buggy, she rounded off the whole show by sticking a horn through the grate mesh and straight into the buggy's radiator. GAME OVER.

So you can understand why four kids were petrified of one cow …

Quite often, once we'd finished school for the day, we would jump in the old ute with Mum and take the lunches out to the blokes while they were mustering. If they were camped out, then we'd also take dinner for that night and maybe the next. Mum would drive, Chooky would stretch out lengthways up on top of the seats (we used to call it 'Chooky's perch'), Nif and I would sit on the passenger seat and Joe would be on someone's lap – Mum's or Nif's or mine. Upon arrival us kids would make a nuisance of ourselves – nah, not really, we were just excited to be joining in, so we would all spread out on the tail of the mob and help bring the cattle along. We didn't like shoes, so we went barefoot most of the time. We got chased and charged at several times from protective mothers warning us away from their calves, and to this day I still get warned by cows that are daughters, granddaughters and great-granddaughters to those old crackers.

Being in the yards was one of my favourite things – we could get close to all those little calvies without getting a snort up our backside. So many cuties! We used to grab our dad's pannikin or a water bottle, fill it up with water and try to convince the calves at the back they had to suck our fingers to have a nice, cool drink of water, such welfare officers we were. Castrating bulls was also great fun – we'd grab the balls, cut the testicles out, run to the fire and throw the knackers on the coals for a bit of a bush delicacy. It's not as bad as you think, unless you have tried it and it's not your cup of tea.

Swinging off the back leg of a calf being branded was a bit of a challenge, especially as a kid, but no way were we gonna let that leg go if Dad was castrating. Dad was always paranoid about us kids being in the draft pens or yards as we were hard to see, so he used to get us to sit up on the rails together. But not for long, mate – we had worms in our bums, so off we would go investigating the cattle until we got told off again.

I remember our first poddy, Bobby, that Dad gave us. When she grew up we used to ride her around. Us kids loved poddies; we would set up makeshift pens under the old tank, yard the poddies up and draft them into god knows what. We would also try to ride around on a few of the bigger ones, but most of the poddies were not in for this idea.

We'd even have a go at mustering the cattle ourselves. We used to round up the cattle on foot at the house windmill and walk them out on the cattle pads like a proper mustering team – until we got caught by Dad one day. Boy, were we in mega trouble! What can I say, we were meant to be musterers!

Back then we used to have a massive old-style chook yard that housed all our cool fowls. (Now we have a new chook house, designed and made by Joe, which we've dubbed the 'Fort Knox Palace' – and it's dingo-proof too.) I remember a black chook called Emma that we were pretty convinced could talk; we'd take this poor chook everywhere around the homestead. Then there was Ducky the one-eyed pirate duck – he lost his eye to his mate Bam Bam the bantam in an argument. We also had two big roosters, Micky Malthouse and Johnny Worsfold (yep, my parents barracked for the West Coast Eagles). Johnny was a bit precious, a bit 'metrosexual' … he was just not quite a full-blown rooster. The chooks, ducks and the bloody horrible roosters – and there were guinea fowls too – thought spurring us kids on was fun.

We also used to have a bomb-proof, piebald horse called Cherry; god, that horse put up with some shit from us kids. We had two other horses that were best mates, Lady and Jane. Jane was an old racehorse and such a sweetheart – if we could climb up her legs we were right for a ride. Lady was a quarter horse and used to have an imaginary line; once she got to it, she would never cross it come hell or high water. When we got older, we had a few other horses and would go for longer rides. If it had rained we would take our horses down the creek and go swimming with them.

Us kids could make a game out of just about anything we could find. We used to set up our old shearers' cyclone beds on their side and pretend we were horses and try to jump them at a flat-out run – pretty easy to do but not so funny when you hit your shin; I still have a few of the scars today. Sometimes we'd set up obstacle courses with the beds and other things that were lying about. I remember when we started at boarding school and were in training for sports carnivals. Our sports teacher commented on our good hurdling skills. When asked where we learnt to hurdle at that level – well, let's just say I don't think the real story was well received.

And *never* leave a mattress, buggered or not, outside in full view with the Paull kids about – it was a trampoline or bouncy castle for us. We may have wrecked a few.

And if you ever get a flat tyre on your bicycle and you can't mend it, rip the tyre and tube off so you can ride on the rim — problem solved. This always happened to our bikes. To get the best speed up we used to start at the top of the hill near the house then go flat cookie and at the end take a sharp left-hand turn — or just hit the fence. Poor Mum!

We'd even have great fun at the rubbish tip. We'd spend countless hours fossicking for broken crockery, coins, steel and whatever else takes a kid's fancy, making things such as 'bang bang sticks' (guns), and dragging old items back to the homestead only to have Mum yell at us to 'take it back, there is enough junk lying around as it is' — to which we'd reply, 'It's not junk, it's useful and looks great, Mum!'

There was an area on the station called North Flat, which used to be an Aboriginal camp back in the day; here we'd find coins, matchboxes, marbles, bottles and old crockery, which would all be carted back to the old cook house and checked out (and once we were there we would of course play with the old Metters stove too). We also used to hide money and trinkets in jars, rags and boxes out on this flat, and dig them up after a time, sometimes after a day, sometimes after a few weeks, though I am pretty sure there is one we have never retrieved. Maybe our own future children will find it one day.

We did have a few stuffed toys too. I soon learnt never to let Niffy near my dolls as she'd massacre them! My Barbie called Rosie with bendable arms and legs, which was pretty unique I thought, was no longer once my darling sibling got hold of it — wires broken, leg missing, and all those glorious locks cut off … that was the last time I let Nif near my toys!

We used to love it when people visited. Woggles was a cattle-truck driver who used to come out and give Dad a hand mustering. Well, when he came it was extra special, because he used to bring us kids a mine satchel bag full of lollies. We were allowed one lolly a day — two if we were extra good. I will never forget that special little treat. Once some army soldiers even came out, tracking down the enemy, though us kids had them ultimately distracted from this task. They showed us their vehicles and other cool gear, and gave us ration packs, which we thought were the bee's knees.

We loved our adventures with Dad too. There was so much fun to be had when you were with him. He used to take us on windmill runs, or out mustering in the buggy, or we'd go off to fix things or just investigate. It was all pretty good fun and we loved helping him. If we saw some cattle while we were driving along and they took off (we had a few wild ladies back in the day), Dad would automatically be off the road and straight over to them to block them up, as this would teach the cattle to pull up and stop, which is pretty important in the education of cattle. To this day that action has paid off for us, as our cattle are easy to handle and block with a bike, buggy, helicopter, horse and probably even with your pet duck if you wanted to. On our drives with Dad we used to play 'I see the cattle first' – us kids would be on constant alert scanning for cattle, just so we could excitedly tell Dad we saw them first.

We were awful to the governesses Mum brought in to give her a hand, as she was a busy lady, my mother, schooling us, mustering, feeding four children and a stock camp, and doing the bookwork. What a champion. But we didn't like governesses so it was our thing to see how long it took to get rid of them with all our little pranks. I think only one governess handled us and that was Georgie from the UK. She had us stumped, but we liked her.

Well, this little story I have relayed to you sounds like I am stuck in my childhood. I suppose I am one very grateful person to have grown up on Noreena. I cherish what I used to get up to and all the time I spent with my siblings. I wouldn't trade anything for my childhood and my siblings and we're all very proud to be involved in station life and agriculture, which our childhoods have made us appreciate.

Noreena's Oldest Biddy

Kate Paull, Noreena Downs Station

G'day you chickees and blokes out there, I am Noreena's oldest known cow – twenty-eight in human years and 165 in cow years. I'm still waiting for the Queen to write to me. It's gotta come soon.

But let me tell you a thing or two, I feel as young as a rock chick. I can still move my hips around and do a quick dash when need be – last year while I was in the mob with my groupies I managed to sneak off in a little bit of wattle on a sand plain, a hundred metres from the homestead yards. I've since tried sneaking off a few times on the wing, but that bloody midget on the four-wheeler, who is my carer these days, keeps catching me out!

One day I heard her tell the riders on those two-wheel motorbikes on the walkie-talkie to keep an eye on me. 'I don't think so, juniors,' I thought, and I did a sneaky dash to the south, heading down to Fosters Bore where I used to live in the drought.

In my twenty-eight years I have seen two horrible droughts, plenty of dry years and a few good seasons where there were plenty of shrubs, grass and weeds to eat. Those years were great because I got to gorge my face. I have also seen so many new things on Noreena: water points, tanks, massive water pannikins, paddocks, and cow highways. The yard used to be an old wooden set, but now I get to waltz through the big steel design. Life's a luxury, baby, live it, trust me.

On Noreena there are six people who have been part of my life for a long time. When I was little and in the cattle yards for the first time, the kids would come into the pen where my calf friends and I were, and they'd pat us and hug us and try to get us to suck their fingers so they could give us water. This was my first interaction with humans. Today one of those kids is my carer.

My old carer was Tex, and he always had respect for us cattle no matter how much we tried to get away with things. I always remember him coming to the back yards when we were trying to put it over everyone and telling us we were old shits. Then he would point his finger to the gate and say, 'Away you go.' This was his serious talk, which meant 'go or be culled', so off we would trot through the gate. Funny old bugger. When Tex passed away last year it was a sad day for us cattle as he was our king, carer and educator.

One of those kids from way back now flies the chopper, so I will have to get sneakier with my hiding plans. The other pops in with much excitement every now and then and another is pretty fast on those two-wheel speedy scooters. They're too quick for me. I also see Tex's partner-in-crime about during mustering, doing the mill run so we have constant water. What a champ!

Each year when I decide to attend the muster, I get on the march to the yards with my groupies and, once passing the draft, I get into the race to get my yearly hair salon treatment. I try to stay really cool and in fashion with all the other girls and get the bangtail bob. It's so my style.

The Lead-up to a Muster

Aticia Grey, Glenforrie Station

There is always great excitement in the lead-up to the first muster of the season. Over the wet season, you've had time to conveniently forget the endless hours spent hauling portable yard panels from one mustering spot to the next, how uncomfortable your bike seat really is and, best of all, just what was wrong with your mustering buggy at the end of the last season. Nothing like a first muster to iron out all the kinks and get you back into the swing of things.

Though the muster itself is always the most anticipated part of the stock-handling process, there is a lot of preparation over the many days leading up to it to make it happen as smoothly as possible. Horses are brought in, exercised and shod; motorbikes are checked over and oil changed. Bull wagons are cleaned out of last year's stockpile of sticks, radios checked and, one by one, the vehicles are shuffled through the workshop and given a reasonably thorough going-over.

The stock truck is fired up again and the trailer deemed usable. The race draft and head bale are loaded up, ready to be taken out to the yard site with the water truck and portable panels. Gear, materials and tools are collected: hessian for the wings, wire and star pickets to hold the hessian up, and strainers; bolts and chains are more often than not forgotten, and avgas is needed for the chopper. We also make sure we have the stock-marking gear, vaccinations, hydraulic dehorners, veterinary supplies, pregnancy-testing gear and the electronic tag reader. The computer is prepared for all the individually tagged cattle to be processed, their wet/dry (i.e. pregnant or not) statuses recorded and ages noted so older cows can be 'retired'.

The camp caravan is given a once-over and restocked with dry supplies for the upcoming musters. Swags are made up and stretcher beds claimed. Radios charged, water bottles filled and then there is the kitchen …

A 'killer' animal is singled out a few weeks before the bulk of the crew arrive to restock the meat freezers. This year, we also lined up a few sheep from down south and got hold of some pork, which is always a welcome change from a fairly steady diet of beef. So begins the slow process of cooking up camp meals: stews, braised dishes, osso buco, spaghetti sauce, stroganoff, ribs and apricot chicken all make their way through the slow cooker or oven in readiness for being reheated out at the stock camp. Though it's hard to beat a feed of steak and spuds cooked in the coals, there is nothing like straggling in after a long day mustering or working in the yards and knowing that all that is between you and a decent feed is a little bit of reheating.

Cold meat in the form of corned beef and roasts is cooked and frozen, ready for numerous sandwiches. Cakes, slices and biscuits are cooked in triple batches for smokos, with extras once again frozen in preparation for long days. And let's not forget the much-anticipated desserts such as the Glenflorrie stock-camp cheesecakes … tough life out here, hey?

As a kid growing up on the station, there was nothing like listening for the beat of the helicopter blades as they flew in the night before the muster. As last-minute jobs were remembered, the station was abuzz with activity. Now as an adult, the excitement and anticipation are still there, but with them, a healthy appreciation for all the behind-the-scenes work that goes into mustering these properties and keeping them ticking over.

A Day in the Life of a Mustering Pilot

Weldon Percy, Fortescue Helicopters

Most of a mustering pilot's work is a long way from home – at least an hour's flying time – so we often go to jobs the night before to be there early the next morning. People often ask why we always start work so early. The main reason is the welfare of the cattle and the people we work with. An early start means we can let the cattle travel at their own pace as we are mustering them. The morning is also much cooler, and during then cattle often travel a given distance in half the time it would take in the heat of the day. If the day goes according to plan, the cattle will get to the yards earlier. If it doesn't and if the cattle don't muster well, starting early gives you the longest possible stretch of time to slow down and work through any problems you're having in any given area before continuing. Starting early is just all round the best way to do things.

When we arrive at the station or stock camp for the night, we normally refuel our helicopters and thoroughly check our machines over for the next day. It's usually easier to do this in the afternoon as it gives you a chance to look over your machine in the daylight, and if any problems are found where the chopper can't fly, it gives you time to get on the phone and organise another helicopter.

We probably spend 60–70 per cent of our year out in stock camps in mustering season. Most Pilbara stations are around one million acres and it's often too far from the homestead to the area that needs mustering, so it's much more practical to camp out.

After we have rolled out our swags and put our choppers to bed for the night, we get a chance to catch up with the mustering crew, have dinner and a couple of cold ones, and relax. This also gives us a good opportunity to talk with the head stockman or manager about the next day's work. Then it's in bed early, around 8.30 or 9 pm, to get a good rest before the next day.

We're up in the dark, around 4.30 in the morning. We roll up our swags and briefly do final checks over the helicopter. Then it's breakfast with the mustering crew, and we are ready to go right at daylight.

The first factor in planning how to do a day's work is working out how we'll muster. Depending on the customer, station crew and terrain, we might coacher muster the cattle or just muster them another way.

The second factor is water, although the two go hand in hand. The plan depends on whether the cattle are living from man-made water such as bores, windmills or solar pumps, or if they are living from waterholes and rivers. To give an example of what I mean, if we have a big, mostly flat area with creeks but no major rivers, the cattle will usually live off man-made waters. Cattle by instinct and by being handled properly generally will move towards water when they hear the noise of an aircraft, so in this type of terrain we gather cattle at waters and the ground crew will walk along beside the mob as 'coachers'.

In terrain where we have big rivers, tall mountains and ridges, and generally less man-made waters, it becomes harder to walk cattle along as 'coachers' and we often use rivers and creeks to bring cattle together and only work them as a mob just before yarding up.

The riverbanks and beds in this type of terrain are generally the easiest places for cattle to walk as they aren't as rocky, so the cattle normally string out and walk along with the ground crew following behind the mob, or 'on the tail', as we say, to keep them walking. The helicopters will then bring more cattle from other creeks and areas.

In either type of terrain, the mob we are mustering gets bigger and bigger as the day goes by. Although a lot of Pilbara soil is richer in nutrients than further south, we do get less rain, which generally means we run fewer cattle in a given area. With the ever increasing need for graziers to be cost efficient, this often means we have two or three helicopters mustering at once, rather than one. This probably sounds more expensive – and it is – but it allows us to cover more area, so more cattle are mustered in a day, which makes for a shorter mustering season with lower labour costs for the grazier.

Depending on how our day starts out and which way we are mustering, our day is pretty predictable to a point. When we are coacher mustering we often get to stop at the bore to have a break, have lunch and boil the billy, while a few of the ground crew are holding the mob. Other times we keep flying all day except for fuel stops every three hours or so, and the occasional brief stop for a sandwich or toilet break.

The first part of the day is usually the most enjoyable from a flying perspective as the air is cool and not so turbulent. The middle of the day is the most tiring as it can be very warm, and thermals and wind often make for a rough ride. The end of the day or yarding up is the most rewarding, to see your day's work accomplished and a mob of cattle in the yard.

Once we get to the yards and the crew have the gates closed, we generally land and briefly talk to the head stockman or manager before fuelling up and heading off to the next station for the next day, where we start all over again.

So You Want to Be a Mustering Pilot?

Weldon Percy, Fortescue Helicopters

As mustering pilots, we often get asked a lot of questions about how to get a job, so I've written a few of them down with some answers that might help anyone out there who wants to become a mustering pilot and learn more about the industry.

My first piece of advice would be to take becoming a mustering pilot seriously, and be committed to making a career out of it – your future employers and customers will respect you for that.

Some people seem to want to be a mustering pilot because they saw one once and thought they 'looked cool'! The truth is, about 95 per cent of the time you're mustering, no one in the world can see you unless you're close to the crew and the mob. So my second piece of advice would be to make sure you want to be a mustering pilot for the right reasons – it's a big commitment and a huge cost to bear if you decide later that it's not for you.

And finally, be patient and stubborn. It takes time – years – to learn the trade and it's a fickle industry to get a start in, but if you're patient and stubborn eventually you will get there and it is worth the wait.

Where should I begin if I want to be a mustering pilot?
I believe a good mustering pilot must first be a good cattleman or woman. Having worked with people with different levels of cattle and flying knowledge throughout my career, I think it's much easier to teach a cattleman or woman to fly than it is to teach a pilot with no cattle experience to work cattle.

That's not to say that someone must be born and raised on the land such as myself to have cattle knowledge. For someone coming from the city, I would suggest working for four or five full seasons as a ringer to have enough knowledge to be able to learn to muster from the air. I'd also suggest spending one or two of those years working in a contract mustering team, as this is the closest thing you can get to being a mustering pilot, minus the helicopter. As contractors move between stations you would get to see how different people do things and learn to accept that and work with the team you're with on the day, which is vital knowledge when it comes to being a mustering pilot. Once you have a good understanding of cattle and the lifestyle of contract mustering then you can look at learning to fly.

How hard is it to fly a helicopter?
Helicopters are complex bits of machinery but you definitely don't have to be a rocket scientist to fly one. If it wasn't so expensive, I think a lot of people would have their licence.

How much does it cost to get a helicopter licence?
This is a little bit like asking how long a piece of string is! By far the most expensive component is flying hours. There is a minimum requirement to complete 105 hours of training in Australia; some of this is flying solo and some of it dual (i.e. with an instructor). Due to recent law changes some schools now have to complete 150 hours of training with students, but I won't go into that here.

The cost to hire an R22 (the most common training helicopter) with an instructor and fuel for one hour is approximately $500 (probably more in some locations). So straightaway you have a minimum of 105 hours at $500, which equals $52,500. Other components of learning to fly are the theory exams and testing, and the cost of these will vary greatly depending on whether you study at home or at a 'theory school', and your associated accommodation and/or travelling needs. So really, aside from the flying, the cost varies greatly depending on your personal circumstances.

How hard are the exams?
There are seven exams you need to pass to gain a commercial pilot's licence (which is what is required to become a mustering pilot). I've often heard experienced

instructors say that they are no harder than high-school exams, and I must say I found that to be my experience too.

What extra licences do you need to be a mustering pilot?
You need to hold a 'mustering endorsement' to be able to work as a mustering pilot. To get this you legally need a minimum of ten hours' training with an approved mustering training pilot, of which there are only a few across Australia. However, in most cases it will most likely take longer than the prescribed ten hours. A few pilots I know have had to pay for this endorsement, but most generally get a job as a junior pilot with a company first, then this company or station will assist them to become qualified.

How hard is it to get a job as a mustering pilot?
There aren't a huge number of positions in the mustering industry; to my knowledge there aren't any publicly available figures on how many helicopter mustering pilots there are operating in Australia, but I'd reckon it would be well below 1000. Like all industries, though, there are always people moving around and positions do come up every year. Generally, everyone works out what they're doing and how many pilots they need for the upcoming year during the wet season, and if pilots move on or are promoted it's usually also during the wet, so generally this is the best time of the year to find a position. Throughout the mustering season there may be pilots whose services are discontinued or who aren't able to fly for medical reasons and jobs do come up then too, but usually not many. If you know the right people, have the right experience and are prepared to work hard most people get their first job somewhere relatively simply.

What do you look for when employing a pilot?
Depending on our requirements at the time we may need a pilot with a minimum number of hours' experience. That aside, in general the first things we look for are professionalism and personality. To our customers our services are necessary but very expensive. They want to know that they are getting the maximum value for

every dollar they spend with us and to do that we need to have the very best people working for us. We believe if someone looks after themselves, they will look after our equipment and, in turn, our customers. So if someone turns up to work and their shirt is untucked, their vehicle's a mess, they're unshaven and smelly, we take that as a sign that they will also present like that to our customers and not look after our helicopters.

If someone presents as clean, tidy and professional, they are off to a great start. A professional attitude and outlook is just as important to us as relevant technical skills.

What do you dislike about being a mustering pilot?
Long periods away from home make it difficult to have a normal personal life, but I think that's something you need to accept before you begin your career. The nature of the job dictates that you might be planning to go away for two days and not come home for two weeks or you might be planning to go away for three weeks and be back in four days – and at times you might only be home for one night! It does put a strain on personal relationships, and makes it hard to organise things. But the nature of the industry won't change to suit you, so you have to learn to change to suit it. The positive side is that through the summer or wet season months there's quite a lot of time to be home with family or away on holiday without it affecting your work.

What's the best thing about being a mustering pilot?
Being a mustering pilot allows me to combine both my passion for cattle and flying. For me, there's nothing I would rather do!

Lights, Camera, Action!

Stephanie Murray, Yarrie Station

Four hundred kilos of bush cow stares me down. I swallow a grating, dust-laden breath. My hands shake, my eyes dilate with adrenaline. I step forward with a confidence I do not feel, and will the mob of cattle to move into the race. Bush cow turns, glassy-eyed – she is not going to go quietly. I hesitate, a life of city living betraying me in that moment, and bush cow sees the ruse. She bursts forth – I am but a speed bump to her if I do not make the safety of the rails in time ...

* * *

It's several days before we muster and no one is around to get the horses in. Being from a country that prefers automatics and the right side of the road (and the car) I have never mastered certain nuances of clutch usage. I am mostly banned from practising my clutch-releasing skills with the station vehicles in an effort to keep our mechanic Wizard's hair from going grey (and gear and transmission boxes in full working order). My only option is one of Yarrie Station's many two-wheelers.

To most people, a dirt bike is a welcome sight, a bit of fun, but it fills my soul with dread. 'Mechanically disinclined' is a kind way to describe me. I pace nervously, eyeing the ripped seat and the worn tyres warily. I wish I could lunge the bike first, make sure it will not buck beneath me when I mount, but it doesn't work like that ... I resolutely shove on a helmet, go through all the necessary safety checks, start it up and climb on. After several stalls in first gear, I trundle around and make the harrowing trip up the gravel drive to the spinifex-laden horse pasture. My confidence builds as I successfully navigate the varied terrain and soon I find myself rocking along in third.

'This might actually be fun,' I think, as the horses gallop around me. Distracted by my four-legged charges I narrowly miss a large rock and begin to swerve badly. My balance is lost; I can feel the bike going sideways …

* * *

I'm happily mounted on a horse. This is where I belong. I'm carefully keeping the riders to my left and right in intermittent view. The sun is shining and there is a light breeze, a beautiful day to muster. We trot along with the pleasant (and reassuring) drone of the chopper behind us. Cattle begin slowing ahead of us and we slow up as we receive instructions from above.

Suddenly a mickey bull breaks from the herd ahead and I desperately try to get in a position that will stop him or at least hold him until I can hail Annabelle in her trusty R22 helicopter. We circle round. The bull holds us in his sights; he's no longer interested in the 'flight' response. I dimly hear someone screaming into my radio to run …

* * *

They say living on the edge makes you feel alive. They say what doesn't kill you makes you stronger. They say glory isn't found in the rise, but in the ability we have to rise again after each fall. They say you never learn if you never fail. I can personally attest to the truth in all these sayings. Yarrie makes me feel alive. Many days I feel weak here, but at the end of each day I feel myself becoming stronger. I fall a lot (sometimes just trying to find a dunny in the dark at stock camp …) but I'm finding it easier to get back up.

I also fail as often as I succeed, but I've never learnt so much. I made it to the rails and out of the bush cow's way, thanks to hours of patient lessons from most of the team I work with. I righted my bike at the last second, thanks to the careful tutoring of Alic and the daily moral support of the rest of the station crew that I received in my long, drawn-out training process. My horse and I scooted out of the way of that mickey bull just in time, thanks to the knowledgeable and protective watch of Ann, who is a true Pilbara legend and who has guided me through my outback orientation process. While Yarrie provides the perfect set in which I can live out my desired adventures and dramas, I have found it is truly the cast and crew who have enabled me to make it safely and successfully to the end of this season, so that this show can go on.

That Day

Caitlin U'Ren, Warrawagine Station

It's the wet season, the days are hot and thunderstorms are rolling in nearly every afternoon with the smell of rain on the wind. The mustering season is over. Most of the crew have gone home for a well-deserved break with Christmas just around the corner. The homestead is eerily quiet, something I'm not used to — no choppers flying in and out, no buggies and bikes leaving at early hours, no road trains bellowing down the driveway. Just the sound of the generator distantly chugging away.

I'm up nice and early to beat the heat, smoko and thermos in hand, out and about on my routine bore run for the morning. I head back home at midday for some lunch and a break during the heat of the day.

It's now 3 pm. The thermostat has hit forty-three degrees, but the day is starting to cool down. The boys are working night shift, and they're just starting to stir, preparing for the night ahead, building a new shed for the road trains. My arvo has begun too, being the cook at night — I'm in the kitchen preparing dinner for eight, listening to the general chit-chat between the crew on the two-way.

It's now 6 pm. Dinner is nearly ready and I'm in the process of washing up when Davo comes bursting through the door: 'Quick, call the RFDS, Dazza's come off his quad bike!'

'Shit!' is the first thing that comes to mind.

Second, 'Holy crap, what did I learn at that first-aid course I did three years ago!?'

I follow Davo outside, thinking, 'OK, maybe Davo is just overreacting and it's not really that bad …'

But when I get to the ute I see Daz is in a huge amount of pain and struggling to breathe. The first-aid training kicks in: OK, so he's breathing — not well, but he is conscious and breathing, that's a good start.

I get the Royal Flying Doctor Service (RFDS) on the phone, explain what has happened and that the patient is conscious but struggling to breathe and in a lot of pain.

'OK, on a scale of one to ten, what would the patient's level of pain be at?' they ask.

'He's in too much pain to talk,' I say.

'OK, so fairly high then. Is someone willing to give a morphine injection?'

'Yep, Beno will do it.' Beno's the head stockman (and my boyfriend).

We grab Beno, then race back into the cookhouse to the RFDS chest and dig out the morphine and needle.

'Right, Daz, I'm going to give you some morphine. This might hurt a bit,' Beno says.

For the next hour or so, we continuously monitor Daz for any change in his condition – so far so good, the morphine is starting to work, and his breathing is getting slightly better. We're keeping in contact with the RFDS in case of any sudden change; they tell us a plane is ready and leaving Meekatharra on its way out to us. But when it arrives, it's too dark for the plane to land.

So we get in the car for the 140-kilometre drive into Marble Bar. Thankfully Dazza's condition isn't dire. The first hundred kilometres is a rough dirt road, and at every bump Daz lets out a grunt of pain. We're trying to get there as quickly as possible, but we can't go fast because it's too painful for him.

The morphine has now fully kicked in and the conversation starts rolling.

'OK, Daz, talk to me, how you feeling?'

'Yeah, pretty good, how's the chickens going?'

'Chickens? What the hell you on about?'

'You know the chickens and the eggs.'

Yep, that morphine is good stuff.

We finally make it to the bitumen – forty kilometres to go. The morphine is starting to wear off and Dazza's condition is worsening. He's having trouble breathing and he's started going in and out of consciousness. The pedal goes down, and finally we're only five minutes from town and the medical attention Daz needs

– five long minutes later we arrive at the nursing post (there's no hospital in Marble Bar). The lovely nurse meets us at the door, makes a quick assessment and Daz is on a bed and wheeled inside.

Davo and I are fairly stressed out by this stage as the nurse calmly does his checks, listening and poking and asking questions. He's also on and off the phone to the RFDS, giving them regular updates of Dazza's condition.

He prepares Daz for the RFDS flight and gets the call – the plane is ten minutes away. We help put Daz in the back of the troop-carrier ambulance and drive out to the airstrip. The plane circles once and then comes in to land. We meet the RFDS doctors and nurses, and they discuss Dazza's condition and exchange notes with the nurse. Then Dazza is lifted into the plane and, within twenty minutes, he's gone.

By this stage it's nearly midnight and Davo and I have a two-hour drive home – plenty of time to think about how Dazza is doing.

The next day, we get a phone call from the hospital telling us of Dazza's condition: broken ribs, bruised lungs and a collapsed diaphragm. He will be staying in hospital for a few more days.

Dazza was very lucky that day – if he had come off the quad any harder, he may not be here today to tell the story. After many painful coughs and sneezes, he is back to his normal antics and avoiding quad bikes like a herd bull on a mustering day.

Home Sweet Swag

Leanna Gubbels, Yarrie Station

Little did I know what was in store for me when I stepped off the plane in Port Hedland that day in 2014. I had just flown over twenty-four hours halfway around the world from my little town of Laurel, Nebraska, to spend my summer – the Pilbara's winter – at a cattle station near a town I had never heard of with people I had never met.

But first I had to find my ride out there. Lucky for me, the station owner, Panze Coppin, could easily pick the lost blonde American through the crowd at the airport. Since most of the car ride back to the station was dark, I didn't get much of a view other than the back of my eyelids, so I was still pretty clueless about what I had just gotten myself into when we eventually arrived.

In 2012, a friend had done an internship through his uni that landed him at Yarrie Station. Having always wanted to go to Australia myself, I asked him about it, and got in contact with the station manager, Annabelle Coppin. Being a pre-veterinary student at my uni, the same internship that my friend had gone through was not available, but if I could find a way out there, Annabelle said, I was welcome at the station. Unfortunately, I was unable to make the trip work for the summer of 2013, but her offer still stood for the next year. I started making plans to come out – including doing double shifts at the nursing home over Christmas break (what joy).

Six months later, I was unpacking my gear (only half of which I used since I quickly found out my dressier clothes would rarely see daylight with all the work to be done) at the Yarrie homestead. Getting up early for work was something I could deal with, but a lot of things I was told to do resulted in a deer-in-the-headlights look since we had different names for things. At the yards, 'taps' were our 'hydrants', and you turn them on differently, so I even struggled with turning on a hose at first.

I am very thankful for how patient Annabelle and everyone else were with me, even though I'm sure they were thinking I had never gotten my hands dirty or seen cattle before, with some of the misunderstandings this 'language barrier' brought about. I had grown up on a farm with cattle (though not nearly as many), goats, pigs, chickens (I later learnt this is what 'chooks' were), horses and crops (corn, alfalfa or 'lucerne', soybeans and oats). I regularly tried to get in on the wrong side of the ute and then had to re-learn how to drive a manual since we're 'backwards' in America and most of our vehicles are automatics. While we don't have swags or billycans back in the States, I soon learnt to cherish both.

After a few musters and a couple of weeks at stock camp, I was finally coming around and getting in the way less.

My favourite days are when we muster. The last one we did, I found myself crawling out of my swag at 4.30 am to get ready in the dark (at least it wasn't as windy as it was at earlier musters). Since I'm not very coordinated in the morning, putting on my boots usually involves me falling into the trees near my camp a few times ... the one downfall of my otherwise perfect campsite. I then meander over to the horse floats to prepare feeds (soaked lupins, meal mix and molasses) for our noble steeds that are lucky enough to tote us around for the day as we chase down cantankerous cows that decide to detour off through the kanji bush for their own enjoyment.

Once the horses are fed, I wander back down to the main camp for brekky and grab the rest of the gear I will need for the day. Once the sun starts coming up (usually around 6), those of us who are riding that day head back up to the horses waiting in their pens to be saddled then loaded onto the horse truck.

On this particular day, Panze and I were driving to where we would be stationed for the day. It was going well, until the cage of the horse truck decided to get wedged on a tree. After trying to back off the branch while avoiding the bank near the front of the truck we had to wind around in the first place, we had to call in the one and only Wizard, the mechanic, to try to help.

Arriving in his 'chariot' (the bull buggy), he made the call to saw the branch off, but since the chainsaw was back at camp, Panze and I unloaded the horses there and headed off on a high-speed trail ride to where we were meant to be. The rest of the day went pretty smoothly, and we soon had all the cattle headed back to the yards at Annabelle's camp.

The muster before that I had torn my jeans open on a kanji bush, and just as we were nearing camp I was thinking I would make it through the muster without that happening again. I was right – it was my shirt that took the blow next time. Upon getting tangled up in a kanji bush and ripping my shirt, I had also managed to squeeze in too close to the cattle, causing them to shoot off in front of me, and earning a good scolding over the radio from Panze.

I quickly tried to scramble out of the bush on my horse while getting out of the way of one of the ringers in his buggy as Annabelle and the other mustering pilot brought around the helicopters to once again pop the cattle back in place for me to direct in towards the yards. Once the cattle were back in line, we were able to yard up without any more breakaways.

The night ends with everyone gathered around the campfire for a home-grown, home-made meal and some good-hearted banter before we each go off to our own camps. I go back to my little 'cave' for a good night's sleep, ready for yard work the next day.

It has been an amazing experience being in the Pilbara and mustering. I have met some of the most wonderful people and learnt so much. I hope I am able to return to do it all over again (with fewer hiccups next time). As I was dozing off in the back of the troopy on the way to Yarrie for the first time, I never thought I would be able to find a new family on the other side of the world so much like those at home, and definitely count meeting each of them a blessing.

A Day in the Life of a Station Kid

Breanna Dorrington, Yarrie Station

Hello, I'm Breanna, but everyone calls me 'Kid', because I am the youngest at Yarrie Station. I'm twelve years old.

Obviously there isn't a school bus I can get on, or a school just around the block, so I do my schoolwork through Port Hedland School of the Air. My school day starts at 7.30 am, and I can finish by lunchtime if I try really hard. I have heaps of activities to do for school, and my mum is my home tutor. We have what we call set work (or sets) to complete in certain time frames in language and maths.

Language sets need to be completed in two weeks, and each set has a different theme. For example, the one I am working on now is called 'Life's a Drama' and I am doing lots of fun stuff about plays and acting. I get to watch movies with this set, which is awesome, because normally I have to do lots of writing.

Maths is my favourite subject because there isn't as much writing, and I have an online section to do each day, which is very cool because I get to use the computer.

I also need to spend half an hour every day on my handwriting, spelling and mental maths, and a new program I have started doing is an online memory game.

My teacher is Miss Boswell and she's from New Zealand and she's really nice. We have online lessons every day for an hour with my teacher and the rest of my classmates (there are seven of us). Mum said when she did School of the Air, they did their lessons by radio, and they couldn't see their teacher like we can now. I also have history and music lessons once a week as well. My teacher comes out to visit me once a term, and spends two days with me doing really cool stuff, like art and T&E (technology and enterprise).

Every term we have at least one school camp, sometimes on a station where one of the students lives. There's also a big camp at the end of the year where we all go to Perth and catch up with all of the other School of the Air kids from Western Australia.

Now, to get to the fun stuff! After school finishes I just want to be me, a little terror and great adventurer.

I love to practise cracking the stock whip, which I have been doing since I was six years old. My favourite trick is cracking two whips at once (which I only mastered a couple of months ago). Everyone gets sick of the noise, so I have to go for a long walk if everyone is home. The Jack Russells (or rascals as we call our dogs) on the other hand love the noise and get very excited, and I normally have to stop once they show up, in case I hit them.

I am always on the lookout for what the station crew are up to as well, because sometimes they are doing cool stuff, and if I have finished my schoolwork, I can go to work with them.

Annabelle (the boss) and Ann, Janelle and Kelsie (jillaroos) look after me like I am one of their own, and I know they will pull me into line if I am naughty, so I make sure I am not. I love it when Kelsie is shoeing horses, because she keeps Banjo, my horse, in for me, and I can gallivant around in the yards. I also help by brushing any manes and tails that are knotty. I also like taking Banjo to the cattle yards with Ann when they are processing cattle, because I can help with the weaners and ride at the same time.

Oh, and the best thing ever — I was able to spend this school holidays out at stock camp because I was ahead with my schoolwork. I was so excited because I was able to go mustering all day on a horse, help process cattle in the yards, have my shower in the river and camp under the stars every night. I was also put in charge of the lollies to hand out to the crew when they needed a pick-me-up.

Janelle takes me mustering and is teaching me to ride properly. When I am with her I always have to stay with her, and I am not allowed to fall behind, or I might get lost. Janelle is also a nurse, so Mum knows she will take good care of me while I am with her. Soon Janelle is going to go back to New Zealand, where she's from, and I am saving all my pocket money so I can go and visit her when I am old enough. She is going to teach me how to play polo cross.

Janelle also gets me to help her near the cattle crush when they are processing cattle. I am still too little to help push up the cattle when they are sorting them, but

I am really quick at passing tags and stuff to her. We always talk and joke around and the day goes really quickly.

I like doing chores for Annabelle too, because you never know when you might get a chance for a chopper ride. I like riding in the chopper because you can see for miles, and it puts butterflies in my belly.

Other things I have been learning to do are drive a car and skin a killer, and now I want to learn to play the guitar, so I can sing around the campfire in the evenings.

I have lived in towns and been to a normal school, so I know the difference between being a townie and a bushie and love being a bush kid. I am never bored, I don't think I will have time to be lazy, and I am learning so many things that lots of other kids never get the chance to.

I think that makes me just plain lucky.

Stories from the Kimberley region of Western Australia

Cowboys, Bulls, Broncs and a Diamond Ring

Constance Wood, Blina Station

My normally cool, calm and collected partner, Matt, was unusually nervous as we headed from Blina to Broome for the last rodeo of the season. He was twitchy, weird and cagey, and I was getting a tad annoyed at his short responses. His hazel eyes, usually looking about and checking out everyone else's patch of country, were instead fixed to his phone screen watching videos of saddle bronco riding, showing no signs of budging. I put it down to nerves about riding in front of such a big crowd.

We arrived at the rodeo grounds on the outskirts of beautiful Broome. Ordinarily I help out with whatever needs doing before and during the various rodeo events, so I thought I'd hang around for a bit and see if anyone needed a hand. Matt told me to have a night off and go to the bar and hang out with my friends. I left Matt and his strange mood at the rodeo grounds to check into our hotel, settle in and have a couple of drinks to start my night.

I was happily singing away, chatting on my phone, sipping my wine, blow-drying my hair and doing all the girly stuff that girls in the bush rarely get to enjoy, when Matt called to check on me. The usual torrent of questions started.

'Babe, did you check-in all right? What are you going to wear? Don't wear that blue-and-white shirt – wear something sexy. Who's picking you up?'

By this time I was thinking, 'Just settle down, Matt!' But after living with and loving this somewhat control freak of a station manager for a couple of years now, I'd learnt it comes with the territory.

'Con, are you going to be on time tonight?' said Matt.

I sighed. 'YES, I will be on time!'

'Well, just make sure you get down to the grounds in good time, babe.'

I hung up, thinking I'd take my time and *would* wear that shirt. Besides, I didn't really own anything that fitted Matt's definition of 'sexy'.

Another hour passed. It was now about 7 o'clock, and I was on to my third glass of wine, and starting to really enjoy the time off.

Matt rang again.

'Where are you? The bronc ride is going to start soon!'

I told him I was still at the hotel.

Matt, clearly getting stressed now, said, 'Constance, you need to see my ride. I'll send Toni to come and get you.'

I told him he was being a control freak.

Matt, having none of it, called Toni and sent her to collect me. Toni is a close friend of mine who'd worked in the Blina stock camp. True to form, she got lost finding the hotel. After a few phone calls and directions, and a slight rise in Matt's blood pressure, she arrived at my hotel. I was sitting on a rock out the front, drinking, not too fazed and blissfully unaware of the stress my partner was experiencing.

We rushed to the grounds, and Jesse met us out the front. We made our way to the bar, and Toni snagged a parking spot right at the front, which had been reserved by our grader driver, Stuey, who was looking pleased with himself.

I told them I needed to go to the toilet. They looked concerned and asked how long I'd be – they didn't want me to miss Matt's ride.

I thought, 'What is with everyone tonight?'

Off I went to the ladies', then got some drinks and headed back to the others.

Toni tapped me excitedly and said, 'Matt's going to ride in a tick – don't go anywhere!'

'Cool,' I thought, and reached for my phone – it's my usual habit to video his rides – but Toni offered to film the ride. Last time Matt rode, I got so excited that I accidentally videoed the tops of the trees around the arena instead, so I handed over my phone.

I spotted Todd Walsh heading over to Matt's chute with the microphone. Walshy is the president of the Broome Rodeo Club and a good mate of ours, who also takes great delight in dishing out public embarrassment over the mic. Matt lowered himself on to the horse. Walshy started his spiel. Except this time he was interviewing Matt.

I was too busy straining to hear Walshy and Matt's 'interview' to notice my friends watching me, trying to contain their excitement. Over the noise of the crowd I managed to hear, 'You are looking pretty nervous, Mr Wood.'

Matt was sitting back in his bronc saddle now, feet in the stirrups, ready to ride.

'Yes, Walshy, pretty nervous tonight, mate. I'm pretty nervous tonight because I've got a pretty big question to ask a certain young lady.'

'What?' I thought. 'What question?'

'Miss Constance Gray: I want to ask you if you will be my wife?'

Is this happening? Did I hear right? What rhymes with wife? I looked at Toni. She had a smile from ear to ear and was nodding at me, confirming my thoughts. Before I knew it, I was up on the rails giving Matt the thumbs up.

YES, of course I'll bloody marry you – now please don't hurt yourself!

Matt nods his head. 'Righto, boys, outside!'

The horse didn't buck hard, so he rode time easily, ending up with a re-ride (another turn to make a better score).

I've never been one to sit back and let things just float my way, so as soon as I saw that bronc thunder past and clear the arena I was up and over the rails, ducking and weaving, dodging the pick-up horses and grinning at the guys as I went, pushing past Walshy. I was running towards Matt to make sure he got my answer before he changed his mind.

I tapped him on the shoulder as he was trying to get a small box out from his friend's pocket. He turned around, surprised. Then he fumbled for the box, lucky not to drop it in the red sand of the arena and there he was, down on one knee, still in the chaps I'd bought him for his birthday.

He said, 'Well, how's this for a bloody grand gesture, Con – what do you say?'

I couldn't wipe the smile from my face. 'Yes, I say, yes, a thousand times over.'

My big, handsome cowboy smiled back at me, jammed the ring on my finger (it fit perfectly!) and wrapped me in his arms. As he kissed me, in true showman style, he threw his hat in the air to the cheer of the 4000-strong Broome rodeo crowd.

The Story of Groomzilla and Bride-dill

Constance Wood, Blina Station

I'd never been one of those girls who dreams about their wedding. To be honest, I thought that getting married and living happily ever after was one of those things that happened to everyone else but me. I was too complex, too torn between town life and bush life to ever find someone who matched me, or would accept my special kind of weird. My vision of myself was the loose, old spinster at everyone else's wedding, getting drunk off free wine, pinching young blokes on the bum, dancing like an old stud and falling in the wedding cake. Pretty good second prize, I thought – at least I would be having a good time.

But when that tall, dark and handsome man got down on one knee, I thought, 'Geez – this is it. This is where my "happily ever after" starts.'

What the hell do I do now?!

True to form, Matt had a plan – he always has a plan. We would get married before Easter and the start of the cattle season. Pretty tight deadline, but perhaps he was as worried as me that the other party would change their mind and decide, 'Nah, actually, my "happily ever after" doesn't start with you.'

This was mid-August 2014 – we wanted to get married in March 2015. I counted it out – September, October, November, December, January, February, March – seven months.

Challenge accepted: on 28 March 2015, we would be married in Broome.

While juggling my job as a human resources advisor at a mine on Ellendale and my duties at Blina, I started the mammoth job of planning our wedding. Big-ticket items first – bridesmaids, venue, celebrant, invitations, caterer – and remember, don't be a bridezilla.

Unfortunately, Matt's idea of a great wedding was vastly different to mine. I remember we were driving across the Erskine Range when we had our first of many wedding arguments. Matt didn't care about things like having pretty chairs or fairy lights. He wanted a huge sit-down affair with lots of rum and a pig on the spit. I could see my Pinterest board of rustic, country-themed wedding ideas going up in smoke – and fast – and Matt was the one with the jerry can of petrol and a match.

I tried to reason with him: 'What about hessian and lace, pretty fairy lights, just a few people, but do it really nicely?'

'Nah, stuff that, forget about all that, we'll just have a few balloons and home-brew rum and everyone can grab a roll and serve themselves.'

I could feel my gut tightening. I was not going to get married at a goddamned B&S Ball! I might not have dreamt about my wedding for years, but now that it was finally here, I wanted a touch of class! I gripped the steering wheel, trying to hold back the tears – *breathe, Connie, just breathe*. I was not going to cry over decorations and chairs. I was not going to be *that* girl. I was not a bridezilla.

Oh god, yep, it was happening – I felt my face go hot, and the tears spilt out and down my cheeks. I sobbed – my fiancé was being a brute!

Matt stopped mid-sentence – he was going on again about home-brew rum and saving money. 'What's wrong? Are you crying? Why are you crying?'

The home-brew rum idea was too much and I wailed, 'I DON'T WANT A B&S WEDDING! I JUST WANT NICE CHAIRS AND PRETTY THINGS!'

Matt laughed at me. How dare he laugh? This was serious stuff!

'Connie, get a grip,' he told me off sternly, as he always does when I become melodramatic or start feeling sorry for myself.

'NOOO,' I cried, getting melodramatic and starting to feel sorry for myself, and wondering how I could possibly marry a man who didn't care about the pretty chairs I saw on Pinterest. 'You don't understand, it's important. I don't want it to be feral. Everything we do is feral. I just want something pretty for once.'

'Connie, do you remember the chairs at Alysha and Blair's wedding?' he asked, his tone softening. 'What about Kate and AJ's?'

My mind ticked over, digging into my memory bank, desperate to prove him wrong – but I came up with big duck eggs. No, I could not remember the chairs, or the decorations, for that matter.

I sniffed. 'No, I can't remember, but I bet they were nice.'

Matt laughed again, sensing he was going to talk me round on this one (as he usually does). 'Connie, do you know what goes on chairs?'

'What goes on chairs, Matt?' I snapped.

'Arseholes, Connie, arseholes go on chairs. Nobody leaves a wedding saying "Oh, wow, did you see those chairs? Forget about the great time we had – all the free grog and dancing, and how happy the couple looked!" Nobody cares about the chairs.'

Despite myself, I knew he had a point. I stifled a laugh and wiped the stupid tears away. I'd just had my first (of very few) bridezilla moments.

It really didn't matter about the chairs – all that mattered is that we got to marry one another in front of our friends and family. After that argument, I promised myself that every time I got caught up in something trivial and superficial, I would just think, 'Connie – arseholes go on chairs'. Whatever it was, it didn't matter. I would think of the big picture.

As a result of this mantra, Matt and I ended up role-reversing – Matt is a naturally organised person and has very set ideas about things. I often joke that my job is to 'manage the manager', and I often had to remind my overzealous fiancé to butt out of it and let me organise this – it was the natural order of things; he wasn't supposed to manage the wedding like a cattle station.

Did he butt out? HELL NO!

At meetings with caterers, party-hire planners and the like, I would sit back and take a few notes, putting my trust in the fact that these people were professionals, while Matt had a list of questions written in his notebook that he would fire at a million miles an hour, poring over every detail to the point that it was sometimes uncomfortable.

That's how he got the nickname 'Groomzilla'.

After my first teary outburst over the Erskine Range, I was determined to be relaxed about this wedding. I wanted to enjoy the experience. Matt, on the other hand, wanted to manage the wedding the best way he knew how. In the same way he scrutinised lick consumption in Blina's weaner paddocks, he scrutinised quotes for the meat and alcohol; with the same keen eye he used to draft keeper heifers, he drafted through suits and shirts in the formal hire place. He even tried to have a say about the bridesmaids' dresses.

He did leave a lot of things to me, like getting a wedding dress, and all of the boring girly stuff like invitations and decorations. But I had to laugh when he would stick his nose in and start making phone calls about items I had already sorted. When I would tease Matt about being a groomzilla, he would retort, 'Well, I'd rather be a groomzilla than a bride-dill like you, you big monkey!' I still laugh at that term; who calls their fiancée a bride-dill?!

Matt and I ended up with a wedding celebration that was the perfect compromise, as it should be. I didn't get nice chairs, but I had a beautiful dress. My bridesmaids were stunning. I managed to get some pretty decorations. Matt got his roast pork, home-brew rum and a full sit-down meal.

Most importantly, we were privileged enough to marry one another, as best friends and partners in this life, in front of people who we love and hold dear. It truly was my dream wedding and I wouldn't have had it any other way.

The Life and Times of the Yellow Devil

Constance Wood, Blina Station

Over the 2014 wet season, my trusty old ride-on lawnmower spontaneously combusted. I swear this thing was the first ride-on mower ever invented, although in all honesty I think she was only about twenty years old. She'd had a tough old life and seemed hell bent on destroying anyone who dared to accept the challenge to ride her. We called her 'the yellow devil', and she was my 'frenemy'.

I must admit I was often a little more frightened of jumping on the yellow devil than I was of jumping on a lively young horse. She had the same sort of temperament: a tad unpredictable and at times spooky. And she needed a fair few things to get her going: about five litres of Rimula fuel, a towel to stop your bum getting pinched by the busted old seat, a set of jumper leads in case she decided to stall, and a screwdriver to start her, as Matt had accidentally broken the key in one of their many face-offs. It needed to be an insulated screwdriver, though, as to stop her you had to pull the spark plug out and risk electrocution.

And all the while I was on her, I would have that 'Hoorang Colt' song, by Martin Oakes, running through my head.

Sometimes if you left her running and hopped off, she would take fright and shoot off at top speed (the speed of a thousand turtles). I would sprint across the lawn and do a flying leap (usually leaving behind a thong) in an attempt to pull the wretched thing's head around before she shot underneath the living quarters and decapitated me.

In the event that the yellow devil didn't bolt and attempt to chop off my toes when I was getting on, she would produce an excessive amount of smoke, which made it impossible to stay in one place for an extended amount of time without being asphyxiated by the grey cloud that would billow out of goodness knows where. She would spit oil all over my feet, though I would try to see the positive side – she was just trying to give me a bit of sun protection, or, in the event I had boots on, she was just trying to oil my boots!

Mowing the lawn was quite an ordeal and she would often just give up the ghost and break down for no reason in the middle, usually just before smoko. I would get off, swearing and carrying on, and attempt to cast some sort of black magic spell or promise my first-born child to appease the devil that lived inside that bloody engine. It was a regular occurrence to see me swearing and muttering and pushing the yellow devil into the shed for one of the boys to deal with.

I was really in two minds about the yellow devil. On one hand she was the bane of my life and a royal pain in my backside, but on the other hand, so long as I could nurse her along, I wouldn't have to push-mow the acres of lawn that seemed to grow exponentially during the wet season.

The day she died, she was actually having a good run. She wasn't shying at trees or randomly bolting in fright; she had a nice, soft feel and was poking along at a gentle pace, with minimal coughs and explosions of smoke. So I decided to have a break. I thought better of turning her off and parked her against a tree in case she got any ideas. Then I jumped off, had a drink, looked over my shoulder to admire her and HOLY SUFFERING MOSES she had burst into flames!

I ran to get the hose (which I had for once rolled up), turned the tap on and tried to extinguish the flames with the dribble of water that came out until I remembered she ran on unleaded fuel, at which point, I ran off, jumped in the car and screamed up the hill to fetch Matt as he would surely save my mighty steed.

Matt just sauntered down, assessed her chances of survival, lit a cigarette and watched her burn, cool as you like. He just wanted to make sure she didn't burn the generator shed down.

I was devastated. As a result, I spent a horrible, sad wet season mowing the lawns by hand.

But all's well that ends well. The yellow devil takes pride of place on top of an old four-wheel drive at the dump. And I now mow the lawns on my brand-new ride-on.

It's the Small Things

Anne Marie Huey, Dampier Downs Station

A major event at Dampier Downs recently was the advent of 24-hour power, achieved by connecting the solar panel system to the generator. This means that during the day the sun charges the batteries, which power all our electrical needs. If the load becomes too great, for example, if someone is welding, the generator automatically kicks in to take up the load. At night, if the batteries are too low, the generator also automatically starts up, charges the batteries and automatically turns itself off once the batteries are recharged.

I posted this happy event on Facebook and one of my friends commented that it is the small things that make the difference.

Believe me, having 24-hour power is no small thing.

No longer is it necessary to get dressed in the dark. No longer do we need to find a torch and head over to the generator shed late at night to shut it all down, wondering if tonight will be the night the brown snake has decided to move back in. Now we can confidently store items like vaccine for our cattle, safe in the knowledge that the fridge will be running all day and they will be kept at a constant temperature and won't spoil. Now it doesn't matter if we fall asleep in front of the TV after a long day, as we won't wake up at 2 am to the sudden realisation that the generator is still running, burning diesel for no good reason.

It takes a lot of diesel to run a cattle station and this was never more obvious than this year. We have a 20,000-litre tank at the station, which generally lasts us a good few months. As we are at the end of 110 kilometres of dirt road, we stock up before the wet season hits and the road becomes impassable for a fuel truck.

The 2013 wet season was unusual. It usually rains from around January to April, but this time it didn't start until March and kept raining until July. Naturally, we ran out of diesel. This wouldn't be a problem as we would call in the fuel truck, but every time we scheduled a delivery it would rain and the road was out. This meant that we had to rely on the 600-litre fuel tank that could be mounted on the back of the ute. Unfortunately, 600 litres doesn't go all that far when you are running a grader, station vehicles and a generator, so we were constantly doing the 250-kilometre round trip to the nearest roadhouse to refuel. While this meant that everyone was able to maintain their ice coffee quotas, it also meant a lot of unnecessary and expensive wear and tear on vehicles. Believe me, slogging through 110 kilometres of mud with 600 litres of fuel on the back is not fun.

So next time you think having 24-hour power is a small thing, try living without it for a month.

The other great technological advance we made is installing telemetry units on a number of our bores. Telemetry is a fantastic system that allows us to monitor the level of water in our tanks from the homestead – or anywhere in the world with an internet connection, for that matter.

Out here, water really is life. Last summer it reached forty-eight degrees on the verandah. That is seriously hot. Dehydration is a real risk for people and animals alike. So during the dry season there is a bore run going on pretty much every day. If there is a problem and the cattle run out of water, the effects can be devastating.

Our homestead is located pretty much in the centre of the station. The furthest bore to the west is about fifty kilometres from the house, and the furthest to the north is about seventy kilometres. The western bore run can take up to five hours, depending on the state of the road and the number of detours required. Obviously, checking the bores is a time-consuming job that is again hard on vehicles. With telemetry, we can do the bore run over a cup of tea in the kitchen in the morning.

Information is fed back to the homestead using radio waves. At a click of the mouse we can pull up any bore on the place and check the level of water in the tank. If there has been a dramatic drop overnight there could be a problem and we know we need to take a drive and check it out. Common problems include busted pipes, broken trough floats, leaking tanks or even the cattle licking the tap at the bottom of the tank and turning the water off (bizarre but true).

Having this information is a huge relief. Before we had telemetry it could have been two or three days before we got back to check. If a problem occurred just after we had visited, we had no way of knowing until we got back a few days later. Just as importantly, we are now able to eliminate a lot of unnecessary bore runs. Most of the time you would arrive at a bore only to find everything was fine, the tank was still full and the entire trip was largely a waste of time and diesel. Now we can make informed decisions as to where and when we need to go, safe in the knowledge our cows are happy and well looked after. After all, that's why we're here.

It's on

Anne Marie Huey, Dampier Downs Station

There's a smell of avgas in the air and the faint 'whump, whump' of rotor blades in the distance. This can only mean one thing – it's time to muster.

The aim is always for a calm, controlled muster where the choppers fly straight and slow, gently pushing the cattle into a 'wing'. A wing is basically two funnel-shaped fence-lines strung with shade cloth that guide cattle into the yard. The job on the ground is to wait at the end of the wing to help move the cattle along, and be ready to leap out and shut the gates behind the mob when they are safely yarded. But not every muster goes exactly to plan.

Not long ago we mustered the northern part of the property, hitting four different bores in one day. The first two yards went relatively smoothly (a little too smoothly as it turned out) and then my partner, Mike, and I were in the trusty Hilux ute at the third yard of the day. As the helicopters brought the cattle up, a couple of crafty old cows managed to slip straight through the fence. Once we'd got the majority of the mob into the yards, the pilot decided to fly around for another go. We had to drive around to the other side of the wing to let the pilots do their job, which involved a bit of bush-bashing. As we were sitting at the end of the fence, we could see the choppers manoeuvring and hear the cattle coming through the scrub. Adrenaline was starting to flow when we noticed the smell.

Something was definitely on fire. It turned out to be the ute. Somehow a small sapling had become wedged in the motor and was smouldering. Mike and I jumped out and desperately tried to remove it so we could be in a position to assist the helicopters as needed. Time was definitely of the essence when we noticed the next problem. The fan belt had been dislodged and with no time and limited tools, it was impossible to get it back to where it needed to be in time. Mike pulled out his Leatherman (a Swiss army knife on steroids) and cut it off. Not the best for the car but we had no option. We had to get down to the yards to shut the gate.

We leapt back into the car and raced down the wing. Halfway along Mike asked me for the radio so he could talk to the pilots. I realised the last time I saw the radio was when we were under the bonnet. But there was no time to worry about it. We got to the gate in time and managed to yard the cattle. As the dust settled, we assessed the situation. The ute was now well and truly out of action. Trotting back up the wing I found the radio and two of its three batteries. So we were now down one vehicle and without any communication, with still one more bore to muster.

The choppers were already on their way to the final bore so we had no option but to scoot up there as quickly as possible. Unfortunately, when we got there we realised that the boys were still a long way from finishing the set-up so once again it was all systems go as we raced to get ready in time. With the Hilux ute no longer operational, I was given the only available option, an old station Toyota, and instructed to wait at one end of the wing, basically to repeat what we'd done previously (preferably without catching on fire this time). The last thing Mike said to me was, 'Remember you don't have any brakes.'

Later I learnt he had also given the boys a lecture on not getting in my way, due to my lack of brakes. Had I known this I would have been highly offended and considered my character personally besmirched, but as it turned out it was probably just as well.

As I was driving to get in position I could see the cattle streaming past me in the trees. This was not good – we were nowhere near ready! Eventually I had the choppers in front of me and started back towards the yards, making sure no cows doubled back along the fence-line. As I got to the yard I could see the pilots had done a great job of getting the cattle in, but there was no one there to shut the gate. This was a disaster, as the cattle were about to hit the back fence. If they turned around we would have lost them all. I kicked it up a gear to get there in time and just as I approached the gate, I saw Mike screaming down the other side of the wing with the same idea. That's when I remembered – I had no brakes. I could see the whites of his eyes but there was nothing I could do. He shot past me and drove straight into the yard with me inches behind until – bang! – I ran straight into the back of him. No time to worry about it as the cattle were starting to spill back past him. I had to get out of there and shut that gate. I threw my car into reverse and backed up only to discover that Mike's father, who I hadn't seen for the last couple of hours, had turned up to give us a hand and parked directly behind me. Bang! Straight into his car, too. The score was now Anne Marie 2, Mike 1, cars 0.

All this, and it wasn't even lunch.

There's One in Every Mob

Anne Marie Huey, Dampier Downs Station

Many have spoken about low-stress stock-handling. At Dampier Downs, this is pretty much the closest thing we have to religion. My partner Mike even went so far as to travel to America to learn from the late, great Bud Williams, a pioneer in the field. Working cattle according to low-stress principles generally results in safer, calmer and more efficient days. Having said that, we still have a lot of cattle that have had very little contact with people, and while low-stress stock handling allows you to deal with these animals, they are by no means as quiet and well-behaved as we would like. You can also bet that if someone from outside the station turns up at the yards something, somewhere, will go horribly wrong.

A while back our neighbour was helping us truck some sale cattle. Mike was working the race and putting in ear tags, our neighbour and his father were loading the cattle onto the truck and I was working the back yards. My job was to ensure there was a steady flow of cattle coming through at all times.

It works like this. The cattle start out in one big mob in a large yard. They are then moved through progressively smaller yards, in progressively smaller numbers, until they are eventually moving single file down a 'race', which leads to the truck.

Obviously, as the yards get smaller you are working in much closer proximity to the cattle. This is where you really need to pay attention as it can get dangerous if the cattle decide they don't want to play the game.

On this occasion, Mike knew there was a really snaky bull in the mob (hence being drafted for sale) and warned me to watch him as he was likely to 'go' (charge) me. I took this seriously as these are big animals and can do a lot of damage.

All was going well until we ended up in the second last yard before the race. This particular yard has three fences made of Weldmesh, a light steel product with a square pattern, rather than traditional post and rail construction. I was watching the contrary bull like a hawk. If he so much as lowered his head or twitched his ears, I would back right off. Unfortunately, I was so busy watching him I didn't notice his mate, who by this stage had also had a serious deterioration of attitude.

He came out of the mob straight at me. I turned and raced for the closest fence, which happened to be made out of Weldmesh. Now, I had often wondered how you would go climbing one of these Weldmesh fences in a hurry, as they are not the easiest to negotiate, but I can tell you, I was up that fence like a little cat.

Unfortunately, once I got to the top, the belt loops in my jeans got snagged on some protruding bits of steel and I was stuck. I couldn't go forward and there was no way in hell I was going back.

Normally, once an animal has put the fear of god into you and made its point, it is happy to put itself back in the mob, at least until next time you get too close. Not this bull. He just wouldn't quit and kept headbutting the fence, which by this time was getting a real sway up. All I could think about was the fact that my father had his ankle pulverised in a similar situation when I was a kid, so I desperately tried to keep my legs out of the way. By this time, I was virtually planking on top of the fence.

Mike was in the yard and, alerted by the commotion, came racing across. He flew up the fence from his side, grabbed me by my britches and hauled me over the fence. Now, though, I was headfirst towards the ground, pretty much eyeball to eyeball with a very irate bull that was still intent on having me for breakfast.

I ended up in a fairly undignified heap on the ground, while our neighbour and his father did their best to not notice anything. I have to say I wasn't sorry to see that bull loaded onto the truck and off the property forever.

I guess the moral of the story is, don't get so caught up with what you think might happen that you fail to see what else is going on around you. Which is a pretty good philosophy for life, really.

Lessons Learnt from a Little Cat

Anne Marie Huey, Dampier Downs Station

When I said 'No more puppies!' I did not expect to come home from town one day to find two tiny kittens in my kitchen. These little cats, one girl, one boy, had been abandoned by their mother and were found – of all places – in the dog run. Normally, Mike and I do not approve of feral cats as we are well aware of the environmental damage they wreak, but these guys were so small and so defenceless we had no option but to adopt them.

It took a couple of days and some serious bribery in the form of mince and milk, but eventually they turned into two very loving and much-loved family pets. They were moved from the kitchen to my office and began growing rapidly.

Being kittens, they were extremely playful and constantly looking for adventure. Before long, I felt they were rapidly outgrowing my office, but with so many dogs, I could not let them out to explore during the day. My solution was to wait until all the working dogs had had their final exercise and feed for the night and were securely locked in their pens, and the pet dogs were chained up. Then I would let the kittens out for a couple of hours to broaden their horizons.

This worked really well until one night when Bitty, the little girl, did not come in for her dinner. By about 9 o'clock I was really worried and began searching for her. Eventually I found her curled up in a spare wheel in front of the workshop. The minute I picked her up she began to purr loudly and I thought we had dodged a bullet. I took her back to my office and put her down in front of her food bowl. It was then I realised something was terribly wrong.

It was like the left side of her body had no power and she couldn't stand up. She wasn't paralysed as she could still move her legs, but something was seriously wrong. I put her into her bed and was cleaning her up when I noticed puncture wounds on her back leg. I could only surmise a dingo had been skulking around the workshop and got hold of her. I hand-fed her a few morsels of mince, tried to get her to drink some water and sat with her until she fell asleep.

At 6 o'clock the next morning, I carefully placed her in the car and set off on the three-and-a-half hour trip to the vet in town. We hadn't had her long but she had firmly cemented a place in our hearts and I was determined to give her every chance. Unfortunately, the vet determined her injuries were just too great and the kindest thing was to put her down. I was devastated, but Bitty's end was peaceful and quick.

Then, there was nothing to do but pull myself together and get on with the drive home. I always find driving a great time for reflection and that day was no exception. I began asking myself if taking Bitty to the vet was really in her best interests, or my own. If I were brutally honest, there was some part of me that knew the night before that she couldn't be saved. But I also knew I would have always had that niggling doubt and associated guilt if I hadn't tried. Was my kindness the right thing, or would a quick end twelve hours earlier have been better for Bitty? Either way, I can at least console myself with the knowledge that though Bitty's life was short, it was happy and filled with love.

I began thinking about how this experience contrasted with some of the standard animal husbandry practices we routinely carry out on our cattle. In particular, how some of our procedures can look inherently cruel on the surface, but when you examine the motivations behind them, they are in fact kind.

Take, for example, dehorning. It is a bloody business that undoubtedly causes pain at the time. The calves bellow and it is not a pretty sight to see blood spurting from their heads as they leave the cradle. However, on the flipside, I have seen old cows come into the yards with misshapen horns growing into the side of their heads or, even more horrifically, into their eyes. I have seen animals in agony that had to be destroyed after being gored by a bull and know at least three people who are lucky to be alive today after run-ins with wild bulls.

I have also seen weaners settling in to munch on a pile of fresh hay and calves happily headbutting mum in the belly to get her to let down some milk mere minutes after being dehorned. This indicates to me that far from suffering an extended period of trauma after dehorning, recovery begins almost immediately.

So, while dehorning may appear cruel, would banning it (as some animal rights' groups advocate) really be in the best interest of the animals and people who work with them, or would it simply serve to assuage the conscience of a largely uninformed public who will never have to deal with the unintended consequences of such a policy?

Even the best-intentioned actions can cause unnecessary suffering. Actions that may appear callous on the surface can actually result in long-term benefit. It is my hope that next time you hear about a farming practice that is cruel or inhumane, or are asked to sign a petition, or to boycott a certain product, you dig a little deeper. Ask questions of people on both sides of the argument. You may still disagree, but at least you will make an informed decision.

And when you get home tonight give your pet an extra pat from me.

RIP Bitty.

Sunday Funday

Anne Marie Huey, Dampier Downs Station

There aren't many days off in the middle of the cattle season. When I lived in town, weekends were a chance to sleep in and maybe wander down to the local coffee shop for a lazy breakfast and a leisurely peruse of the papers. These days it's different.

Take last Sunday, for example.

My day started at 5.30 am, just as the sun was coming up. My first job was to let the dogs out for their morning exercise. It's a beautiful time of day and despite not being a morning person I can't be too grumpy as the dogs are always super excited to see me.

Once the dogs were safely back in their cages it was time to do a bore run. This means driving out to the bores to make sure there is enough water for the cattle. Those bores that are getting low need to be pumped, troughs checked and a general scout around for any potential problems. I also had to drop off a drum of diesel for my husband, Mike, who was frantically grading along fence-lines, clearing the flammable vegatation in an attempt to ward off a major bushfire burning next door.

The bore run took care of the rest of my morning, then it was back to the homestead for a quick bite of lunch and another let-out for the dogs while I cleaned out their cages. Then I headed to the yards to help with the branding of a few weaners.

I got the job of bringing the cattle up, which is my favourite job in the yards. You might have to walk a few miles and eat a lot of dust, but I do enjoy working the cattle through the back yards all the way to the race. It is a great opportunity to practise my low-stress stock-handling techniques. Things were running smoothly, the sun was shining and the cattle were flowing nicely.

The team doing the actual processing (branding, ear marking, castrating, vaccinating and dehorning) was doing a great job, even with the new hydraulic calf cradle that took a bit of getting used to. This is a great invention that takes a lot of the hard work out of branding. It does, however, require a bit of practice to perfect the timing when catching the weaners and on this day one or two managed to escape. This was not really a problem, though, as they would just end up in the back yard again and I would simply bring them round once more.

Now, as cattle evolved as prey animals, they don't really like being on their own, particularly in stressful situations. Their first instinct is be part of the mob, which means it is often easier to move a large number of animals than just one. Unfortunately, late in the day one heifer escaped and found herself on her lonesome.

She was fairly unimpressed with proceedings thus far and being on her own in the back yard brought out her feisty side. Mike often criticises me for not being enough of a coward, but I believe that if you've worked with cattle long enough you become a reasonable judge of when an animal is just bluffing, or if it is seriously going to hurt you. As I walked into the yard to move this heifer, she ran straight at me. Every instinct I had screamed that she was not going to stop, so I did the only sensible thing and turned around and ran. I picked out my bit of fence and flew up it as quickly as I could. Unfortunately, the heifer had the same idea and (even more unfortunately) picked out the same bit of fence.

I hit the fence, she hit the fence, and we both promptly fell off the fence. I now found myself boxed into a corner with an increasingly irate heifer shaking her head at me. I followed the only course of action open to me and started squealing like a schoolgirl at a One Direction concert.

It wasn't until I saw the look of total surprise on her face that I realised she hadn't even seen me in her headlong rush to the fence. Her sole aim was to get out of the yard and she was surprised to find herself confronted by this strange caterwauling creature. Being a sensible heifer she gave one final shake of her head and trotted off to the far side of the yard.

I let the dust settle, then checked myself for damage. My arm was a bit tender but my ego took the biggest bruising. Fortunately, she was one of the last for the day, so I was soon able to take myself back to the homestead to lick my wounds — then feed the dogs, cook dinner, sort the laundry, check emails, pay a few bills and get ready to do it all again the next day.

So You Want to be a Ringer

Anne Marie Huey, Dampier Downs Station

You've heard about the big horizons, the scrub bulls, the horses and all the adventure of living and working on a remote cattle station. You've got the Wranglers, the boots and the ute, and you've decided to head north to give ringing a go. Good decision – one of the best ways to experience all the north has to offer is to get amongst it on a cattle station.

Before you roll your swag and dust off the Akubra hat there are a few things you should know. Being a ringer is not for the faint-hearted. The days are long, the work is physically demanding and the pay – when compared to the mining sector at least – is not great. You will be hot, dirty, uncomfortable and at times find yourself doing things you really don't want to do.

So why would anyone want to work on a cattle station?

People are one of the most valuable resources on a cattle station. When you are managing a large area and are reasonably remote, you need to know that you can rely on your staff to get the job done, even if they are at the opposite end of the property. Good staff make all the difference between a well-run, efficient business that is an enjoyable place to work and a time-consuming, energy-draining exercise in frustration that is akin to mustering cats.

Over the years, we've had all sorts at Dampier Downs. I could probably write a book about some of the more dubious characters who have come and gone, but we have also had some brilliant staff, many of whom have made lasting contributions to our business.

One of the best things about the pastoral industry is that most employers are willing to give you a go, even if you don't have all the necessary skills at the start. Skills can be taught, but it is essential to have the right attitude. Some of our best workers in recent times have been a lawyer, a classically trained trumpet player and a fashion designer. Despite having little to no experience when they started, by the time they left they were driving trucks, welding end assemblies, servicing motors and operating machinery. These are skills they will have forever and will stand them in good stead wherever they go in life.

So what are the qualities that make a good ringer?

Strong work ethic
Some days you will find yourself doing jobs you would really rather not be doing. That's unfortunate, but the reality is, those jobs are just as vital to the running of a successful cattle business as the actual cattle work. So if you find yourself cleaning troughs, digging holes or cementing posts, the only thing to do is get on with it and do the best job possible. Chances are the result of your labours will be there years – or even decades – after you have moved on. Do it badly and the boss will offer a silent curse every time he drives past that crooked post, but do it well and it will be a lasting testament to your hard work and ability.

It is also important to understand that the only way the boss can afford to pay your wages is if you are out there making money every day, so you need to work hard. This might sound a bit mercenary but margins are tight in the cattle industry and if you're not making the business money then you are costing it, and nobody can afford that. Bludging, shirking and doing a half-hearted job are sure-fire ways to find yourself at the top of the 'do-not-employ' list (and believe me, that list travels).

Initiative and a willingness to learn
No one can predict every possible scenario that may occur. Being a ringer is about keeping your eyes open and your wits about you. If you see a potential problem, don't just drive off and hope the next person will come along and fix it. See what you can do about it yourself. If you don't know how to do something, ask. You'll rarely get into trouble for asking questions, but going off half-cocked can end in disaster.

And even if you have experience under your belt, appreciate that there are many ways to do a job. Be open to new ideas and if you think you can see a better way of getting the job done, offer suggestions. However, it might be wise to pick your moment. Down at the yards, when the uninvited tourist has just turned up with a fluffy city dog that has just latched on to an old scrub bull, who in turn has just knocked out the newbie backpacker and is on his way to taking out the portable panels and therefore spilling the entire mob, is probably not the best time to discuss the finer points of yard design.

Loyalty

At the end of the day, wherever you find yourself, you have chosen to work on a particular cattle station. At the end of the fortnight, you also receive a healthy deposit in your bank account. For that reason alone your boss deserves your loyalty. If you're truly unhappy working where you are you can always leave. Done the right way (with sufficient notice and not leaving the rest of the crew in the lurch), no one will begrudge you moving on if it is just not working out. Bitching, moaning and constantly complaining, however, is a whole different story. Amongst the camp it can lead to seriously eroded morale and you will probably end up with a reputation as a whinger. Done off-station, it marks you as the sort of person who would rather complain about a problem than fix it, a serious red flag to potential employers.

A sense of humour

You'll need it. Chances are you'll find yourself far from home, living and working with a diverse bunch of people – some of whom you would probably not associate with normally. This doesn't have to be a bad thing. Look at it as a way to increase your circle of friends or, at the very least, an opportunity to gain an insight into different ways of life. You'll also need tolerance, patience (note to self) and the ability to move on from disputes without bearing a grudge. When everyone works together there can be great camaraderie within the camp, and that can make even the dirtiest jobs that much more enjoyable.

In summary, if you're a clock-watching, self-serving, blame-laying wannabe who thinks the boss is only there to provide you with a lifestyle, being a ringer is probably not for you. However, if you're willing to give it a go, prepared to do the hard yards to get the rewards and keen to learn the business from the ground up, it could be the start of a whole new adventure.

And the pay-off is really rewarding. There is a real sense of freedom in the Australian bush. You get comfortable in your own skin. You might have to learn the hard way (most of us do), but by the end of the season you will have a good idea as to what you can achieve.

Spectacular sunsets, glorious sunrises and stars so big and clear you would swear you could almost touch them are there to be savoured. New skills, new abilities and bragging rights over your 'soft' mates in the city are all there for the taking. And you will go to bed each night knowing that what you did during the day really mattered. You're feeding the world, and that's something of which to be genuinely proud.

So You've Got the Job –
Now What?

Anne Marie Huey, Dampier Downs Station

As another busy year kicks off, there will undoubtedly be many first-time jillaroos and jackaroos heading north to try their hand working on a cattle station. For most, it will be a huge change and, despite what you may think at the time, a leap into the unknown. This can be a tough industry, but also a rewarding one. Your ability to succeed rests largely on the attitude you bring to the job. The fact that you now find yourself on a property is due to someone, somewhere, seeing something in you that convinced them you were worthy of a shot. However, just because you have a start does not mean you have a guaranteed free run to the end of the season. You have put your toe on the very bottom rung of a ladder that, with commitment, some common sense and a whole lot of effort, will result in the experience of a lifetime. Whether that experience is a positive one, or whether you end up sent home with your tail between your legs, is entirely up to you. It will take grit, determination and sacrifice and will probably result in coming to grips with a few hard truths about yourself.

So what can you do to give yourself the best shot of coming out the other end of the season (relatively) unscathed? For what it's worth, I have jotted down a few bits of advice that may (or may not) be helpful for those new to the job.

Be honest with yourself.
First, it is important to ask yourself the tough questions. Why do you want to work in the pastoral industry? If your primary reasons include any of the following:

- Because you think cows are cute
- Because you like the idea of riding around on a horse all day

- Because you want to impress the girls/boys in town
- Because of all the fishing/camping/pig hunting you can do on your days off
- Because your current job/school is boring and you've spent most of the day checking out Facebook pages such as 'Ringers from the Top End'

Then, no, you haven't thought this through and you're in for a rude awakening. The first thing to understand is that working on a station is nothing like the television series *McLeod's Daughters*.

It is a tough job. You will screw things up. You will receive the odd rocket or two from your boss and there may be times where you will find yourself in tears, wondering why the hell you gave up your life of air-conditioned luxury to pull dead cows out of bog holes.

You will be battered, bruised and filthy at the end of most days. Your muscles will ache and your hands will blister. You will see more sunrises than you ever have before and there will be times when you will still be going long after the sun has set.

You will miss out on friends' birthdays, parties and music festivals. You will not have every weekend off and, when you do, your new social calendar will revolve around rodeos, camp drafts and race meetings, with maybe the occasional visit to the neighbours (who are likely to be at least a couple of hours' drive away) if you are lucky.

But you will also challenge yourself as never before and, when it works out, you will be rewarded with a huge sense of pride and self-achievement. So, even if it is nothing like you imagined and you are tempted to quit within the first week, take a deep breath, calm down and understand this is an opportunity you may never be given again. Give yourself at least a month and if it is still not for you, walk away knowing at least you tried. Quit any earlier and you are likely to sell both yourself and your employer short.

Find someone you trust.

It's understandable to be nervous and there will be times when you feel like you can't cope. As an employer, one of the most frustrating things is when you know a staff member is having trouble but they simply won't tell you what is wrong. If we don't know, we can't help. Hopefully, your boss (or his or her spouse) is approachable, so if you are struggling, talk to them about it. If you don't feel comfortable talking to them, find someone you trust to act as a mentor. Of course, you might be told you are being a bit of a sook and to toughen up (tough love is sometimes required in this industry), but bottling things up can be destructive. Most importantly, when having the conversation, don't approach it as a whinge or blame session, just as an honest discussion. If you can come up with potential solutions, even better.

At the same time, understand that your boss is exactly that – your boss. They are not there to hold your hand, or be your parent. Develop a strong sense of self-reliance. It will stand you in good stead, not just in the pastoral industry but wherever life should take you.

There are no free rides.

If you want to be successful in this industry don't look for excuses. It doesn't matter if you are not the tallest, strongest, most athletic or experienced in the camp, what does matter is giving every job a genuine and determined go. The one phrase every employer loathes is 'I can't'. Don't say 'can't', just try. Hiding behind the rest of the team may work in the short term, but it won't go unnoticed. Not only will you find yourself deeply unpopular with the rest of the camp, it won't be too long before you find yourself heading down the road with a poor reputation to boot.

Additionally, if you are one half of a couple, and your partner is skilled but you are new to the industry, still expect to start at the bottom. Even if your partner is head stockman it doesn't mean you get to pick and choose your jobs. Fixing tyres, cleaning troughs or cementing posts – these are all jobs that need to be done. The most respected person in the team will be the one who rolls up their sleeves and just gets on with it.

Be accountable.

The best advice I can give is to pay attention, ask lots of questions and – most importantly – listen. Make sure you understand what is expected of you with every job you're given, as mistakes can be expensive. Take care of gear, no matter how old or battered it may appear. In fact, the older the gear the more care it probably requires. Understand that every dollar your boss has to spend replacing something you've lost or broken is one dollar less he or she has to spend on things like fencing, water infrastructure, hay, cattle vaccines – and wages.

You will make mistakes. It's inevitable. Admit them, take responsibility and, most of all, learn from them.

Enjoy it.

Whether you're just there for a gap year or aiming to make a long-term career working in the bush, take time every day to appreciate the unique opportunity you have been given. Yes, you will work hard but there is a certain satisfaction to be taken in kicking back at the end of the day and feeling the ache of muscles you never knew you had. Take pride in the knowledge you have put in a solid day's work and I'll bet you never look at a gym membership in quite the same way again.

Chances are you will find yourself in an area very few people will ever get to see, spotting the wide variety of birds that visit while you fix a trough, or the odd frill-neck lizard sunning itself on a newly erected picket while fencing. So savour the quiet moments in your day, appreciate the untouched nature of your surroundings and count yourself lucky to be amongst the few who get out of urban Australia and back to where it all began – the bush.

Welcome to the Top End.

A Day with Mrs Plains

Helen Campion, Anna Plains Station

It won't be the longest walk I take today, but the walk from the house to the camp kitchen will be my most important. Many things run through my head. Is the crew awake? Is the crew ready for the day? Is there avgas at the yards for the chopper? Are the two-way radios charged? Are the vehicles ready? What's the weather doing? My head has started spinning and the sun hasn't even poked its nose over the horizon yet. Oh, and where's my hat?

Breakfast is usually quiet – everyone is thinking about their role for the day and going over the plans. Most are also thinking about why they are up at this ungodly hour. Then the chopper fires up, and suddenly everyone is wide awake and ready to go. We're off.

The drive out to the cattle goes pretty quickly. I'll chat with my offsider for the day. It's a good way to calm the nerves and stop the spinning in my head for a brief time – there's still a million things running through my mind. It's hard not to worry about a muster. I have to be prepared for the worst, so I'm ready if something goes wrong, whether it's equipment not working or, god forbid, someone getting hurt. The whole time I'm on edge, hoping for a smooth and safe run.

The cattle are found, the chopper is buzzing like the flies that have found us, and it's game on. We let the chopper do most of the work, but we have to be organised and in constant communication on the ground to keep the herd together. In a cloud of dust the colour of rust, we point our livestock in the right direction. Hopefully.

After hours that are never counted, we reach the yards, and the cattle wander in, just how we want them to. You'll get the odd one that doesn't like the look of a crew member, or one that decides it would rather be out in the scrub, but most times it all goes to plan.

With the cattle in the yards, it's time for drafting. What to keep? What to send? This is all part of the yearly plan, and hopefully there's enough to send to town.

The yards can be busy – there's cattle, there's dust, there's people, there's more dust, the cows are chasing stockmen, the stockmen are moving the cows, and there's plenty to do.

But it can be totally peaceful, despite the roar. It can be beautiful to watch.

Crew and cattle love the lunch break. There is a wonderful sense of relief, and so much curiosity from the cattle. It can be strange watching a cow watch you eat. This is the time I get to sit back, reassess what's going on, and think about what's next.

The crew are amazing, working through until the sun drops and the temperature eases. The latter part of the day can be the most stunning, but it's also when I need to be extra diligent as we are all tired.

If breakfast is quiet, then the drive home is absolutely silent. But my head is still spinning, because now it's all about what's happening tomorrow …

City Girl Goes Bush

Emma Hawkins, Anna Plains Station

Born into and blinded by the bright lights of Sydney, all things waxed, bleached, brand-named and manicured were highly regarded. If you didn't spend half an hour each morning putting on your celebrity-endorsed war paint, you stood out like a sore thumb.

So relocating to the opposite side of the country to a station two-and-a-half hours from the nearest town seemed appropriate. Whatever it was that put the idea in my head, I'll be forever grateful it happened.

I've not been here on Anna very long. In this short time, though, I feel I've gained more life lessons and moral values than any classroom could ever teach me.

It's about pregnancy-testing a cow for the first time instead of getting pregnant. And fighting fires and battling the weather instead of hiding in the air-conditioning. It's also about handling the occasional snake and wishing your mum were here, even if it would age her a decade. It's about ensuring the poddy calves are fed, the cattle have water, the fences are secure and the utes are packed.

I don't even know what a 10 am wake-up is any more – sparrow-fart o'clock is more like it, though watching beautiful sunrises together with the crew definitely makes the early rises worthwhile.

The lingo can sound like a foreign language, but being part of such an amazing team, and getting to meet many other people considered family and friends to Anna, is a great highlight of my job.

My lunch is now eaten on a crate next to the yards to the sound of cows. My make-up time is down to five minutes. I don't give a damn about my thighs and I'm not sure I remember what a manicure is, and I don't care anyway. Go stick your make-up where the sun don't shine.

* * *

A typical day at Anna is long and exhausting.

I'm up at 4.45 am to get ready. First job is sorting clothes to determine what's dirty and what's not. This is followed by slapping on make-up and trying to tame my hair into something that doesn't resemble an afro. At this point I'm finally awake, ready to brush my teeth and shuffle over to breakfast.

After a 5.30 am buffet breakfast, plus coffee, we are told the day's activities by the head stockman and then we are on our way.

Come 8 am we are settled and working hard. It is mustering one day, fencing the next. Walking out cattle, ear-tagging calves, putting out fires and wading through knee-deep mud are in the job description, with the occasional pregnancy diagnosis of cows to liven up the day. My advice? If you're pregnancy-testing, do your washing that day, not four days later.

We have regular smokos and lunch is from noon to 1 pm, so we can tune into the *Country Hour* on ABC Radio. We park our backsides and scoff food like we haven't eaten in weeks. Being spoilt, we hook into beautiful gourmet wraps and brownies with a Diet Coke in hand. Bellies full, we get up and begin the hard slog again.

Come 3 pm, we are now smashing through the work with thoughts of our first beer motivating us. Often at this time of day, you look back and realise how much you have done and learnt – a proud but tiring moment.

At knock-off time, the crew is well exhausted. Pulling into the homestead, it is time to fill our water bottles for the next day, have a shower and crack open a beer. After dinner at 7 pm, the crew relax together and chat, talking of the day's activities and having a good laugh before heading off to bed around 9.30 pm, a long day behind us.

Mrs Boss always quotes that there is never a dull moment on Anna. She is definitely not wrong.

The question is, why? Why relocate to a remote station to do long days in the middle of nowhere for a season?

The answer is simple – we love what we do. From showering with frogs to 'bush bathroom' stops, it is all worth it. Crawling into bed feeling like you have done something with meaning makes for a restful sleep.

Though station work can be tough, we get treats too. On Anna, the crew recently spent an afternoon tagging birds for research. Trips to Cape Missiessy (the northern-most point of Eighty Mile Beach) for a picnic, or along the beach for a sunset are often taken, and occasionally we get spoilt with ice-creams from Sandfire Roadhouse. Whether it's people going buttocks-up in the mud, or getting a dirt moustache and dust monobrow, the atmosphere is always fun and entertaining.

So after another truly exhausting day spent working on the Plains, I can sit here in dirty jeans, eyes falling out of my head with a 'fro underneath my cap and assure you there is no rocking needed to get me to sleep.

What Do You Do When There's No Cattle Market?

Nikki Elizovich, Country Downs Station

As with most couples that run their own station, I take care of most of the admin stuff including the books and the budgets, making sure that they at least look the part so that 'Mr Banker' is more amenable to our advances during the hard times.

And what hard times we have been having since the Live Export Ban in 2011. It was a huge transition for us as a small, developing family business to suddenly have to find some other way of paying the bills. I will admit that due to our own little niche within the livestock market (we had great access to the Middle Eastern markets as well as Indonesia), we were probably not as hard hit initially as the majority of pastoral operations in the Kimberley. But since 2011 and the ongoing debacle with our political relationship with Indonesia, other producers in our area are now doing everything they can to access the same markets that we have always had – and rightly so, as their traditional market is no longer reliable. However, as we are such a small operation in comparison to these much larger enterprises, we found that we started to miss out on many of the opportunities that in the past had saved us.

In 2013, things came to a head for us. As of September, we had only managed to sell 121 head of cattle, nowhere near enough to cover our annual expenditure.

What do you do when there is no cattle market any more?

We diversified.

To pay the bills, we (well, I should say my husband, Kurt; I had the job of making sure the station kept ticking over) had to go out and do earthmoving contracting with our machinery, which we were supremely lucky to be able to do close to our property – it didn't cost us much as it would have if it were a further distance from our base. That was a short-term diversification we had undertaken as – for obvious reasons – we would much prefer to spend our time with cattle. We could never have done the contract jobs without the help from our family. Kurt's folks and a very close family friend came up and spent months here. Kurt's dad, Jack, was Kurt's offsider, driving a backup vehicle on the big contract job, and Norman spent most of his time fixing our broken-down machinery. We are indebted to them for giving their time and efforts to help us out.

Another diversification project we undertook was cropping or, more accurately, fodder production. A couple of years ago we received a permit to clear about 230 hectares to plant improved pasture in order to produce supplementary feed for our sale cattle. We can use this fodder in two ways: we either cut it and bale it as hay to feed our sale cattle or weaners (or any cattle really) in the yards, or we can put the cattle that we want to be fattened up on the 230 hectares to graze the pasture down.

Our project is relatively innovative in terms of the Kimberley region, mainly because we are not irrigating our pasture. We are doing what is termed 'dry-land crop production'. This means that we are relying on our annual rainfall to grow the improved pasture. With a 980 mm annual rainfall average, one would think this wouldn't be too hard. Wrong again. I was reminded that when you rely on nature, anything can, and usually does, go wrong!

Despite a couple of setbacks from abnormal seasonal events, we actually undertook a project with Rangelands NRM, an NGO that encourages the sustainable use of natural resources, to trial different varieties of improved pasture grown under dry-land conditions. To us, even the failures were a success as without the support and contribution from Rangelands, we would have had to spend years (and lots more dollars) figuring this out on our own. Now we have some great preliminary results that can be shared with the entire pastoral community so they can also consider their diversification opportunities. We are hoping that it leads to a situation in the Kimberley region where everyone can move ahead again – well, as long as the government doesn't keep holding us back. But don't get me (or Kurt, or anyone in our industry!) started on that subject.

While not technically considered diversification, the other method we used to give ourselves a long-term benefit was increasing the genetic diversity of our livestock. We started developing a composite herd structure in the anticipation that one day in the (hopefully not too far) future, instead of having a good-looking, perfect line of classic Brahman stock that limited our market access, we would have a more physically disparate line of animals with the potential to fit into any (or even more miraculously, all) markets. Kurt has spent numerous hours on the internet and talking to stud producers, researching what I call his 'porn' – different breeds of cattle. This has led to us buying bulls of different breeds that we can put over our high-quality Brahman and Brahman-cross breeder cows. So hopefully in the next few years we will be able to reap the benefits of a successful (albeit intrepid) business plan. Optimism: it's not for the faint-hearted, but it obviously works.

The other form of diversification that we, and Kurt in particular, believe in wholeheartedly is adaptation. We must, individually, be able to adapt to ever-changing and new situations, whether they be environmental, economic or social. A recent workshop in Mataranka that Kurt attended had Allan Savory as the guest speaker, renowned worldwide for his expertise in holistic management. The one thing that was pivotal to our understanding of it was that nothing ever stays the same. The relationship between all organisms in nature (and, as a biologist, this is the crux of it) is complex and in a continual state of flux. The whole concept of holistic management is to know and accept this, and therefore be adaptable to these changes.

Kurt's two favourite quotes of Allan Savory's were:

1. 'Plan, monitor, replan', which basically means deciding on a management practice and enacting it, but constantly reviewing to make sure it is still working. If it isn't, develop another management practice to achieve your end goal.
2. 'Don't face problems, face solutions': deep, but apt when you consider the mental attitude behind it.

Both these quotes sound simple until you have to put them into practice. But, as they say, nothing worth having comes easy.

All this has served to remind me of the big picture of what we are doing. As we all know, it is good to take a step back sometimes and look at the forest, not the trees.

Fire on Country Downs

Nikki Elizovich, Country Downs Station

On a Sunday in early August 2014, we noticed fire to the east – not unusual for this time of year. We thought it was about forty kilometres away, so we weren't overly concerned, but we kept an eye on it. On Monday, the south-easterly winds decided to create havoc so by Tuesday night, we knew we were in trouble.

On Wednesday morning, after Kurt and Josh had left at 3 am to do what they could to keep the fire at bay, we called the Department of Fire and Emergency Services (DFES) out. This was a good move because by midday, we had a fifteen-kilometre fire front heading directly for the homestead – it had travelled about forty kilometres in two days. To make matters worse, the 'fingers' of the front had travelled to the north and south of the homestead, and the fire had jumped the Cape Leveque Road, so it was also west of us. By that afternoon, the homestead was completely surrounded by fire – and uncontrollable fire at that.

For three days DFES and the Broome Volunteer Bushfire Brigade came out each day to help us fight the fire. When the fire got to within 500 metres of the homestead, we started back-burning about fifty metres from the house, which helped to save the homestead and improved pasture area. Once we were assured the homestead was safe, we focused on trying to stop the fire in the surrounding paddocks.

Unfortunately, we didn't succeed. On the fourth day we made the decision that the fire was just too dangerous. When you are trying to fight twenty-foot flames with a powerful and continuous wind pushing them towards you, all you can do is pull out your resources and head back to the homestead. We lost up to 95 per cent of the pasture on the property.

What did this mean for us? It meant we had to sell and agist what we could, and bring our five-year development project to completion in about three months! We had to go flat out every day just to try to relieve the pressure on the livestock.

We are so lucky to have some great friends who gave up their time and put their own lives on hold to come and give us a hand for a few weeks. Close friends quite literally set up camp on our back lawn and some drove 2500 kilometres from the south for a week and offered to 'do the stuff you don't have time to do'. For those who aren't station savvy, these were the crap jobs of grading and repairing fence-lines where burnt trees had fallen on them and, in our case, bulldozing new tracks and dams so that we had the option of alleviating the current water points of their stocking densities and spreading the grazing impact of our herd over a larger area, which would provide the animals with the best possible chance of surviving until the wet hit. Needless to say, we worked our friends like dogs. But I think they had a good time! Still more friends of ours provided us with the space (and pasture) to agist our weaners and younger cattle.

In a time of crisis you realise that there are some absolutely fair dinkum lovely people out there in the world. We have been blessed to meet and know some wonderful people who have done massively altruistic things like not only donating hay, but transporting it to our property.

Just to say 'thank you' seems lame, but what else can you say? The truth is, if the tables were turned, I realise now that I would do the same, if I could, and a 'thanks so much, that is so kind' would actually suffice and make me feel it was worth it. So THANK YOU to those who helped us out without asking for anything in return! I am looking forward to repaying the favour one day, whenever we can. (Hopefully we won't have to.)

I said to Kurt after DFES and the volunteer fire-fighters had helped us out: 'If we ever move back into a town situation, I am going to volunteer as a bushfire volunteer!' Those guys were more than great. They do so much for their community, without people realising the dangers they are exposed to. And they do it for nothing. If I could give back to them what they have all provided us, I would be proud.

Our Indonesian Holiday, Ahem, Work Trip

Nikki Elizovich, Country Downs Station

In late 2013, my parents, being the wonderful people they are, offered to look after the property – and the kids – for a couple of weeks so that Kurt and I could have the honeymoon that we never had. Naturally, so we wouldn't offend my folks, we jumped at the chance to have a break! I was dreaming about a relaxing week or two by a pool, with a bar nearby selling cheap cocktails, and the sound of waves pounding on the beach in the background.

But even on holiday, Kurt is always searching for new things that are related to agriculture and keen to see how things are done in different areas and countries. So I emailed Lisa Wood, who works in Indonesia in the cattle import business and has written a weekly blog for Central Station for a couple of years. I told her Kurt and I were heading to Lombok, Indonesia, to visit a friend and if she knew of anything to do with agriculture – cattle, cropping etc. – that we might be able to have a look at. Lisa told us that if we happened to be in Sumatra, she might be able to help us.

This simple email set up a chain of events that saw us go to Bandar Lampung, Sumatra, in March 2014 to look at the facilities and places where some of our cattle end up when sent to Indonesian feedlots and abattoirs. We packed our bags, kissed and hugged the kids and took off in an aeroplane, laughing at how silly my folks were to take on all that 'home stuff'.

We arrived in Bandar Lampung at around 6 pm. At 10 am the next day, Lisa picked us up to take us to visit the Way Laga project, which had gone from feeding breeding cows palm oil and palm waste products (as well as other feed waste products), to feeding the progeny of those breeders on the same food source. The first project was shown to be a great success and the second one was looking pretty great too. The weaners were fat, happy and completely calm. The company Lisa worked for had also undertaken another side-project that used some of the waste in a bio-fuel set-up that produces enough gas to power a couple of gas lamps and a couple of gas barbeques. Kurt and I were keen to take that information home and see how we could save energy this way.

After lunch, Lisa took us to the Juang Jaya feedlot in southern Sumatra. This was a professional set-up on a massive scale, working in a holistic permaculture fashion whereby they were producing other useful, commercially viable products that helped to support the local community. This was great as the cattle used the waste products from the other products, and the waste products from the cattle were put back into the land as fertiliser. This was such an environmentally sustainable system that we began looking at ways to implement some of the ideas on Country Downs.

On the way out of the feedlot, we stopped to look at another little project that was being done with the Banteng, a local cow breed – such gorgeous cattle. Kurt and I really enjoyed our day, and Lisa was an excellent tour guide.

The next day, after an early dinner and a quick couple of hours of sleep, we dragged ourselves out of our comfortable hotel bed at about 11 pm and headed out to an abattoir with Lisa to see how they kill and process the beasts before heading out to the wet market. It was amazing! The cattle were brought up the race, one at a time, put into the crush with absolutely no fuss and stunned with the stunner. The side of the race was opened up so the beast could fall down the ramp and be slaughtered according to Halal tradition. This was all very efficient and done in about five minutes. There was also an animal welfare officer on site who made sure that each animal was unconscious and slaughtered according to the practices put in place for ESCAS (Exporter Supply Chain Assurance Scheme) requirements.

But what truly astonished us was the efficiency, speed and dexterity with which each of the butchers' teams (there were three different butchers at the abattoir) skinned, quartered and processed their beasts. A team of about four small but very strong men would take only about twenty minutes to completely process their beast down to quarters – a task that takes us over an hour when we're doing killers ourselves – and then maybe another fifteen minutes to process it into smaller pieces to fit in the back of the ute. That's efficient!

They also did not waste any part of the animal, which was so refreshing to see compared to what we had witnessed back home. The only part of the animal that was not loaded onto the back of the ute was the contents of the digestive system. All the stomachs and intestines were emptied into drains and washed out completely with water. They loaded the head, hooves, guts and all other sundry body parts and drove to their little butcher shop in the wet market.

Before they left, we had a fantastic discussion with the abattoir manager and other workers (which provoked much laughter at our inept Bahasa Indonesia) and showed them a few photos of our property and the way we do things. They were absolutely astounded at the size and space of what is an average-sized property in Australia. They could not believe that we had to travel for over an hour to get to the nearest town. The funniest thing that I remember is that they could not believe that we were able to take a photo of not only one, but over a hundred of our cattle with no fence between them and us.

That night we were especially lucky in that we were able to follow one of the butchers to their stall in the wet market and get a sneak peek at how they go about portioning and storing the cuts of meat. Apparently the most sought-after cut is the head! We also found out that only a few cuts sold for a higher price; for the most part everything on the beast is the same price per kilo. Each person comes along and orders whatever they want, so it's a first-in, first-served scenario, which was why it was so surprisingly busy at 2 am.

We saw an excellently run, excellently managed, clean and efficient slaughtering facility that demonstrated to us that these procedures *are* done properly in Indonesia. Now we can honestly say to people that we do know where our animals are going and that we are happy with the way they are being treated and slaughtered.

In fact, I felt that many of the practices we witnessed surpassed many I have seen in Australia. These lovely people allowed us to watch and observe their facility and I can only hope that we gave them something in return, if only to show that not everyone who visits them is there to find a problem with what they are doing. We learnt so much from them in that one night. I feel that if all I can do to repay their kindness and trust is to let everybody else know what a fabulous job they are doing, then this is the time and place to do it.

The Vegetarian Backpacker

Barbara Camp, Kalyeeda Station

I live on Kalyeeda Station in the East Kimberley with my husband, James, and his family, the Camps. We raise Brahman-cross cattle for sale, primarily via live export, on our 120,000-hectare property, which spans from the edge of the Great Sandy Desert to the Fitzroy River.

Before I tell you a bit about my life at Kalyeeda, let me introduce you to the girl I was when I first arrived, because she was very different.

Until I was twenty, I lived in Edinburgh, the capital of Scotland, and had been a vegetarian since I was ten years old. I had just finished an equine science degree and wanted to work in researching thoroughbred horses, but first thought I would do a year's backpacking.

So when my cousin mentioned she wanted to travel to Australia, I thought, 'Why not?' We had the working holiday visa sorted in two weeks, booked our flights and merrily headed over to the other side of the world. The first job I was offered was in the middle of nowhere mustering cows on horseback. My only previous experience with cows was riding past them in little fields on my horse, or occasionally being chased by them if I had jumped the wrong gate. But the whole point of this travelling malarkey was to try something different, right? It was a seasonal job – only three months. What could possibly go wrong?

To say I experienced culture shock would be an understatement. I arrived in Broome, home of blue skies and turquoise waters, and was picked up by a good-looking, burly cowboy-type boy who loaded me and my backpack into a busted old ute. It was piled up and roped down with unidentified lumps of car innards, unexplained lengths of pipe and enough canned goods to feed an army for a year – or so I thought! He drove me out past the end of sealed roads and mobile reception to dirt tracks and ant beds. We drove four hours out towards the centre of Australia and a very different life.

My first weeks of station life were a blur of new experiences – finding lots of things I'd never done, or even considered doing before, and living in the most bizarre circumstances. There were no walls on the 'house' that I and the other dozen or so workers stayed in. We had green, see-through shade cloth for walls and a tin roof. The boys slept on stretcher beds and swags out in the shed. My pampered city self had never experienced anything like this.

I'll be honest: I hated it. The life was hard. I was terrified, out of my depth and felt utterly useless. If something breaks or goes wrong when you're hours out from the nearest expert, you have to fix it yourself. I had never even changed a flat tyre, let alone serviced a motor. Sure, I knew how to look and see if my farrier at home had done a good job shoeing my horse's feet, but I didn't have a clue how to do it myself.

But I learnt – oh, how I learnt. Out there, you cannot call for back-up. It's up to you and the crew you work with to fix it. If the generator you rely on for power stops in the middle of the night, it's up to you to figure out why and fix it in the dark. If a pipe connecting the windmill to the bore has sprung a leak, there's 500 head of cattle relying on you to notice and fix it before they perish. Life was a constant challenge. I learnt some awesome skills, but more importantly, I met some of the most inspiring people on earth.

These Kimberley station types – they're a breed unto themselves. These men and women can problem-solve their way out of any situation. They think big and dream bigger and are always looking for ways nature and humans can work together to survive in one of the toughest, wildest places on earth.

They have a sense of humour and irony like you wouldn't believe – and they need it because when things go wrong out here they can go very wrong. But you still have to pick yourself up and carry on because there's always a job that needs doing and thousands of animals relying on you.

I'm now very different from that sheltered, slightly naïve vegetarian who came out here for an adventure. The good-looking cowboy who picked me up from the airport all those years ago is now my husband, and I've been lucky enough to be absorbed into his family and their life.

I've been a part of the whole picture of rearing beef cattle. I've raised them from orphaned, poddy calves sucking milk off your finger through to having my ribs bruised by the horns of a cleanskin bull as I sat on my horse. (And wasn't I lucky that was all I got from that encounter?)

I've caught, killed and prepared my own meat, literally from paddock to plate. And I have been lucky enough to follow our cows to Indonesia to see the whole story of this industry that has become my life. My vegetarianism rapidly became a thing of the past when I came out here – I learnt that respecting and loving animals is about how you deal with them when they're alive, not what you do with them when they're dead.

I know what it's like to ride a bucking horse at a rodeo, and experience the awesome power of the wet-season floods and the responsibility of trying to move your stock to safe ground before it's too late. I've seen the heartbreak of drought and watched animals you've fought to keep happy and healthy get weakened and stuck in bogs as waterholes dry up. I've felt the fear of watching a raging bushfire you're trying to fight turn with the wind and head straight towards a ute full of your friends.

Life out here isn't always easy, but it's full of passion and promise.

Cattle Sense and People Skills

Barbara Camp, Kalyeeda Station

Cows and horses are large, unpredictable animals and they can be pretty bloody dangerous. It's a fact that more people are killed by cows than sharks every year. So when you're working with animals, you need to understand them. This is central to any job that involves dealing with living creatures, especially when working cattle through the yards.

An animal that is happy and healthy will not try to fight you and therefore be less likely to hurt you. Humans are supposed to be the intelligent ones, so it is up to us to try to think like the animal so it knows what we are asking of it.

Life would be easier if we could make a bovine–human dictionary. If you could get a megaphone and say to all of the animals in the yard: 'Excuse me! If you could just proceed in an orderly fashion through that gate there and wait in whatever pen you've been assigned, we will be with you soon. We just want to do a quick tally and give you your vaccinations and then you can all go back out again!'

Or, in the case of the sale cattle, 'Congratulations! You have just won an all-expenses-paid cruise to China for you and 500 of your closest friends! All-you-can-eat buffet and fully serviced apartments included!'

Unfortunately, despite my best efforts, I've never managed to get that off the ground, so we have to work our stock the old-fashioned way.

We do that by working with their instincts – they are herd animals who will respond to predators with a fight-or-flight reaction. Generally speaking, a cow will want to stick with its mates and be away from you. The quickest, most efficient way to move a mob of cattle through the yards is to take things slowly, logically and steadily.

Let's think it through: if the cow is staring at you at the back of a pen when your mate is opening a gate at the front, then she did not see that the gate was opened – she assumes it is still closed. So when you start running towards her, she responds in panic by either running away blindly in circles, and still does not see the gate because she is too stressed, or decides she has been backed into a corner and needs to fight her way past you.

On the other hand, if you are to enter the yard with your mate via the gate, the cow will see this escape hatch is open. If you then move to the side and circle around her to the far side of the gate, just close enough that she will want to get away from you, but not so close that she feels the need to panic and run blindly (trust me, you learn pretty quickly how to read when you've crossed that line), she will move away towards the escape hatch. This works even better with a bigger mob of cattle. It just takes one bright spark to go through the gate for the others to watch their mate, see it's safe and follow suit.

Animals almost always take the easiest option. It's up to us in working them to make what we want them to do the most appealing option. This concept of low-stress stock handling is important from every angle. Happy cows mean fewer injuries to other animals and to people. It means better use of time because you're not literally chasing a stressed-out animal in circles. It makes sense financially because a cow that has come through the yards steadily and happily is not going to lose a heap of weight or potentially abort a calf through worry.

This attitude pays off through the generations. If a calf's first contact with a person is being walked quietly at his mother's heels into a set of yards, and moved quietly from pen to pen with no yelling or mad galloping, he learns to stand with the mob when the horsemen are positioned around them. He will be easier to deal with when he is mustered in next year as a weaner. He has done it before and it wasn't so bad. You know you've done a good job as a ringer when, at the end of a day's drafting, you see a young cow with her first calf lying down by the rails of the drafting pen contentedly chewing her cud.

The end result of station life is to produce beef cattle to feed people, but there's so much more to it than that. We do this job because we love and respect animals and what they give us – food and this wonderful life in the bush. The only way to get the most out of our animals is to look after them and their habitat to the best of our ability. For me, station life is all about happy cows.

* * *

I had an interesting discussion with a friend once about what working cattle taught young men. She had only seen stock whips and poly pipe used in the yards and didn't understand the context in which these tools are used. In her mind, it taught boys to bully and shout and use violence and force to get what they want.

I think it teaches the absolute opposite. To work stock successfully teaches respect, patience, teamwork and sound judgement. Let me explain why.

Imagine you have a group of cattle to draft. The aim of the game is to move them through the yards as quickly and efficiently as possible. It's not rocket science. Cows are like people in that they work best when they are calm and alert, not stressed or scared. If we were to run in screaming and bullying, then we would be removing the brain from the equation. The saying 'to work out the IQ of a crowd take the IQ of the stupidest member and divide it by the number in the crowd' holds true for cattle too. It's up to us to be smarter. Quite simply, hostage negotiation and siege tactics take a long time to work and are dangerous.

Cattle are generally bigger and faster than us, so bullying and chasing don't work. The basics of low-stress stock handling is to be quiet and efficient and work on common sense. A group of animals is more likely to do what you want when you lay out their options in a way that makes the right choice the most attractive option, and the crew has to work together to achieve this. I think that is a brilliant lesson for young men to learn.

This would be a beautiful note on which to finish. What a lovely moral to the story. Unfortunately, I can't stop there in all conscience. I absolutely stand by all of what I just wrote but I'm not going to lie and leave it all sugar-coated and lovely.

You cannot escape the fact that, like some people, some cows are just real – to put it politely – arseholes.

When you have a mob of 1000 head of cattle, there's bound to be a few idiots in the mix. These are the ones that we tell exciting stories about. If they were humans they would be the hoons that you see on reality-TV cop shows heading down the wrong side of the highway in high-speed chases or getting drunk and disorderly outside a nightclub.

This minority take the happy-cow, low-stress philosophy and trample all over it. They are the bad apples that can spoil the whole barrel, and they are the ones that give the bad impressions to people like my naïve friend. I suppose that's another life lesson we all learn: you get the best results out of life with respect, patience, teamwork and sound judgement. But every now and then, you need a stock whip and a bull catcher.

Not Just Cats and Dogs

Barbara Camp, Kalyeeda Station

One of the best things about living on a station is the animals we get to have around the place. We've had orphan dingo pups and injured wallabies; corellas that have fallen out of the nest and brolgas that like living in the machinery shed; a 600-kilogram ex-poddy steer that can only walk in circles and a one-winged galah that makes the dogs run in terror – we've certainly had some interesting creatures sharing our home!

When you're moving more than 3000 breeding cattle twenty-one kilometres for vaccination and tagging, it's inevitable there will be some mismothering. We do our best to make sure all mums and bubs are reunited at the end of the day, but sometimes we're not successful. These babies that don't find mum come home and get bottle-reared by us – these are our poddy calves. These calves grow up and progress onto the reticulated green lawns of the homestead before joining the main herd when they are old enough to look after themselves.

Of course, sometimes we get poddies for other reasons. For example, Dingo.

Dingo is a 600-kilogram Brahman steer with a large set of racks on him who lives in the homestead paddock with the killer cattle (those which we keep for our own meat). Not that Dingo is a killer, though. He's a bit of a mascot. We found him as a tiny baby calf, all big ears and eyes – and covered in blood. Wild dogs had attacked him, chased him away from his mum and ripped into his back. We bottle-fed him and treated his wounds as best we could but it was pretty touch and go. Miraculously, he pulled through. The attack left him permanently disabled, though. He has some form of damage to the nerves in his back and cannot coordinate his back legs to move faster than walk. It can be rather amusing to muster him as his front end might be trying to follow the mob but his bum is heading in the opposite direction.

Also in that paddock we have Will and Grace, the donkeys that think they might be cows. They were both orphaned as foals. Grace was picked up as a baby by one of the chopper pilots and given to a ten-year-old Wave, my sister-in-law, to look after. She grew up with the poddy calves and thinks that's what she is. Will was mustered in the following year with a mob of cattle. We had seen him out and about when checking the bores around the property and knew he had lost his mum too and that he had taken protection from the savage wild dogs by living with the cows. Now that Will and Grace are older we use them for the same purpose – as our poddy calves get older we send them out to the paddock with their donkey minders to protect them against feral dogs.

One of the greatest characters we've had living with us is Fred. Fred is a galah a family friend found on the side of the road in a sorry condition with a broken wing. After a trip to the vets and the amputation of his left wing, he was alive but incapable of going back to the wild. Instead, he became the station guard bird. Fred ruled the roost. He would wander around the floor of the shed of an afternoon and cause chaos, homing in on people he didn't like and biting their socked toes as they came back from lunch to put their boots on. If one of the dogs was caught napping unawares he would give them a merry nip on the tail to send them off howling. Unfortunately, Fred met an untimely end on one of his afternoon strolls when he wandered under the wheel of a trailer. We will always miss his evening chant of 'Fred wants a beer!' as we get in from work.

Fire and Flood: A Land of Extremes

Barbara Camp, Kalyeeda Station

The weather in the Kimberley is very different to my native Scotland. It has only two seasons: the wet and the dry. To explain this in terms of the daily ABC weather report – there are only two variations that they play on a loop. For about eight months of the year, they will tell you it will be clear skies and sunshine. For the next four months you will get a vague 'hot with the chance of a thunderstorm'.

We are situated on the edge of the mighty Fitzroy River. In a big wet season it will burst its banks and can flood all the way up to our homestead and leave us marooned on a sand dune. Our roads become waterways and our cows can be trapped and swept away by the creeping water. We try to be smart about moving them onto sandy desert countries before the floods arrive but sometimes we are unprepared. In those situations we rely on helicopters to push the cattle to higher country to wait for the water to recede.

These floods can be spectacular, but the rainfall is not a dead 'cert'. Some years we may get far below our yearly average of 450 mm. Those are the tough years. Much of our country has no artificial water supplies like bores and dams, so we rely on the natural billabongs and waterholes that are filled every year by rain and floods. If we have a dry year or – god forbid – a couple of dry years, then the water that the cows and wildlife rely on will dry out. We have to be diligent about checking waterholes and the corners of every paddock for cattle perishing from thirst or stuck in bogs. Moving weak, dehydrated cattle in the heat at the end of the season is slow and heartbreaking, but no one can control the weather. Installing bores and dams is an ongoing process at Kalyeeda, but it takes time and money and is not always foolproof. Sometimes the pumps just can't keep up with the demands of the animals and sometimes they break down. It's a full-time job to check and maintain them, and the consequences for not doing so can be dire.

There's another big seasonal danger that affects us every year – fire. After six months of no rain and baking hot days, the vegetation becomes dry tinder, ready to spark up at the drop of a hat. Before the wet comes the build-up period of hot winds and lightning with no rain to show for it. If that lightning hits that dry grass and is picked up by the wind it can rage out of control within minutes.

Fighting fires out in the bush can be full-on and dangerous. We treat it like a wild animal, which usually means trying to get around it and hem it in by cutting off its food supply. We do this by creating a fuel-free border with no vegetation. We use heavy machinery to scrape big tracks clear of grass, then back-burn off these. This involves lighting a fire downwind of the oncoming blaze that travels out to meet it and in the process takes all its fuel and pulls it up.

Nature's a tricky mistress, though, and the wind can change direction in seconds. Suddenly your back-burn is picked up by the breeze and can turn around on top of you. Our fire-fighting utes are loaded with 500-gallon water tanks and hoses, but when a big blaze comes at you, you may as well spit at it. These fires are dangerous. I've seen blazes three storeys high roaring down towards a ute-load of my friends when, seconds before, the fire was heading in the opposite direction at a crawl.

Every season bushfires, sometimes started by lightning, accident, carelessness or by deliberate vandalism, can rip through and destroy massive swathes of land. Bushfires are not fussy whether it's your property or your neighbours', and the longer they blaze uncontrolled, the bigger and more damaging they get.

These are the times the remote Kimberley community pulls together. Your neighbours will come and help, as will their neighbours. It's a tough, tiring job and teams of people can be fighting for days on end, twenty-four hours a day, catching sleep in shifts, whenever the blaze dies down enough to allow it. Fire is everyone's problem, and everyone pulls together to beat it and hopes the next one doesn't threaten their livelihood.

From the Other Side of the Stretcher

Barbara Camp, Kalyeeda Station

It is 6.04 am and I am woken by the sound of my mobile buzzing into life next to my ear.

'Hello, Barbara. We've been tasked. Would you like to come flying?'

Well, ask a girl a silly question! Of course I do!

In every station and remote outpost throughout Australia there is a large, green locked box with RFDS – Royal Flying Doctor Service – and a phone number stamped on the top of it. It's a box we all hope not to have to use. But when you are so far from the nearest hospital and live in a world of dangerous machinery, unforgiving flora and fauna and – let's be honest – sometimes silly accidents, it's a box you become familiar with. In here is stored a range of medical supplies ranging from triangular bandages to strictly controlled vials of morphine, and everything in between. This box is the first line of defence for health emergencies in the bush.

In my time in the Kimberley I've had a fair bit of contact with this iconic and essential service. Sometimes the reason can be minor – I've woken in the night to find my hayfever has progressed to uncontrollably itchy hives. Time to call the RFDS. Not a condition that merits a visit, but the doctors will diagnose you over the phone and walk you through the box ('Go to shelf two, find the red bottle with sticker 226 on it …') and follow up on your care.

Sometimes it's more serious.

Some of my scariest days have involved motorbike stacks, horse and rider falls and car accidents. I will never forget standing next to my good friend on the back of the bull catcher, watching him lose his balance and fall off, only to be run over by the trailer we were towing. A little bit of bush bandaging had his badly broken leg splinted to some canoe paddles and he was transported to the airstrip on the back of an old door to meet the RFDS plane.

Now I am experiencing life from the other side of the stretcher. As part of my training as a student nurse I am taking a rotation with the RFDS in Port Hedland.

Western Australia is a big state, but the only tertiary hospitals we have capable of dealing with acute problems requiring specialised surgery, or with critical care units, are in Perth. Even getting to a local hospital can take hours down a rough, bumpy dirt road. Sometimes help just can't get there quickly enough.

That's what the RFDS is all about. There are fourteen PC-12 planes and one jet based around WA that are there to provide medical services to the most remote areas. This goes from flying out regularly to organised GP clinics in remote communities, to the 24/7 on-call doctor, nurse and pilot team who will perform remote retrievals for ill and injured people across the bush. They then transfer the acute patients from the smaller regional hospitals down to Perth for specialised treatment.

Imagine this: you live in Kununurra – a reasonably big town in the north-east of WA – and your little daughter has just choked on a carrot stick. She cannot breathe and is turning blue. You perform basic first-aid and manage to drive her into Kununurra Hospital, where the doctors and nurses intubate her and get oxygen into her little body. But the carrot is still lodged in her lung and she is relying on a ventilator to breathe. She needs surgery that can only be performed 3000 kilometres away in Perth.

In Derby – the closest RFDS base – a phone is ringing. While your little girl is being stabilised in Kununurra there is a pilot checking the plane and finalising the flight plan. The doctor and nurse on call are deciding what equipment will be needed to maintain your child's life and loading it onto the plane. Inside a space that is not even big enough to stand up in are oxygen and ventilators, a full array of monitoring equipment, defibrillators and drugs. That tiny metal cylinder is a pressure cooker of a critical-care unit with everything necessary to keep your little girl's body functioning long enough to get her to the help she needs.

Meanwhile, in Port Hedland, another phone is ringing. This time it's a retrieval. This means someone outside a hospital needs to be rescued. A grader driver on a station has got chest pains and he's going grey and struggling to breathe. It's another Priority One call, so the team has an hour to assemble their equipment and get in the air. Even as the plane is being loaded, the doctor is on the phone talking to the fellas looking after the driver and asking the important questions: is he conscious? Is he taking any medication? What is his pulse? The doctor will be directing the station people on how to sit the driver and what drugs to get out of the big green RFDS box. When the plane arrives, he's immediately put onto oxygen and cannulas are pushed into his veins to deliver him the medication he needs to ease the strain on his damaged heart.

These are just two examples of what the RFDS might experience, but there is no such thing as a typical day in the job. Like station life, this is not a nine-to-five job. I was warned on day one to take a bag of essentials with me because you never know where you might end up.

I wish I had taken that advice seriously as I am writing this at midnight from a faceless hotel in Perth where all I have is my empty lunchbox, the scrubs I'm standing up in and a hi-vis vest. Let me tell you, it's a damn sight colder in Perth than it was in Hedland this morning. We loaded the plane to pick up a man with suspected appendicitis at a remote Indigenous community and transport him to Karratha Hospital. From there we were tasked, redirected mid-flight and sent here, there and everywhere. Since this morning I've been off the plane at two mine sites and the Onslow airstrip. We were supposed to have a 'meet' at RFDS Meekatharra, but a Priority One diversion for a broken pelvis caused us to miss them.

All up, we were at work today for fourteen hours and nearly eight of them were in the air. Strict guidelines protect the RFDS crew from fatigue and, except in exceptional circumstances, the pilots can fly for only eight hours. That means we're grounded in Perth for the night for a break before flying home tomorrow. I'm exhausted, but exhilarated after such intense monitoring and patient care in the cramped, noisy, little plane.

The RFDS staff are without doubt a special breed of people. The nurses and doctors have a strong background in critical care or emergency medicine and the nursing staff are also trained midwives. They deal with intense and acute issues in the smallest of areas and are used to adapting to unusual and difficult circumstances without ever losing their heads. They never know if the day will end with them getting home to their families or whether they'll find themselves thrown into an emergency situation with no warning. But, like most bush workers, they will be smiling and thriving on the adventure, and maintaining a good sense of humour and a high regard for teamwork throughout.

When I ask the staff what attracts them to the job, they tell me how they love the challenges that remote work involves. No day is the same as the last, and you can travel all over this big and rambling state while using your skills. It is fulfilling work – and definitely not your typical nine-to-five.

Club Kalyeeda

Barbara Camp, Kalyeeda Station

We call it 'Club Kalyeeda', and, to be honest, it's a bit of a big deal. They say the crew that parties together stays together and I know I've partied with some of the best friends you could hope to meet on the verandah out at Kalyeeda. When you work from sparrow's fart to past dark, day in day out, with the same crowd – love 'em or hate 'em, you're gonna get close. And what you tend to find after living in each other's pockets for that length of time is that you learn to love each other like some sort of weird family. We sometimes considered that, instead of advertising for stockworkers on the station, we should put it out there as a dating camp – more than a few couples started their lives together while sitting around the campfire at Kalyeeda!

The social side of station life moves in a spiral. First, there's your core unit – the workers. With up to eight people using one shower of an evening, it is a bit of a ritual to sit and have a cold beer while waiting your turn. It's the perfect way to end a hard day – sitting around covered in red dirt and comparing stories from the day. With 5 o'clock starts being the norm we generally all hit our beds straight after dinner.

Things are a bit different on Saturday nights when Club Kalyeeda opens its doors. After a long week of work in the dust and sun, and looking forward to a relaxing Sunday off fishing or watching movies in the aircon, people tend to linger for a chat after dinner. Whether it's sitting around having a few beers on the verandah in the warm weather, or huddled around a bonfire when the desert chill sets in, it's always good to have a gossip with your mates.

Usually there's music – a bit of country and western always goes down a treat. Sometimes we're lucky and there's someone who can play a guitar.

Sometimes Club Kalyeeda gets a bit wilder. We've had some awesome nights riding practice bucking bulls made out of 44-gallon drums set on big suspension coils, or climbing the house water tank to check out the sunrise after a long night partying.

The social circle spirals out more when you meet up with other stations. When there's a bit of a lull in the mustering we might get some time to get off the property for a proper catch-up with other people in the area. Our next-door neighbours are Nerrimah Station – a mere forty-minute drive away. They host an annual cricket match for the local crowd. It's a long day of hard-out rivalry followed by an awesome barbeque of home-grown beef – a great day's wind-up at the end of the season.

But the gold standard of station socialising will always be the rodeos. Whether you watch or participate, this is where you catch up with other ringers, make friends, let your hair down and blow off some steam. Almost everyone who has worked on Kalyeeda has had a go at riding a steer at a rodeo. Some, like me, have a two-second career at rough riding before they meet the dirt and decide it isn't for them. Others, like my far more athletic husband, carry on for the elusive belt buckle awarded to the cowboy or girl who can hang on in style for eight seconds.

Either way, rodeos are a great way of catching up with mates or making new ones in an area where there's no phone reception to be constantly making Facebook status updates or cruising Tinder. It's the ultimate weekend getaway after weeks of only interacting with the same half-dozen people.

Funny though – when you do make it out into the wide world, you always end up gravitating back to your crew. That's what Club Kalyeeda's all about.

Business Diversification, aka the Kayleeda Outback Dating Service

Barbara Camp, Kalyeeda Station

A common theme in any conversation about the sustainability of outback station life is diversification. After the 2011 Live Export Ban, many families and businesses were suddenly faced with the loss of their livelihoods. It's only natural we would want to safeguard our futures and make sure we have alternative sources of income. This is to look after not only our families, but the land and livestock that relies on us. What seemed to be forgotten when live export was frozen overnight was that the land and livestock did not freeze along with it – cows were still standing in yards looking for hay, and diesel was still needed to drive out and start the bores so they had water. All this takes money, and so we started to look to alternative means of securing income. This has given rise to some wonderful new enterprises in the Kimberley.

Some people turned to cropping and installed huge pivots to grow their own hay and fodder. Others opened their homes as station stays to embrace the growing tourist market in this beautiful part of the world. I'm a great believer in playing to your strengths, so I proposed setting up an outback matchmaking service.

I know what you're thinking – it's hard enough to find Mr or Miss Right in a city where your pool of prospective partners is considerably bigger. Even now in the days of speed-dating and Tinder, trying to find that one-in-a-million fish in that big ol' sea is a challenge. So what are the chances of finding them when that sea suddenly becomes a pond cut off from the rest of the world, with a population of a dozen or so fish?

Maybe that's why it works so well. When you work together in a stock camp it can be a little like a pressure cooker. You are with a small group 24/7 in all sorts of circumstances, so a lot of the usual dating etiquette and practices go out of the window. You see them sleepy and grumpy after a week of 4 am starts, and you see them covered in muck and dust after an eighteen-hour day. Your 'first date' might be driving three hours into the desert to fix a bore, or riding together in the lead of a mob of cattle – there's certainly plenty of time to talk, but no time to worry about whether your lipstick has smudged or whether you should wait three days to text him.

Maybe it's the magic of the desert stars, or maybe there really is something running in the waters of the Fitzroy River, but Kalyeeda seems to be a bit of a hotspot for creating lasting romances. I would even go as far as to say it breeds true love. I'm certainly happy with my own outcome from using the Kalyeeda Outback Dating Service, but don't just take my word for it – let's hear some testimonials from some of our other happy customers.

Justin and Julie

This lovely couple met while working on the stock camp back in the 1980s, when the north-west really was wild. Kalyeeda's resident horse guru recalls the time he watched this feisty cowgirl chase a rogue cow into the scrub on her horse, only to emerge from the other side of the bush a few minutes later sitting on the cow instead – she was so determined she would not lose the beast. Justin's eyes get a sparkle when he talks of Julie's fighting spirit and determination. 'She's one tough girl,' he told me.

Josh and Emma

Described by many as perfectly suited, this beautiful couple met at Kalyeeda more than ten years ago when Emma was the station cook and Josh was head stockman. The talented bush-poet and his beautiful lady are now married and raising their two gorgeous kids the outback way.

James and Sarah

A chippy and a student nurse, James and Sarah met when they worked the stock camp together in 2012. They first bonded through their shared passion for racehorses. Love blossomed as they grasped for each other's hands while falling off their horses' bums trying to pose for the above photo … just kidding! They now live in New Zealand where they are featured regularly in the best-dressed pages in the society press.

Jeremy and Angharad

The Welsh city girl with a masters in chemistry met the professional Kiwi feral with a degree in agribusiness that he'd rather not mention in the 2013 stock camp. It was a steep learning curve for both of them: he taught her to ride a motorbike; she taught him how to make a salad dressing. Beautiful. This comedy-act duo continue to keep it real wherever they travel, be it playing cricket on the lawns of England or busking on the streets of Christchurch.

Darren and Diane

It worked for German backpacker Diane like a letter to Santa. She requested a tall, good-looking Aussie bloke on the store order one month and then fell in love with Darren, the local mechanic, who brought the boxes of veggies out to us. Two years down the track they're still madly in love and she's helping him run his business in Broome.

What will the next year bring? Will the magic of the muster bind another young couple together in the hobbles of love? Perhaps you would like to try out the Kalyeeda Outback Dating Service and would like some more information on this nascent business enterprise?

Watch this space.

Postscript: I pitched the idea of the Kalyeeda Outback Dating Service to my father-in-law, big boss Peter Camp. As I see it, all we would need do is tweak the wording of our 'Stockperson Wanted' advert and perhaps ask applicants to enclose a photo – then we could start charging for our services! Unfortunately, Peter was not particularly receptive to the idea.

Peter Camp would like it to be known that he will not be hiring staff based on romantic availability. He prefers to hire based on such characteristics as a good attitude, appropriate experience and enthusiasm. Other attributes he looks for in a prospective stockperson include physical capability, a good sense of humour and a love of animals.

Is it just me or do the attributes of a good ringer sound quite similar to what you see written time and again on the 'searching for' section of dating websites?

The Stuff-up Jar

Barbara Camp, Kalyeeda Station

Everyone makes mistakes. We're only human. Unfortunately, living and working in remote areas means that what might be a minor error can turn into a pretty big deal. If you forget to buy coffee when you live in town, it's not so much of an issue. When you forget to put it on the store's order for a station and don't realise until you get back from an eight-hour round trip, this can cause a problem. Station work involves being in close quarters with a small community of people who, apart from being grumpy without caffeine, are usually keen to exact punishment for small errors.

Enter the birth of what I will call, for the sake of polite company, the 'stuff-up jar'. It's a fairly simple idea, and functions like a swear jar. On the sideboard at Kalyeeda, next to the industrial-sized bottles of sunscreen and insect repellent, sits a large jar that contains a load of coins and notes and a few crumpled IOUs. Next to it is a book with two columns – one labelled 'Crime', the other 'Dubious Excuse'. It's a standard fee for an oopsie: five dollars, which goes into a communal bar tab whenever we get time off for a night in town or a rodeo.

Looking back at the stuff-up book there have been a range of crimes – not to mention some humdingers of dubious excuses. The most common one is the standard 'bucked off my horse/motorbike':

> Name: Barb
>
> Crime: Bucked off Cowboy the stockhorse. Again.
>
> Dubious excuse: Can't ride cowboys.

Also included are some truly bizarre 'how on earth did you ever think that was a good idea?!' situations:

Name: Gareth

Crime: Sprayed himself in the eye with a gas-powered drench gun.

Dubious excuse: Looking to see why the nozzle was blocked ...

Name: James

Crime: Losing an entire wheel from the ute while out on a bore run.

Dubious excuse: I could swear I'd tightened those wheel nuts ...

And then there's the endless 'bogged this or that piece of machinery':

Name: Peter

Crime: Bogged the dozer while getting carried away making a creek crossing.

Dubious excuse: None – he's the boss. You don't laugh. You just don't.

Most of these 'crimes' are fairly minor and – in hindsight at least – pretty funny. Sometimes, however, a small slip of the mind can end up with big repercussions. I will never be allowed to forget the time I had a blonde moment and took the wrong turning with the horse truck when heading out to pick up the mustering team and their six stockhorses.

Unfortunately, while I blithely assumed the road would be suitable for the height of the truck, it was not.

Unfortunately, in the argument between a low-hanging branch and the truck crate, the branch won.

Unfortunately, the crate and truck parted company. That was the only crate we had that was able to transport the six stockhorses.

Unfortunately, the team were literally a full day's ride from home.

When you have to explain to half a dozen ringers, who are saddle-sore and tired from a week of hard riding and camping out in their swags, that they will not be heading back to the homestead for a proper shower and bed, but instead have another day's walk ahead of them, you are not a popular person.

Five bucks, Barb. And then some.

Mustering and yard work are hotspots for these little slip-ups that become a big deal. The biggest culprit? 'Who left that gate open?!'

When working cattle through the yards, the basic idea is quite simple. You start with a huge pen full of all of the different cattle that make up your paddock – herd bulls, breeder cows, calves, youngsters ready for weaning, cattle ready for selling and so on. They are slowly filtered down, one at a time, into different pens with their peers and tallied accordingly. This is a time-consuming job that we aim to do as quickly as possible to minimise the time the cows have to be stuck in the yards.

Picture the scene: you've been up since 4 am to start drafting on daylight, and managed to sort 800 head of cattle into six different lines before smoko, intending to walk the first mob out to their new paddock after you've gone up to the homestead for a break. Everyone is tired and keen for a feed and a cold drink, so you pack up quickly and jump onto the Toyota to head home. Unfortunately, someone has not latched the gate between two pens properly and one of the curious little weaner heifers has gone to scratch her head against it … Looks like we're re-drafting.

Variations of this situation crop up again and again. It's bad enough when just two pens get mixed up. Just imagine spending the whole day with choppers, horses, bikes and bull catchers cleaning out a paddock, only for someone to leave the gate open for the next vehicle coming along to close – but no one does. The next day, all the cattle are back, chilling out around the waterhole, and everyone is denying being the last through the gate.

Stuff-ups will always happen and they say experience is the best teacher. Once you've messed something up and paid the price – whether it's scraping yourself off the floor after stacking the motorbike, digging a vehicle out of a bog hole or living another week without any coffee – it's great to know your mates will be there to fine you for it as well.

Hey, at least you know next time you go for a night out there will be a few drinks waiting for everyone on tab.

Our Kimberley Experience

Jed O'Brien, Liveringa Station

My first year here was pretty flat out. It took a while to find my feet and work out what the role entailed, then longer again to work out how to do it. So it was a little chaotic for that while. I found myself doing a lot of things twice, finding out the hard way what worked and what didn't. I seldom saw our front yard in daylight (it was only at the end of the dry that I finally got to see the great job my wife, Karen, had done with the gardens).

Of course I need to remember (and I am often reminded!) that managing Liveringa is my dream, not Karen's. After spending nearly twenty years in the north, a few as a young ringer and about eight in northern cattle research, I thought I could have a crack at managing a larger cattle station myself. In January 2010, we left the comforts of a government job and the great little NT community of Douglas Daly and arrived at Liveringa to the sweltering heat, the driest wet season on record and twice the working hours.

While I was busy in the cattle yards, Karen was as busy at home, on her own with the three kids. Dealing with school, nappies, the Kimberley heat and dust, isolation … She once told me that 'she could be a single parent anywhere; why on earth would she pick Liveringa Station, in the remote west Kimberley?' Good point. We have four kids now so I must have made it home at some point that year (even if it was just for a short while). Mind you, four kids under seven is enough to keep anyone away from the house!

But after nearly four years, I'm a lot more organised and less stressed about all the stuff that still goes pear-shaped every day at Liveringa, and the seven or eight kilograms that I lost in my first year has managed to relax its way back on.

That said, a day at Liveringa still never ever goes according to plan and there are always countless things left undone.

Here, we are responsible for 22,000 head of cattle, each needing to be mustered, drafted and counted (twice a year if possible); calves weaned and branded; weaners trucked to the station yard; older animals and culls pulled out to be spayed; and sale cattle sorted and trucked to market. Most years we will brand 8000 to 9000 young cattle. The sale program is substantial. Every Friday between April and September 2013, we trucked three road trains of cattle to market or agistment – about 3500 cows and nearly 6000 weaners in total.

Because we live above the 'tick line', nearly all the cattle we sell need to go through the plunge dip as part of their preparation for trucking. Then they are checked for ticks, and dipped again before being trucked to market. Cattle dipping is a bit of a tourist attraction at Liveringa; if you visit you can't leave until you watch some cattle go through the bath. After dipping more than 10,000 head twice each, the 'tour guides' have become a bit weary of it, though, and the novelty has worn off.

There are five sets of cattle yards on Liveringa and we muster surrounding paddocks to each of these yards. Because they are so far away from the main station, Inkata yards, the ringers need to camp out at these yards until the muster is complete. We have station horses that the stock-camp ringers ride when working the cattle, but given the sheer size of the breeder paddocks (between 50 and 300 square kilometres), the helicopter is an essential part of our operation and we have a contractor's machine and pilot based here throughout the dry.

One week we set out to walk 1200 weaners thirty-five kilometres from an out yard to the station trucking yard. The mustering, drafting and segregating took three days and it's a two-day walk home to the yard. On the night of the first day's walk, the weaners took fright, smashed the fence and 'went bush' into a fifty-square-kilometre paddock with 1100 breeder cows in it – leaving eight ringers, bridles in hand, scratching their heads! So much for next week's trucking instalment. Those weaners had to now wait in that paddock until we did the second muster the following month. Like I said, things seldom go according to plan and a good sense of humour is the best defence.

During the dry season every week is busy; some more than others. In August 2013, with no notice, we had a contract to supply a shipment of 800 heifers and

1000 steers. At the time, prices were pretty ordinary – but a sale is a sale and every opportunity had to be taken. We got the phone call on Sunday night saying that the road trains would be here to load on Thursday and Friday.

'Thursday, you reckon – of course we can handle that …'

It takes two days and three helicopters to muster the heifers out of the bush paddock and half a day with two machines to muster the steers. So in six days, with little sleep and no time to miss it, we mustered and pre-drafted about 2500 heifers, then re-drafted 1000 of them to secure the sale line. We then walked the remaining 1500 heifers seven kilometres to their new home. Then we drafted 2200 steers, trucked 400 and bushed 700 near the yard. We dipped, fed and redipped the 650 weaners and sale cows we still had in the yard waiting to go south. Then we drafted, weighed and dipped the 700 weaners and cows for next Friday's trucking, pregnancy-tested 200 heifers (in the dark) and branded 150 feedlot weaners, just for fun.

We ended up trucking out eight road trains of sale cattle that week, plus the obligatory three trains of Friday's cattle to go south, leaving about 700 head to truck south the following Friday and a further 700-odd in a holding paddock for trucking the week after. So by the end of the week the contract was filled. And at 4.30 pm on Friday, when the blunt end of the last truck disappeared, in replica of my own thoughts, Brent, one of our staff, turned to me and asked, 'What the hell just happened?' The Rec Club Bar seemed like the only logical place for the reply.

The dry season is the time when we get everything done, but the wet is my favourite time of year; it can be a time to slow down a bit. The build-up to it is hot, humid and often unbearable, but that is the price we pay for the rain. And when it rains here, it rains; the grass becomes green overnight, the cattle are healthy, dams fill and streams rise.

It is generally late in the wet when the Fitzroy River can become a big problem. It has a huge catchment and when the river floods it makes Liveringa look like an inland sea, with water for miles. We have about four days' warning before the floodwater at Fitzroy Crossing makes its way to Liveringa. We usually carry about 6000 head of cattle on the river country and it can become a mad rush to move the cattle to higher ground or they will perish. Depending on the amount of water coming down, this can mean three helicopters for five days. In the 2011 flood, we were only one day ahead of the water as it spent four days spreading across the landscape, paddock by paddock.

The river country, by the nature of its thick tree growth, creeks and channels, is very hard to muster cleanly at any time of the year. Consequently, there are many feral bulls and cows (two- to ten-year-old 'cleanskins' or unbranded bulls and cows of questionable genetic composition) along the river system. While constantly trying to improve the breeding of our cattle herd it is important that these undesirable cattle are mustered and sent to market, or they can affect the quality of the herd. But they are wily, cunning and reluctant to relocate. They can hide under vegetation and ignore or run underneath the chopper or simply stand defiant.

Flying over the flooded river you might see a cohort of these defiant ferals 'suffering in their jocks' as they stand on a small piece of high ground, belly deep in the rising floodwater. They will need to stand there for six days or more. I have heard it said that if an animal stands in water for a week, their hooves will fall off. Well, they must grow back too, because I'm sure these same mongrel cattle were still trying to outrun the helicopters again the next year!

Another part of my job that I really enjoy is working with and teaching the younger members of staff: the jackaroos and jillaroos, or ringers. They keep me entertained to some extent with their antics, and often 'out there' conversations. They also help to keep me fit as I try to outrun or simply keep up with them. I think it's important that the staff enjoy their work; I reckon you get more out of them that way. I try to make sure that they go home having learnt something. I'm au fait with all the mod cons now – I know all about iPods and iPhones, Snapchats, FaceTime and Bookface. These guys help me to recognise what's cool and hip and what's not. Usually they are, and I'm not.

Karen and I are both gregarious, and while we live a long way away from our immediate families and old friends, for the most part, we have both enjoyed the job and the lifestyle in the isolation of the West Kimberley. We both appreciate the space, the landscape and nature. And although it doesn't happen often these days, we both enjoy a chance to get out on the horses.

Maintaining a happy and harmonious life on the station depends a lot on the people around us, those we live and work with. Usually we have the mix pretty close to right, with a good blend of old and young (at forty-six, I'm still not real sure which category I'm in).

Some people work a nine-to-five job that they don't really enjoy, but it pays the bills. I think for most people in our industry the opposite is true: we enjoy the job, but it sometimes barely pays the bills. I reckon I'm one of the lucky ones; I have been in the livestock industry my whole life and I can't remember having a bad day at work. In a lot of ways my work is my hobby. I can't imagine working in another industry. And as for the next four years at Liveringa, well, it's like they say, 'happy wife, happy life'. I guess I will be wandering around the cattle yards at Liveringa living the dream, as long as Karen and the kids are still happy with the deal.

Pressure and Release

Jed O'Brien, Liveringa Station

It's all about keeping things low stress; it's vital to the operation. We want calm cows, horses and people. It's a simple principle: you apply pressure to get some movement and release the pressure after the desired response. That's how we get cattle through the yard, horses through a turn and ringers through the year. Pressure and release.

The way we work cattle at Liveringa is taken very seriously. New staff are inducted to the low-stress stock-handling principles and we talk about it all the time throughout the year (well, I do, ad nauseam I suspect). Every year for the past six years Jim Lindsay has also been invited to teach and reinforce the methods and principles of low-stress stock-handling.

The cattle-handling stuff is a bit old school in many ways, stuff that may have been lost over the years due to the transient nature of our industry. Jim puts in a modern take, a few new ideas and a fair bit of animal psychology. I won't go into all the principles but one is important, which I apply to the running of the whole business, not just the cows. Pressure and release.

Generally the pressure comes from simply being in a cow's personal space (or flight zone). It's a bit like that weird and annoying guy at the bar who stands so close that you need to keep moving away. Well, that's me in the back yard with the cows. Perhaps we're all a bit weird and annoying over here at Liveringa …

If done properly you end up with a method of moving cattle without sticks and whips, without noise and frustration, and without getting cattle and people stressed and injured.

We don't get it right all the time. There are times when the cattle do get stirred up and we need to quickly climb, or get lifted, over the fence. There are 20,000 cows on Liveringa and there's gotta be a few that woke up on the wrong side of the boab.

But we keep trying. We learn and use these stock-handling techniques because we care for the cows, we give a damn. We want to get the job done efficiently and safely. Cattle that are under stress place people under stress (and vice versa).

Horses can come to work in a bad mood too, so it's important to teach the staff techniques to enhance their riding ability, and help them be kinder to and get higher performances from the horses. We have had a number of horsemanship schools with staff over the years and there's one or two old hands here as well that can assist the ringers along the way. Riding a horse is a bit like moving a cow. You apply pressure or discomfort to ask it to do something and release the pressure as a reward for doing it. Although don't try this technique on the back of a cow as it seldom works …

We still have the odd worker's compensation claim because of horse-riding accidents, so we haven't got this a hundred per cent yet either. But getting a buster from a horse gives a young ringer something to brag about at the bar, and that's important too.

There is a difference between pressure and stress. Stress is pressure with no way out or no foreseeable release. Pressure needs to be released before it becomes stress. That release can come in different ways; for the cow it can be an open gate, for the horse it's one step sideways and for the ringer it's the rodeo in two weeks' time.

Now let's put some pressure on the people. The speed at which we can do the first weaning round is vital to the productivity of the station. Weaning the calves takes the nutritional pressure away from the cows. This improves reproduction rates and reduces cow mortality. Increasing breeder nutrition or maintaining their condition through the long dry season is our greatest challenge and weaning is our greatest tool. We start weaning round one in April and work paddock by paddock until we finish in July.

The stock camp works flat out from April. If we are to take time off work between April and July it is under sufferance from me as there is always something more to do or get done. However, while often difficult to achieve, it is important that the odd day off is forthcoming; again, it's a low-stress principle. We need to take some time to release the pressure and have a bit of fun along the way.

In the past we have held various events at and through our social club: quiz nights (that was a pretty short party), 'Liveringa has Talent' (we all got to bed early that night too), mini Olympics and the odd birthday party. Flyboarding is one of the latest crazes to hit the country and last year we got in on that craze. Yep, Liveringa, too cool for school. The jet ski arrived on the dam ten kilometres from the homestead and the jet boots were strapped on. Everyone got to have a go at flying and had a heap of fun, although the cows and crocs were a bit annoyed with us for turning their social gathering place into a theme park.

Through July and August I find myself organising the work program around rodeos and race meetings. This weekend is the annual Derby campdraft and rodeo. Into the truck we load the best horses, swags, some tucker and the town hats, and test our skills in the campdraft, rodeo and dance arena. The team has a great time at the drafts and rodeos – they can get off the station, let their hair down, drink some beer, and catch up and fraternise with staff from other stations – we go to three or four throughout the year.

July through August is the Broome Race Carnival and for the next few weeks it's the humble fascinator that will be dictating Liveringa's mustering program. This week it's also Ladies Day, and Karen will need to spend two nights in Broome to get ready for and over it. What's worse is that she is taking Cath, the governess, with her. So I will be under a bit of pressure, with little release, looking after our four kids for three days.

Next week is the Broome Cup and the entire team will be going to that one too. Karen has a good friend in Broome who designs and makes headpieces and fascinators. You know the kind that matches your shoes and handbag but offers little shade to your face? Well, apparently she is very good at it and is taking her wares to a New York fashion show in September.

'Great,' I thought when I heard about it. 'Oh shit' was next when Karen told me she was going too.

A trip to New York is a great opportunity for some well-earned release from six years of pressure at Liveringa. Ten days with the kids: I'm pleased she's not taking the govvie to this one. That much pressure on management should be a sackable offence for both of them.

But let's not get too carried away with how much socialising we do at Liveringa. The staff at Liveringa work pretty damn hard; they love the job (that's what they all say anyway) and their commitment doesn't go unnoticed or unappreciated. Taking time out for socialising allows them to enjoy a different side to their job in the Kimberley and life on the station. A contented team has a healthy balance of pressure and release. That's important to me as a manager. We need to look after these guys – I want them to come back next year!

Extreme Childhood

Karen Forrest, Liveringa Station

Visitors who often come during the dry and stay for a few days or weeks will tell us how lucky we are to be living this life. They fail to remember that they are on holidays, and that for many months of the year I can't even get my kids to leave the house because it's too hot outside, which pretty much restricts me to these four walls too!

For most of the mustering season I feel like a single mother – and in my rather less than positive moments, I sometimes think that if I were going to be a single mother, I would at least elect to live near friends, family or at the very least a town. I realise that many husbands don't get home till dark each day – this is not exclusive to the Kimberley station life. However, I don't know anyone else (in my old life, that is) whose husband also works every weekend with perhaps half a day off on a Sunday – during which time he still needs to go and feed cattle.

Apart from the obvious challenges – nowhere to pop in for a coffee; nowhere to wear, let alone buy, current fashion; no opportunities to wear a cupboard full of great knee-high boots; old friends live in another timezone; new friends live more than two hours away … I'm finding it increasingly difficult to stop this list … – I consider raising kids out here the biggest.

We have three boys and a girl aged two, four, seven and eight. The boys all do school through Kimberley School of the Air (KSOTA), based in Derby. We are lucky enough to have Catherine, a trained teacher from the UK, acting as our home tutor and governess. She does a great job with the kids, and I'm sure they've really benefited by having this 'one-on-three' time in the schoolroom every day. However, I worry about the things they are missing out on by not being able to attend a 'mainstream' school. While I feel happy that we can protect their innocence and play a greater role in nurturing the values we deem important out here, there are valuable social and resilience skills I fear they will not learn through not being part of that 'schoolyard culture'.

Occasionally, because we live in the bush, I actually forget that the kids don't always know how to behave in town. What is acceptable and totally normal out here is not always OK in amongst the general populace! About three years ago, I confused my three boys enormously when I turned around to see two of them relieving themselves from the top of the ramp outside the front doors of the supermarket and was clearly mortified.

'But, Mum, you said it was OK to wee on dirt!'

Well, I guess they were aiming at a patch of brown earth … Obviously, bush rules don't apply in all situations and one must endeavour to be clear about this!

Apart from the concerns regarding potential social ineptness, I also worry about all sorts of things in relation to them living this life: is the schooling system 'through the air' good enough? How do they compare to kids in the rest of Australia? Will they ever get to enjoy team sports or learn valuable musical skills? Where will they go for high school? Will we have to send them to boarding school? Can we possibly afford to? Will they have the necessary skills to make friends in a mainstream school?

But in reality my concerns aren't dissimilar to those of parents everywhere. Same worries, just in a slightly different context – and, let's face it, I am in the privileged position of being able to be essentially a stay-at-home mum because my work here can be done from home within school hours and in between our daughter's naps.

Really, life for the kids here is pretty awesome – they are all learning to ride motorbikes and horses. They get to swim most days in the station pool. They have limited access to the abundance of technology that drives so many other parents crazy. They get to compete in the rodeo gymkhanas and have learnt to cope with long car trips without the need for technology. They have mastered patience while I spend over an hour-and-a-half shopping for groceries. They don't experience peer pressure and remain gorgeously innocent. And through this lifestyle they have formed an incredible closeness as siblings.

So, you know what? Maybe those visitors are right. Apart from the fact that we still have to deal with snakes, perhaps life up here isn't so bad after all. Once again (it happens annually) I have talked myself into the realisation that life out here on a Kimberley cattle station really isn't that bad at all … and my husband will be super impressed that he didn't even have to be part of this conversation!

The 'Don't Do' List

Catherine White, Liveringa Station

As a teacher, detailed planning becomes part of your daily existence. There are lesson plans, plans for where you would like each student to be at the end of the week or term or year. You plan for field trips, assemblies, camps and performances. Then you evaluate your plans: did everything work out OK? Were the targets met? What should be done differently next time? The children are expected to get in on it too. Plans are there for a reason: they help us get to where we want to go, be it in a story or in real life. It's good to be prepared.

In early January 2014, I stood, swaying slightly, in my friend Phyllis's London home. 'I'll see you in six months,' I said for the second or third time. We'd agreed that Phyllis shouldn't get up the next morning to see me off, partly because I was getting a very early flight to Perth, but mostly because the sensible plan of going to bed at a reasonable time had turned into a lot of wine-drinking instead. Our conversation had started to become circular, with me insisting I'd see her soon, and Phyllis being equally insistent when telling me, 'You never know what might happen; stop writing things off.'

I stumbled off to bed, wondering why she didn't believe me. Couldn't she see that I was a woman with a plan? This plan was to spend half a year in Australia as a kind of career break. After six years' teaching in various countries, I felt burnt out and disillusioned with my career choice. I thought I'd try out a few different jobs and see some of the country before heading back to Europe, maybe with a new career path.

Accompanying this plan was a mental list of things that would not be happening – a 'Don't Do' list. For starters, there would be no teaching. I wanted to leave my job behind for the whole six months so that I could gain some perspective. I was also adamant there would be no relationships and definitely no falling in love. To add to this, I'd pretty much decided against living in a remote area after a recent bad experience living and working in Borneo. Finally, I had absolutely no desire to stay longer than six months in Australia; it was too far from friends and family and I couldn't see myself moving to any country on a permanent basis.

I arrived in Perth safely, and my trip started well. I moved into a great house with lovely housemates. Then I picked up a terrible job as a charity fundraiser, which involved a lot of high-fiving. I lasted three days – that was all it took for me to gain a little perspective on teaching. Standing in a shopping centre harassing strangers for money – money that will more than likely end up being used to pay someone like me to stand in a shopping centre and harass more strangers for money – makes you realise how good it feels to have a normal job.

I'd heard about governess jobs and it seemed like it might be a kinder form of teaching. Maybe it would help me to remember my reasons for wanting to be a teacher in the first place. Maybe I didn't need to adhere to my 'Don't Do' list quite so strictly.

My phone interview with Karen confirmed that Liveringa was the place for me. Her enthusiasm for her children's education and the way she spoke about past governesses gave me a good feeling about my tentative steps back into the field of education.

I said a sad goodbye to my lovely Perth housemates.

'I'll see you in six months,' I continued to insist.

'Bet you fall in love with a jackeroo and don't come back,' they replied with a laugh.

I laughed back, mainly because I didn't know what a jackeroo was.

I arrived at Liveringa, still trying to decide if I was making the right decision. I'd made so many questionable decisions in the past, I wasn't sure if I could trust my gut instinct telling me that this was a good idea.

It was February, still baking hot but beautiful, green – and wet. The floodwater surrounding the station gave the impression of the sea being nearby and it soon felt like home.

'Wow, I'm going to find it really hard to leave in six months,' I thought to my idiot self, still somehow convinced.

The remains of the plan went down the drain a few weeks later, when I met someone who changed things quite dramatically. Yes, I went and fell in love with a jackeroo called Jake Weincke.

A year-and-a-half later and I am still at Liveringa and Australia is looking a lot more permanent for me. Clearly nothing really went to plan, and my 'Don't Do' list became more of a shopping list, but I'm very grateful as I genuinely love my life. I live in a beautiful home, in an incredible part of the world with someone I love. I get to see the sunrise every day and spend weekends fishing, horse riding or just exploring. I've realised how much I love living in a remote area and how my past experiences are just that – in the past. I go for runs with my dog and stop to take endless photos that do no justice to the landscape and I often wonder what luck brought me here.

My job as a governess is the balance in teaching that I was looking for. Don't get me wrong, there are frustrations, but not having to deal with school politics, classes of thirty, staffrooms and general interference has its real upsides.

I often think of my friend's drunken advice and how insistent she was that I stay open to all possibilities. There were times when I almost forced myself to stick to my original plan: I nearly refused to look at governess jobs, even though they interested me, and I nearly stuck to my original six-month term at Liveringa, for fear of the decisions that I would have to make later down the line. But in the end I'm so glad that I threw my 'Don't Do' list out the window.

All the Small Things

Tom Robertson, Liveringa Station

Waking at 4.30 am to the familiar 'knock, knock, knock' of the generator springing to life signals the beginning of another day at Liveringa stock camp. No doubt today will be similar to many that came before it, and many that will follow.

Whether it be tailing the mob as the chopper pilots work their magic above you, yarding up, drafting or branding cattle, fencing, assisting in pulling a bore or loading a road train, you can guarantee no matter what day of the week it is or what task you are currently undertaking they will all have some things in common.

They will most likely be long, hot, sweaty, dusty, windy, noisy, chaotic and a whole range of other emotions all rolled into one and at the end of the day you'll crawl into your swag and do it all again tomorrow. For a split second I may have even caught myself wondering, 'What the bloody hell am I doing this for?'

So what the bloody hell am I doing it for? It's simple. During my time studying agricultural science at Charles Sturt University I heard endless yarns from fellow classmates about how they spent their gap year learning the ropes of being a 'Ringer from the Top End'. Instantly I added it to the bucket list and knew that before too long I had to get my fix of the North Australian cattle experience that I had heard so much about.

It was a bold decision to leave my career as a broad-acre cropping agronomist, the town I had called home for the past six years, family and friends so that I could venture to the opposite corner of Australia to become a ringer. Was it the right decision? Absolutely.

For me it seems to be all the small things that constantly remind you of why station life is so unique, and truly an amazing experience. Little things like the stock-camp crew piling in the LandCruiser troopy before daylight, not many words being spoken as most people feel it was only five minutes ago that they were climbing into bed. We begin the fifty-kilometre journey out to McCreas yard and as we drive over the levy bank you begin to see the sunrise over the flood plain with Moulamen Hill standing tall in the background. Inevitably camera phones begin to flicker and a mumble from the back seat says 'first-world problems, hey'. A swift reminder that if the truly stunning sunrise is the biggest of our issues at that moment, then there isn't much to complain about.

Or it could be the solitude that comes with being based at stock camp. No phone reception means no Facebook, emails, phone calls or messages and this can sometimes last for weeks on end. At first it seems like quite a daunting prospect; however, you soon get used to it, and after a short while come to enjoy it. It puts you back in touch with the simple pleasures of life such as sitting around the campfire reflecting on the day's events, reading a book, showering under the stars, or flicking through the iPod and playing your favourite tunes as we eagerly await the delicious feast that Linda is about to serve up.

A personal favourite stock-camp activity is 'Around the Grounds with Woodrow', a segment that takes place during dinner whereby each member of the stock camp must take it in turns to describe the highlight of their day. It may sound a little silly, and some of you may think, how could you possibly find a highlight in every single day? You soon realise that no matter how dull or uneventful your day may have seemed, with a little thought you can always find a highlight.

It is all these tiny little things that amount to so much, and in no way leave me questioning the decision I made to venture to the Top End. As our illustrious leader Jed O'Brien would say 'It all adds to the romance'. Those long, hot, sweaty, dusty, windy, noisy, chaotic days all pale into insignificance when you stand back and take five minutes to reflect on why we are all so lucky to be living the lifestyle we do.

70 kilometres/hr and 180 bpm

Katharina (Tini) Wachholz, Lochon Contracting

Y̶ou catch wild bulls?
How?
Where?
Why?

I am sitting in the passenger seat of the 'blue dog', one of our bull buggies. The terrain is rough, the grass is high. Locky spots the 'flat' in the distance and while radioing the helicopter pilot to see how far away he is and how many bulls he is bringing out of the scrub, he heads for the bull-catching flat. We have to get out of the long grass. It would be suicide run chasing a bull in this. Ant beds and gullies, tree stumps and logs are hiding in the thick undergrowth. Hitting one of these at high speed would be incredibly dangerous.

Seeing the chopper in the distance, we suddenly spot the first bull trotting out of the wattle. 'Here we go', I think. Locky watches, slowly approaches the bull from an angle to encourage him to keep walking onto the flat. There's no grass, no trees and plenty of room to circle the cleanskin (unmarked) bulls. I pull my hat down, push my foot against the frame of the buggy and hold on tight for the high-speed chase ahead of us.

My heart starts pumping and the adrenaline kicks in, all senses super-sharp. There is no room for error. And I am only the passenger. I have never felt unsafe sitting next to Locky. There is an art to driving the buggy and I know he has the skills to do it. He watches the animal closely, he scans the ground, he looks out for obstacles, and adjusts his course and speed accordingly.

The right moment to roll a bull is easy to miss. Experience is what you need to determine this moment. The bull must not be fresh, so you chase him around on a clear flat with good vision. He must not be fully exhausted either. When you see

Running repairs

GLENFORRIE STATION

YARRIE STATION

COUNTRY DOWNS STATION

Nikki and a bovine friend

KOORDARRIE STATION

KOORDARRIE STATION

The de Pledge family's life on the station

BLINA STATION

Constance and Matt get married

DAMPIER DOWNS STATION

Anne-Marie and Mike

ANNA PLAINS STATION

KALYEEDA STATION

James and Barbara: honeymooners on horseback

Need that bovine–human dictionary!

LIVERINGA STATION

Karen, Jed and family

All in a day's work
at Liveringa

LIVERINGA
STATION

LOCHON CONTRACTING

Downtime

Locky, Tini and team

Chris Daniell

MYROODAH STATION

Station staff and trainees

THE McDONALD FAMILY

Mel, Judd and baby Trent

Cooking ribs the outback way

YEEDA STATION

STEPHANIE COOMBES

Steph and Snooki

Steph changing her first tyre: it fell off 30 minutes later as she chased a rogue cow

MT BUNDY STATION

Ben, Kasey and Bec Witham

YOUGAWALLA STATION

Doodie showing Angus where to find conkerberries

Jane Sale

Jane and Haydn

Matilda

'Pink Lady'

The Yougawalla team

YOUGAWALLA
STATION

ALEXANDRIA STATION

Weaner yards

Head stockwoman Stacey Haucke

EVERSLEIGH STATION

Jenny Underwood and Goliath

The life of a single mum/station manager

WHITE KANGAROO STATION

The view from horseback

him slowing down, starting to look back while running, you prod him on the hip with the tyres mounted to the front of the buggy and roll him.

The extended frame at the buggy's front sits over the bull and holds him down on the ground. This is the moment I have been waiting for. With a strap in hand, I quickly jump off and put my foot on the neck of this huge cleanskin bull (no brand, no earmark, he is a free roamer). It is a strong bull with sharp horns and an attitude. Locky is right there. He puts his foot on the neck too and grabs one of the bull's horns. I bend down and start wrapping the strap around the knuckles of the front legs as quickly and tightly as I can. Restrained by the strap, we leave the bull and jump back in the catcher.

The dust hasn't settled yet, and the helicopter is already bringing out another few bulls. It's on again. Another chase, another bull. While we pursue the next cleanskin, the other bull buggy, which has been sitting back in the distance, comes in and holds the rest of the bulls to keep them from running back into the scrub. Dust is swirling, bulls are getting chased, rolled, tied and left sitting there, wondering what just happened.

Before we have even tied off the last bull, the other buggy has already started loading the first one onto the truck. This is what you call teamwork and a reliable and alert crew. Everyone in the team should be able to take any position, therefore we rotate. So, today was my day as the strapper, tomorrow we swap around. The only consistency is Locky as the actual bull catcher, the operator of the 'blue dog', and if necessary he can be his own strapper.

Although bull catching may sound like a big adventure with a thrill element to it, it is hard work and requires the greatest care when carried out. It must be done quickly to limit the stress on the animal, and it's hugely important not to damage the bull. We don't want to damage either the animal or the people – or the gear, for that matter. As with everything you do, you have to be careful.

So, that's the 'how'.

Why do we do it?

There are various reasons why.

Kimberley cattle stations can be as big as one or two million acres (and bigger), with cattle spread all over the place. Creeks and rivers, thick bush and mountain ranges, sandy deserts and salt flats can make certain parts of a station inaccessible. Not all corners can be reached by road. Helicopters are often the only force during a muster. While cattle in general tend to stay in mobs and follow a herd that is being pushed by a chopper, male cattle can be quite hot-headed and stubborn, but also smart and creative. Some of these bulls and mickeys get left behind simply because they don't want to go. They hide in creek beds and under big leafy trees or stand in the middle of a flat just staring at the helicopter. There is only so much a chopper can do without losing the main herd, which is their priority.

In these particularly impenetrable areas of a station, where cleanskin bulls roam that have been getting away with their little tricks for years, it is a good idea to bring in a buggy and a small 4×4 truck to take these scrubbers out of their scrub.

Some stations in the Kimberley have been reverted to a national reserve with native wildlife dominating the landscape. With a history as a cattle station, however, and neighbouring places still operating as such, the place must be cleared of all cattle first before the kangaroos can reign again. If these properties haven't been mustered regularly for some time, many of the cattle would be cleanskins. They would have never seen a helicopter and never been mustered. This is paradise for cleanskin bulls, and the right time and right place for the bull catcher to come in and take control of the situation.

No cattle station wants too many cleanskin bulls on their place. These bulls teach younger mickeys their behavioural pattern, thus spoiling them. They stir up cattle during a muster, and they can jumble the healthy cow–bull ratio on a cattle station. Sometimes it is simply unavoidable to catch wild bulls.

Now, do you remember my tight grip I had on the buggy as Locky chased the big bull with the sharp horns?

It wasn't always like that.

A few good years ago, when most stations still mustered on horseback, ringers lived in their saddle for most of the year and formed a unity with their horses. A horse plant had to be brought along as each ringer had to swap their horse every so often to give them a spell. The ringers mustered the free-ranging cattle, held them and walked the growing mob. A plane gathered cattle from remote areas in the hinterland and brought them in from afar. Stockmen walked them to the nearest yard. These musters took weeks or months.

Bulls were just as headstrong then as they are now, but the methods of getting them (back) into the mob were quite different from today. The ringers didn't 'roll' a bull, they 'threw' it. They didn't hang onto a steering wheel, they hung onto their reins.

In those days, Locky and his mates were 'bull mad'. They didn't let a single one get away. If they saw a bull break out of the mob, they didn't think twice. They chased the bull for a while, slid out of their saddle and grabbed the bull by the tail. Another ringer had already come in to 'work the head'. He distracted the bull and made him turn slightly to the side. That was the moment the tail had to be pulled hard to throw the bull to the ground. He lost balance and fell. The legs were strapped and the horns were tipped (the sharp ends were sawn off). The mob of cattle was then walked to the bull. They unstrapped him and shouldered him back into the mob. By then most bulls had given up and accepted their defeat. The muster could continue, until the next bull challenged the handy horsemen.

Even though most modern ringers have swapped the saddle for an engine with two wheels, planes have been replaced by helicopters and time has become a major factor in the cattle industry, the reality of it all remains the same. The herd has to be mustered and cattle have to be processed. Techniques and operational procedures have changed in the face of the challenging demands of the industry, but skills, dedication and an unconditional love for the land keep this wheel spinning and the spirit alive.

Bush Baby on Board

Katharina (Tini) Wachholz, Lochon Contracting

This time last year I was pregnant. Locky and I were preparing ourselves for a new chapter in our lives, which we are in the middle of now.

Locky runs a contract mustering business, which takes us all over the Kimberley. It has taken us to Haydn and Jane Sale's stations for the last few years.

Last year, we were mustering Bulka Station, when I had a little passenger on board. I was still out in the camp until just a few weeks before our little bundle was born at the start of August. Although I was on 'light' duties, I was still out in the yards every day. There really wasn't much I did differently or 'lightly'. It's hard to change one's habits, especially when you don't feel much different. I just couldn't help myself.

I stayed out of potentially dangerous situations like getting in the yard with fresh cattle, as climbing the rails took me a little longer, and I did allow myself the luxury of having the occasional rest. I would also count the cattle that went on the truck sitting back in the bull catcher (a cut-down Toyota LandCruiser). This made me feel like the queen of the cattle yards. From my throne I had a great overview of the truck, the race and the yard. Naturally, I was trying to be helpful by yelling out to the crew: 'Quick! Shut that gate' or 'coming back', 'push 'em up' or 'two more'. I'm sure my commands did nothing to improve the process of loading the cattle. If anything, they probably just annoyed everyone. But nobody said a thing. They were kind enough to allow me to feel needed and an efficient member of the team.

Now that our precious little baby girl has hatched, there is a whole new set of things to consider. She is on the 'outside' now and I can't just take her with me anywhere at any time without having to worry about the heat, the flies, sunburn or missing her nap time. It would be a much greater challenge now to be an equal member of the mustering crew.

I am not even trying. My preferred challenge and new adventure is that of being a mother. It is the hardest but also the most rewarding 'job' I've ever had. The journey of parenthood is full of surprises. To watch your baby develop into a 'real' person and to see her character emerge and her personality form is such a joyous and wonderful experience. Helping her become this person is our responsibility as her parents and makes for many great moments and memories.

Moving around the Kimberley to do contract mustering, fencing and yard building, we have always lived relatively basically, compared to the standard in town or the city. Our house was a tent. Tent plus baby is not exactly a parents' dream. So we upgraded. We now live in a caravan. It is a good shelter from the harsh elements of the outback and offers a lot more comfort than a four-square-metre fabric pop-up home.

But apart from the luxury of a home on wheels, our girl is very much a baby of the bush. She gets her baths sitting in the shade of a tree, listening to the birds chirping and the leaves rustling in the wind. We go up to the yards and watch the crew draft cattle. She chases cattle up the race sitting on my hip. She goes for a cross-country joyride in the bull buggy with Locky, steering and speaking, er, chewing the mouthpiece of the two-way radio. Her days start and end sitting around the campfire, listening and laughing (!) at the yarns everybody is telling.

However, like any other kid, it is essential for her to be with other children and babies. Our social outings take us to Bulka homestead where she gets to play with Yulia and Gazza's little boy. Occasionally we go to the 0–3 group at the Wangkatjungka Community school. And we go back to town to catch up with other friends, children and grown-ups.

All in all, Locky and I are trying hard to be the best parents we can. We want her to experience the best of the world we live in: the outback, small-town Australia, my home country Germany, and the rest of the world.

We can only hope that she likes it. She seems to enjoy life so far and that's all we can ask for.

The Simple Pleasures

Katharina (Tini) Wachholz, Lochon Contracting

When you live out bush you learn to recognise and appreciate the most simple and common amenities that you take for granted when you live in town. A hot shower, a cold drink, a room with four walls and a door to shut suddenly become luxuries that you long for occasionally. On the other hand, it becomes clear that they really are just that – luxuries. In our bush camp, we have lifted our standards so much over the years we even consider some aspects of it 'luxurious': the washing mashine, power on demand (you gotta love the little suitcase generators) and comfortable camp chairs in the shade under a massive tarp.

But in the end what is most precious are the simplest things: sitting around a campfire at night, mesmerised by the flames and the sound of the crackling wood, with a stew cooking in the camp oven; a good night's sleep in a cosy swag with the stars shining above you and the sound of nature waking you in the morning; a good coffee and toast cooked over coals as the day is dawning.

You can bring all the luxuries you want into the camp, but what is most enjoyable are the things you can't pay for.

It is always quite amusing to watch the transformation of people who come to work for us for the first time. Some might have been keen campers for years, some have never even pitched a tent in their life. What most of them have in common is that they are virgins to a full-time bush-camp lifestyle. It takes a few days, sometimes a week or two, for them to rid themselves of certain expectations and surrender to the pleasures of a basic lifestyle.

A hot shower at night does not have to involve a tap, a shower and unlimited water supplies. Try a bucket, a dipper and a few litres of cold water with some boiling water from the fire. A dinner does not have to be a fancy fish dish one night, an Asian stir-fry the next and a chicken parmigiana the night after. How does oxtail and kidney stew with rice cooked on the fire sound? Have you tasted home-made, fresh salt beef and damper or a barbeque T-bone steak, rib bones on the coals (all fresh and unprocessed beef from the free-range cattle around you)?

And who needs a lap pool or spa when you can jump in a cattle trough on a hot and dusty day of drafting (before cattle have been slobbering all over it, of course)!

Life in the bush can be as good or as bad as you make it. We are always trying to make the best out of it and truly enjoy what it has to offer. And when it is time to go into town for a break, we indulge on the easy luxuries of an urban life, knowing that the bush is not very far away.

Just enjoy life, wherever you are!

Why I Get out of Bed

Chris Daniell, Myroodah Station

I have had the pleasure of growing up in the Australian bush, more commonly referred to as 'Outback Australia' by our city-dwelling cousins. It's an environment full of hardworking people with common goals and a purpose in life. Everywhere I looked as a young boy I saw Indigenous role models before me, going to work in some of the harshest conditions this country can throw at you and taking it all in their stride.

It is only now in my early forties that I fully appreciate the foundations they laid down for me. From my parents, grandparents, uncles and aunts, I learnt about respect for Elders and the importance of a good education. I was not alone in this environment. Every cattle station we lived and worked on had a large Aboriginal workforce, with lots of young kids my age seeing their fathers and mothers go off to work every day and they all had a purpose in life, a reason to get out of bed.

Thirty years on and you see a totally different scenario. Why such a big change in such a short time?

Most of the men in the stock camps working for my father in the late 1970s and early 1980s have either passed away or have drug and alcohol problems. I have memories of these same men in their prime – fit, athletic and full of pride. I looked up to all of them. They taught me so much about the land and how to survive in this unforgiving environment. They had everything they needed – a job and, more importantly, they were surrounded by family. As for their children who would now be in their forties, I know of only one family who still has some connection to the bush way of life.

It has become too easy to get money through the welfare system and that is one of the main reasons for the lack of respect towards Aboriginal Elders and the law. Three years ago I was struggling to find a purpose to get out of bed. I can only imagine how it feels for people with depression to try and get through the day, just to go through it again tomorrow.

I needed to find a reason to get out of bed and a reason to continue in the cattle industry. I made a commitment to myself to do all I could to provide opportunities for fellow Aboriginal people. This decision led me and my young family to my current role as manager of an Indigenous-training cattle station in the Kimberley. This is something I never saw myself doing three years earlier. How life can change!

I now have the opportunity to pass on what knowledge I have and provide an environment for young Aboriginal people to prosper. This environment comes packed with strict guidelines and plenty of support. I make no apologies for raising the bar and challenging these young men and women — it is the least I can do. To see them rise to the occasion and follow in their grandfathers' footsteps gives me great satisfaction.

I have seen firsthand what their forefathers were capable of. They deserve respect, and the last thing they need is a handout. I have a great support crew around me, from my wife Pam, little offsiders Will and Sam and all my staff at Myroodah and within the Indigenous Land Corporation. There is no way this could be done alone.

An Impatient Little Boy, Tragedy and Gratitude

Mel McDonald

After two years with Rangelands NRM, a non-government organisation that promotes the sustainable use of natural resources, I'm now in a job where you create your own work. I had created myself a mountain – I not only had to finalise a series of projects before the end of June (because it was the end of that funding program), I was also going to need to start slowing down and preparing for the arrival of our bundle of joy, due in mid-September.

Our little boy, however, had other plans. During the last week of May I had a cold. My partner Judd was mustering at Springvale Station, so I did my best to look after myself. I was preparing for a phone meeting and a day out visiting a couple of stations with potential projects. I had the humidifier on and the chicken soup going and somehow managed to feel human towards the end of the week.

On Friday morning I said goodbye to the homestead 'yardy' who asked if I was going to Springvale for the weekend. It had crossed my mind earlier in the week, but Judd was meant to be home before now, so I had dismissed the idea and then been so tied up I hadn't given it another thought. But why not, I thought to myself – it was a long weekend after all, and I will be halfway there (Springvale Station is 600 kilometres by road from Yeeda Station). So I pulled up at our cottage on my way back, threw some clothes together and was off. I had to ignore the state of the house after being sick and busy. I remember thinking I'd freeze that yummy home-made chicken soup on Monday. Little did I know I would not be home for four months!

I had a lovely weekend up at Springvale. I was able to go out mustering, getting a lift out to the yards in the helicopter, before jumping in the passenger seat of the bull buggy (an old ute to help with the muster). Even though the bull buggy broke down and I spent most of the morning sitting in the bush with it until the cattle were in the yards and Judd came back to pick me up in the helicopter, I was just happy to be out there.

On Sunday night I felt uncomfortable and was in a bit of pain during the night, but I had been reading that Braxton Hicks contractions start at about my stage of pregnancy, at about twenty-five weeks. In the morning I left Springvale at 5.30 am, heading to Derby Hospital with Will, a worker who had broken his leg. He was actually from Yeeda, so Derby was close to home if he had to stay in, rather than stopping in Halls Creek or Fitzroy Crossing, which both have small hospitals.

My pains continued through the morning but as they came and went I kept kidding myself they were getting better. I don't know why, but it never crossed my mind that there might be something wrong with my baby. So there we were, without knowing it: a woman in labour driving a guy with a broken leg six hours to hospital.

By the time I arrived at Derby about noon I thought I had better get myself checked out. When a doctor examined me, I was in labour and it was too late to stop it. Poor Judd got the message that I was in hospital. He thought I was just taking Will to hospital and didn't realise I was having the baby. By now he was actually at a station halfway between Yeeda and Springvale, helping with their muster for a couple of days. He jumped in his helicopter and flew to Derby in record time. He would have landed on the lawn outside the hospital if he could.

The Derby hospital staff were great and able to slow the labour enough to get me on a Royal Flying Doctor Service plane to Darwin. I am so grateful the Royal Darwin Hospital accepted us as patients because it was only a three-and-a-half-hour flight away. There was a storm in the Pilbara and going around it to Perth would have taken at least eight hours. Unfortunately, with the added passenger of a baby doctor in case of a birth on the plane, there was no room for Judd. He had a long, lonely night and day until the first available commercial flight from Broome to Darwin the following afternoon.

As much as I was crossing my legs, little Trent did not wait for his daddy to arrive. He was born at 10.30 am at twenty-five weeks' gestation, fifteen weeks early. I was told he would probably only weigh about 500 grams. I was so happy he gave a little cry when he was born and weighed in at 831 grams – he was huge! At the birth were about four nurses and doctors in the room for me, and even more for Trent. Immediately he was whisked away for the doctors to keep him alive. I had to have an operation to remove the placenta so I did not see him until about six hours later. He was so tiny and fragile with tubes everywhere, but even then, as during the whole labour, I knew he would be OK.

Judd was a wreck when he finally arrived at about 6 pm. He had not slept the night before and had been keeping busy on the phone updating everyone. He was so happy to see his son, although he did describe him to one relative as 'looking like a shrivelled-up piece of steak'.

For the next sixteen weeks we rode the emotional life-and-death roller-coaster of the neonatal unit. Trent's early arrival gave me a new appreciation for humanity. In the months after his birth, we received overwhelming support from countless friends and strangers, which has literally left us speechless.

It did not take long for reality to set in that Trent and I would be in Darwin until at least his due date, nearly four months away. One of the nurses at the hospital helped Judd find a furnished unit for me to rent only five minutes' drive from the hospital. This was lucky as accommodation in Darwin is not easy to find. The cost of this would have been a huge financial strain were it not for the fantastic Patient Assisted Travel Scheme, which in Western Australia receives the state government's Royalties for Regions Fund support, and so is more generous than in other states.

My mum came up from southern WA – 'just try to keep me away', she said – to help me settle into the unit, while Judd flew home to get my car. This was a 2000-kilometre drive but even including stopping to have drinks with friends to wet the baby's head, he and his mate who came along to provide moral support managed it in two days.

Both Judd and I received fabulous support from our workplaces. Judd kept busy with work, flying up to Darwin for about four days a fortnight. It was hard as when he was on the station he just wanted to be in Darwin, but when he was in Darwin he felt helpless, and was constantly on the phone sorting things out back at the station.

Rangelands NRM was very supportive and allowed me to keep working remotely from Darwin. The plan was for me to drop back to part-time after the birth – it just came a bit earlier than we intended. Being able to continue working kept me busy in between hospital visits and maintained a connection to home. I spent time at the hospital at least twice a day and a few times even visited in the middle of the night – I was up expressing every three hours anyway.

I simply cannot believe the support we received from friends and acquaintances. A girl I had met only a few times collaborated with a good friend to organise a fundraising raffle, with tickets sold at the Broome rodeo and the Willare 4 Hour Enduro motorbike race. They then travelled out to Yeeda Station and used the money raised to paint and furnish Trent's nursery. This was finished off with the most comfortable nursing chair you can imagine, which many friends had put in for. I don't know how Judd managed to keep it a secret, but it was the most wonderful surprise when we finally got home.

Something that makes me so proud to be a part of the Kimberley community was that a hat was passed around at a meeting of the Pastoralists and Graziers Association's Kimberley Division. This, along with a very generous donation from the Ord Valley Country Women's Association, amounted to quite a sum. Most of these donations were anonymous and we are humbled by the help and generosity.

All this is in addition to the wonders of modern medicine and the delightful staff of Derby and Darwin hospitals. The nurses in the neonatal unit are so patient and gentle with the tiny babies and their parents. I will be forever grateful for the assistance from two girls volunteering their time at Royal Darwin to support parents of premature and sick babies through the Miracle Babies Foundation. Talking to someone who has been through what you are going through to help you come out the other side is invaluable. These girls are now good friends.

There are countless others who helped both Judd and me through this traumatic time. We hope we can pass on such kindness to others in the future.

We count our lucky stars every moment of every day that we have a healthy, happy little eight-month-old boy. He has just a few scars from hospital procedures and will have his first birthday in less than a month's time.

* * *

How time can fly and drag at the same time. Nearly two years ago I wrote about impatient little Trent coming into the world fifteen weeks early and how overwhelmed we were by the support we received.

Today Trent is a very healthy and happy two-and-a-half-year-old who keeps his mum very busy. Tragically his dad only lives on in our memories and in his little man's appearance and happy, sociable character.

On 25 August 2014, when Trent was just fifteen months old, Trent and I kissed Judd goodbye and headed to Perth for a week for work. Judd was to fly from Yeeda Station to Springvale Station to muster, but he never made it to Springvale. The day got away from him, it became dark and his helicopter was found crashed the following day.

Judd was a natural horseman and a talented stockman with great passion for the pastoral industry. Although each property does things in their own way, Judd was lucky enough to experience one extreme to the other. When he first headed to the stock camp at fifteen years old, they lived and breathed their horses, moving weaners and sale cattle all on horseback. They slept out in swags for two months at a time with the only vehicle being an old tractor to cart the cooking gear from camp to camp. Helicopters were used during mustering, but there were no hand-held radios and the helicopters left once the mob was together, leaving the horsemen to walk them to the yards.

By contrast, the last job in Judd's career used only helicopters and trucks to muster and move cattle. Judd used to call his helicopter his 'horse'.

Judd was a genuine character who had friends from all walks of life. He loved a laugh and was always having fun. His sense of humour could get him through the most mundane of jobs and he loved a beer at the end of the day.

My heart breaks daily as I see so much of Judd in Trent. More than anything, Judd wanted to be a dad. He would hold Trent and, with a crack in his voice, say, 'How could you love something so much?' He could not wait until Trent was no longer being breastfed (and even more so was walking and toilet-trained!) so he could take him to work and teach him everything he knew.

The way I have coped is to practise gratitude and to never ask why. I believe tearing yourself apart with questions cannot change anything. All I can do is try to be grateful for the time we had together and for the incredible gift of little Trent.

I had previously written about all the amazing people who supported us following Trent's birth. The support from family, friends and the community at that time was dwarfed compared to the support I received following Judd's accident, which is a tribute to both the community in which we live but also to Judd's charismatic character and the depth of his friendships. Even now we often talk about the laughs and good times we had with Judd. There are certainly no shortage of stories to tell!

Trent is a happy, kind and sociable 'Junior Judd' who makes everyone around him smile. He loves animals, adventure and the outdoors, just like his dad. He has amazing men and women in his life who want to teach him everything they know. He is a very special little man who keeps a smile on his mum's face.

Judd's plaque at the Helicopter Pilots' Memorial in Halls Creek:
JUSTIN (JUDDY) ROBERT MCDONALD
29.06.1980 ~ 25.08.2014

A fearless, wild and spirited kid who never really changed
Born to muster wild stock, with horse blood in his veins
Young Juddy grew up quickly in the stock camps of the north
He held his own and learned the trade of bovine, hoof and horse
He loved a laugh, he loved a joke, he loved good times and beers
But underneath was a level head mature beyond his years
For Juddy was respected by the good folk that he knew
He was rough around the edges but his character was true

A noted stockman of the north, amongst the very best
A brother, husband, father, son and a good mate to the rest
And the land he loved is where boabs grow,
may his soul forever fly
Above the open plains of the Kimberley runs,
farewell but not goodbye.

Nerrima, Mick and Sal

Mick and Sally Courtney, Nerrima Station

Welcome to the desert and Nerrima Station! My wife Sal and I moved to Nerrima in early 2012, with our two girls, Grace and Lilly, and then young Jack came along before Christmas. Before that we had spent two years at Liveringa Station. Once we decided, the move had to be made in the wet so we could get settled in before the season kicked off. We worked around storms and the wet in January 2012, and after three days of bogged removalist trucks, graders, tractors and a big hand from Shane Bailey at Yakka Munga, we arrived to find cattle grazing on the metre-high lawns at the homestead. The place was quiet, the generator wasn't running, there was no water to the station complex, and UHF, internet and TV were all non-existent. The kitchen was flooded from a pipe that had broken sometime during the week, but at least the phone worked, albeit inconsistently.

A few days later the caretaker 'Pigsy', who was responsible for looking after Nerrima before we moved, came back. Pigsy is a law unto himself. We set about restoring some order and normality to the place. It was at this time I realised Pigsy was one of the most likeable and hardworking characters I have met. The next two months were lively, to say the least, but it would have been an incredibly hard transition without him here.

We found that the amenities and infrastructure were somewhat more basic at Nerrima, and as we are reminded regularly, 'Nerrima ain't no palace, but we love it'. I'm sure the basic infrastructure and amenities both at the homestead and in the paddock motivated me the most. As strange as it sounds, I clearly remember saying, after having a close look around, 'What an opportunity', much to Sally's amazement and confusion. What I actually meant is that Nerrima is a great opportunity to put our own brand on something that is reasonably undeveloped. Sal and I then embarked on the rebranding.

In a short time I found myself with a growing 'wishlist', containing everything from new yards, machinery, bores and upgrading dilapidated water infrastructure, to bringing Nerrima up to its full potential. Currently the focus is on developing new water infrastructure for previously unused pasture. This has been ongoing since our arrival. Water is the most important resource on any station and has always been number one on my priority list.

For Sal and me Nerrima has been a welcome change of pace from Liveringa and previous properties we have worked at. Mainly, as we have a young family, the work schedule can be a bit more flexible if I want it to be. We feel the kids have a much wider range of experience growing up with this lifestyle, and although there are some harsh realities of life out here, it is a more genuine representation of real life, which we don't think is detrimental to them in any way. They are confident, outgoing children, with plenty of manners when they decide to use them, but importantly they have developed a love and appreciation for the outdoors and animals.

You can't beat the simple freedom that bush kids enjoy outdoors and the opportunities they have to become adventurous little people and use their imagination to amuse themselves. The kids are lucky this year as they are attending a Catholic primary school in Derby and enjoying all the social activities associated with school, but spending as much time as possible back at Nerrima. This may sound unusual, but for the kids' sake we were happy to make a few sacrifices. We feel that the social interaction for the kids in town is invaluable, even if it's only for a year or two.

I first came to the Kimberley in 2000, after leaving agricultural college in Western Sydney and our family property in central-west New South Wales, to work on contracting camps and in stock camps. After spending time at Carlton Hill, Springvale and Moola Bulla stations, I met Sally while I was head stockman at Moola Bulla Station in 2004. When Sally turned up to work at Moola Bulla, my first impression was that I already had too much to worry about without adding a woman to the equation. I'm sure Sal thought my ego was out of proportion, and it possibly was. The comment was also made about my aspirations far outweighing my abilities. Little did I know that I would spend the next three months working hard to convince her she was wrong.

Two years and a couple of stations later, we found ourselves married and living in Darwin where I was employed as an Elders agent covering the Katherine and Darwin area. Sally went back to marketing and public relations, and started as marketing manager at the Darwin Entertainment Centre. A couple more moves later with Elders, including being based in Katherine, then Broken Hill (the last place we thought we would end up) we drove across a lot of country and met some great station people throughout Cameron Corner, and the Strzelecki and Birdsville tracks. Even so, the desire to head back to the Kimberley only increased over time. Incidentally, we accepted a job at Liveringa Station in late 2009 and made the move back to the Kimberley, where we knew we would be happiest.

I credit a lot of my understanding of running an efficient, well-structured, animal welfare–focused station to two of my earlier employers at Springvale and Moola Bulla stations, Damien and Kirsty Forshaw. Damien is a hard man, but fair, and brought me from a young, carefree wannabe ringer with no real direction to showing me the responsibility of running camps and the junior management of breeder and sale cattle programs, and the economic benefits and consequences of our actions as managers in the cattle industry. It was at this point I knew I wanted to achieve higher goals within the industry, and the Kimberley was where I wanted to do it.

Having the opportunity to manage Nerrima lets me get back to basics with high emphasis on best practice. Being a traditionalist, coach mustering, solid horsemanship and low-stress stock-handling, along with animal welfare, are high on the agenda. Since my association with Jim Lindsay, which dates back to 2004, low-stress stock-handling has become more than just an obligation to the company, it has become a keen interest of mine, and our staff would probably tell you it's an obsession.

I believe the economic benefits and consequences can be quite significant. Because we manage the station for someone else, it would be easy to cut corners in cattle management, husbandry and welfare with no one looking over your shoulder daily. Although having a solid grounding and confidence in my abilities I do, at times, find myself second-guessing a lot of what I do nowadays. I feel an obligation to our company and the rest of the industry to do our part in animal welfare, due to bad publicity in the live export industry in recent years. The cattle here will reflect our work ethics and practices for years to come, and it is a legacy that we and our staff are proud to be a part of.

A word from my wife Sal …

Two-and-a-half years ago, while living at Liveringa Station, Mick put the question to me: 'The manager's job is coming up at Nerrima, would you consider going over there?'

He then said, 'It is over the river and a bit tricky at times to access in the wet and a bit further south. However …' then he proceeded with a long list of what Nerrima had to offer and why it would be good for us to make the move. I wasn't that convinced, but continued to listen, thinking simultaneously, Mick does have a good sales streak in him at times and can talk anything up if he wishes to.

Looking for a change at the time, and having learnt from history to never say never, a decision was made soon enough, and we were off to Nerrima. I remember once saying to a friend, 'I will never have three kids and live on a station and do school remotely.'

I knew it would always be hard to get out of the house and to keep working. Well, that was life for us last year and it wasn't so bad, and it was a great experience to be part of the Kimberley School of the Air.

Now in our third year, Nerrima is operating well. Overall numbers and calving rates are above average, the general infrastructure is at a good standard and we have good staff. Everything is where we want it to be and it's a nice stage to be at, where the focus can be more on cattle-breeding strategies, increasing carrying capacity, expanding new paddocks and bores and improving water infrastructure. Initially we were trying to run an operation that was constantly interrupted with the bores breaking down, and machinery experiencing major water and power problems at the station. In the first year, we were grateful to have the staff that we did, as they played a big part in making improvements to the station. We had electrician Tom and plumber Joe, who both worked in the stock camp and proved invaluable as they brought their trade experience with them.

In the dry, Nerrima is just two hours from Derby, a straightforward drive on the Camballan Road and over the Fitzroy River. In the wet, however, it is a different story. An alternative route has to be taken via the Gee Gully Road, which is 160 kilometres of dirt road all through paddocks, as opposed to the ninety kilometres on the Camballan Road. It doesn't sound like much, but getting the gear in and out over the four months has its challenges, because your travelling time is twice as long and you run the risk of getting bogged or stuck at the Gee Gully if it's up.

Making our move in March in the middle of the wet was pretty stressful. When the removalist truck arrived at Liveringa, I suggested to one bloke that he stay the night when he got out to Nerrima. He thought he'd be back to Broome later that night. He didn't realise it was five-and-a-half hours one way from Liveringa to Nerrima, then they had to unload and it was another five-and-a-half hours' drive back to Broome.

'I hope you brought your toothbrush,' I said half-seriously.

Three days later, the poor two fellas made it back to Broome, after getting bogged on the way in, seventy kilometres still from Nerrima, and again on the way out. They slept in the truck both nights with little food.

Since moving to Nerrima, we've had some time in town as well, so our girls can attend school in Derby. Over many years, I've tried to have the best of both worlds: bush life and being involved in the cattle industry, combined with what town offers. My interest in the cattle industry kicked in when I made the move to the Territory at twenty, and since then, I have tried balancing a life in the bush while pursuing a career in marketing.

I spent ten years throughout the Northern Territory working as a governess at Camfield Station and as a station hand on a large export depot/station in the Douglas Daly region between Darwin and Katherine. I also completed a degree in business and marketing at university. My next station was 120 kilometres south-east of Darwin towards Kakadu. A few years later, I was at Alberta, Canada, where

I worked on a ranch for six months through a rural exchange program, an awesome experience.

Back in the 1990s/2000s the live cattle export industry was booming. After four years with a company, I had an opportunity to fly to Sarawak in East Malaysia and meet my fella (the manager of the depot) who had gone on the boat with 200 buffalo, the first shipment to Malaysia. He didn't know I was coming; a fax was sent to the boat that he was to meet me at a small airport north of Sarawak.

The buffalo were domesticated, but still wild, and the idea of going over was to help with the animals. We spent ten days with local vets looking after the buffalo. It was an eye-opener, seeing how they managed the buffalo with basic yard infrastructure and trying to transport them on little body trucks with only portable panels or bamboo tied together, five head at a time. They were then placed straight onto a barge with no panels, just pallets lined up to make some kind of laneway. It all seemed to work, but only over there.

While working at the Department of Asian Relations and Trade a few years later, I represented the government at a trade show in Jakarta. Even though I was just starting out in the department, I learnt much about the government's role in building relations with neighbouring Southeast Asian countries to try to develop new markets for the live cattle trade and other industries. I am fortunate to have had great experiences in the industry and to meet and work with motivated, likeable characters.

It wasn't until 2004 that I headed to the Kimberley and worked on Moola Bulla, supposedly as the camp cook, but also as self-appointed station hand. Arriving later in the season, I only worked there for four months, but it was one of the most memorable experiences I've had, and the hardest work I've done. But I'll never forget the captivating country and rugged landscapes. It wasn't just about meeting you, Mick.

Now, many miles later, perhaps going through a car and tyres a bit quicker than Mick would like, and having a bad track record for getting unwanted scratches and dents on our vehicle, our way of life at Nerrima incorporates both worlds. I've had some hairy trips over the Myroodah crossing, at times with just the kids, via the Gee Gully Road, and slipping sideways off roads on the black soil, dodging cattle and driving through the Gee Gully River at high levels. We did this trip on a weekly basis. After three-and-a-half hours and finally arriving in Derby on a Monday morning after dropping the kids off to school, it almost got to the point that I felt like asking for a shot of rum instead of a latte to calm the nerves at the local cafe.

It is great to have the flexibility of running our own show at Nerrima as managers. The flip side is that you can no longer rely on someone else to fix things as at previous places. We have no designated handyman, gardener or mechanic, so everyone has a diverse role here and is expected to turn their hand to most things.

I soon realised that applied to me as well. I couldn't go asking Mick every time something broke down as he was busy. At times, I would be by myself when the water stopped running to the house, the cold room almost died again or the generator went off. On many occasions I gave my diagnosis to Mick when something wasn't working and he quickly replied, 'Just look at it, Sally, and work it out.' It wasn't the answer I wanted, but I had another look and, much to my surprise on a couple of occasions, I did work it out.

I clearly remember having been on a lovely holiday down south and getting back to Nerrima in the middle of the day after a four-hour drive from Broome. (In October it was up around the forty degrees Celsius mark.) I had only been home a quarter of an hour when silence. The generator was off. Both the 'govvie' and I spent the next three hours trying to get it going again. No one was here and I was cursing dusty, dry, powerless Nerrima – just when you need a little air-conditioned comfort. I wanted to get in my car and leave again but finally got the generator going again. I soon discovered the beer fridge had remained cold and a couple of rums went down very nicely. Things were looking up again. It's the simple things you have such an appreciation for – power and alcohol!

Living on a station as a mum with three little ones is completely different to the days of being a carefree station hand. Getting out of the house for more than three hours seemed like an achievement, let alone getting on a horse. It is becoming easier now that the kids are older. My role here has incorporated doing things from home: office work, ordering anything required from food to parts, recruitment and also fighting fires, cooking for staff, offering first-aid to injured staff and trying to be of some help when vehicles, trucks or graders are bogged (and knowing not to ask any questions on arrival!). It's the simple things – going mustering or walking cattle away and seeing a mob of cows mother up with their calves – that are really rewarding.

I love that our three children can experience the freedom of the bush. It's an environment that encourages them to be adventurous and curious, to learn about their surroundings and things such as the life cycle of animals, how to look after them, the seasons and just understanding where our water and food comes from. That, combined with having their mates in town, breaks up the isolation of living with just adults. We have been fortunate that, in this close environment and regardless of age, our staff have been so good with our kids over the years and a positive influence. All except you, Baydo Adams!

Shipped off to the Big Smoke

Minna Burton, Yeeda Station

G'day, my name is Minna Burton and I'm from Yeeda Station. My parents, Jack and Vicki Burton, own Yeeda and brought me and my brother William up on the land and taught us to love it as much as they do. I've always been a keen station hand, running beside Dad, helping him in every way, from handing him spanners while he's under a ute to sitting beside him in the chopper spotting cattle.

So many things make me love country life: the early mornings and late nights, camping under the stars, helicopter flying, yard work, horse riding and the bull catching, not to mention the people. My whole life, I've grown up and lived around blokes of all measures: ringers, bore men, chopper pilots, truck drivers and even cowboys (and yes, they do come under a different heading).

So you can imagine the culture shock when I was sent off to an all-girls' school in suburban Perth.

Apparently swearing was actually only meant to be done in the yard, blowing your nose out of one nostril was totally unacceptable (even when outside), jeans didn't cover every dress code and hats were a fashion statement rather than a lifesaving component. Heck, talk about life-changing! To survive this chapter of my life, I was going to have to make some large changes.

First thing I learnt was that the girls I went to school with weren't the blokes, so don't talk to them about home stuff, they just wouldn't understand. This rule changed not only my life but the rest of the Yeeda crew as well, as I was constantly on the phone to our truck drivers and chopper pilot making sure they were working hard in my absence and finding out what was going on. Then I'd talk to Dad that night and fill him in on anything *he* may have missed on the day, from 2500 kilometres away.

'Yeah, Dad, muster went well today, the boys said there were a few good bulls too, going to be flat out drafting, processing and trucking them to get them to town in time for the boat. Maybe I should come home to help, since you're short of hands? They are on their last drum of avgas by the way, should probably get one of the fellas to shoot to town to get some more before we muster again on Thursday.'

In my first years of school I think I stretched a few friendships with my 24/7 need to know. This is where I inherited the nickname 'Miss Boss'. Not that much has changed really; I think the crew is just used to it.

Presbyterian Ladies College (PLC) would definitely not have been my first choice if I had had a say in where I went to boarding school. It's probably safe to say it wouldn't have even made the shortlist, but like all good parents, mine wanted me to have the best education to give me all the opportunities that the big wide world has to offer.

PLC found it had to accept that, unlike the rest of my cohort, I did not want to go to university or take a gap year and travel to other countries to volunteer in an orphanage. I did not want to get a part-time job while living at home and waiting to gain a bachelor's degree.

I want to live a 'gap life', as my dad often refers to it, a life where you succeed by watching, listening and slowly learning. Producing beef to feed the world is what I want to do, and it is just as important as being a brain surgeon or a prime minister.

The day-to-day life is what really hooks me – working alongside people who are from all walks of life and have somehow found themselves in the bush, who love station life like I do. There is the satisfaction of hard work, the blood, the sweat and – when I have to go back to school – the tears!

After my first three years of boarding school I got into the swing of it. I started enjoying the school side of things and the sport. Although nothing quite met the adrenaline spike that bull catching offered, I stuck with some winter sports that near on killed me! Perth winters are pretty different from Kimberley winters. I got better at making friends with girls once I realised that, unlike the blokes, they didn't care who rode the most bulls or had the most buckles.

I feel a bit like Hannah Montana, like I live two lives that do not cross, with two separate wardrobes that, still to this day, have not crossed (and never will).

I like talking about riding horses with the girls from school, because even though dressage and camp drafting are different, I still get to talk to the girls about something we mutually love.

My plans for the future are probably quite predictable. I have 127 days, 10 hours and 32 minutes until Yeeda Pastoral becomes my full-time employer for the 2016 season at Springvale Station (north of Halls Creek). After that, I hope to travel around and work on different stations across the top end of Australia, gaining experience and as much knowledge as possible. Then one day, much to my mum's horror, I hope to take to the skies as a mustering helicopter pilot, the best job in the industry, if you ask me.

Now that I am nearly finished school, I can look back on my time away and say that it was worth the pain of being away from home. I've made great friends I know will stick with me for the long run, and had once-in-a-lifetime opportunities. If anything, it has proven to my family and me where it is I want to be, and where I will enjoy my life the most – in the outback.

Working with Our Indigenous Neighbours

Haydn Sale, Yougawalla Station

Yougawalla Station is bordered on two sides by Aboriginal-owned stations. One is Carranya Station, owned by the Indigenous Land Council, and the other is Bohemia Downs Station, owned by the Bohemia Downs Aboriginal Pastoral Corporation and run by Doodie (Alan) and Selena Lawford for the local Bohemia community of around thirty-five people.

It has always frustrated me to see productive land not being used and effectively going to waste, as well as Aboriginal communities living on this land with no work and no part in the production process. For many reasons, many Aboriginal-owned stations have fallen into a state of neglect or are operating on not much more than a self-sufficiency basis.

Bohemia Downs is a more developed station and was operating commercially, mainly through the toils of Doodie and Selena. It still struggled financially due to lack of scale and ongoing funding and operating expense issues. I got to know Doodie over a few years and respect him as a cattleman and a person.

During the immediate aftermath of the suspension of live exports to Indonesia, and the reduction in trade that followed, we found ourselves in a very precarious situation. Being so remote from the rest of Australia in the Kimberley, we had little chance of selling our cattle elsewhere, due to the logistics of transport over massive distances – it was 2750 kilometres to our nearest abattoir in the south.

Financially, this was a disaster, as our revenue to run our business, pay our staff and our suppliers dried up overnight. Of greater concern to us was the immediate future for our livestock. Every year we need to sell animals to get them off the station to make room for the calves that have been born the year before. If we do not do this we are immediately overstocked and quickly run out of grass to feed our cattle. With everyone else in the vicinity in the same boat, we were facing a potential animal welfare disaster.

Looking over the fence to the neighbouring Aboriginal stations that were understocked with relatively low numbers of cattle on them, I thought there has to be a solution here. Due to our financial circumstances, we were going to struggle to pay an outright agistment fee to run cattle on these properties. And often money has to be spent on the stations to bring fencing and waters up to scratch to run the cattle. In nearly all cases the Aboriginal stations don't have the funds to do this, so are left in a catch-22 situation.

We decided to approach Doodie and Selena about an agistment deal to run cattle on Bohemia Downs, where Yougawalla could provide services to help run their station in lieu of agistment. These included mustering, grading, providing fencing material and steel for yards, a bulldozer or loader for cleaning out dams, and trucks to transport cattle around the property. This would allow Bohemia to rid itself of its major costs, make its cattle operation profitable and at the same time allow us to use machinery, labour and materials we already had to offset our agistment.

With Doodie and Selena's great leap of faith three years ago, we have been able to ride out the storm with extra space for our cattle over the last few years and they have been able to survive the cattle downturn and go ahead with their business. We have also forged a great friendship between our families.

On the back of this, Doodie introduced us to the Elders in charge at Louisa Downs Station, which borders another of our properties, Margaret River Station. Last year we were able to strike a similar deal to run cattle on Louisa Downs Station. We've already seen new infrastructure go into the property and the start of its economic recovery. There are certainly bumps in the road and difficulties that need to be worked out, but I firmly believe we and the local communities that own the stations are getting a great benefit from these arrangements.

I find it very satisfying to see young people excited about going to work and seeing some pride in the stations returning. While not all people stick it out, there is at least opportunity there for them now, and some will go on to be a success.

In time, the communities will benefit financially from the renewed cashflow for community projects. Most importantly, there will be opportunity and a chance for them to work there if they choose to take it.

We have found Aboriginal stockmen and women to be very good, with a natural sense for working and handling cattle. They are proud of their history in the pastoral industry and its development, and in some small way we are extremely proud to be helping to revive this. We are also fortunate to have the opportunity to run cattle on these properties. Without them, we would have struggled for survival ourselves. As some cheesy management consultant once said, it has been a win–win outcome for all involved.

Farewell to a Friend

Haydn Sale, Yougawalla Station

Life in outback Australia can be very hard. Until you have experienced the depths of isolation, droughts, unrelenting extreme heat and loneliness, it is hard to explain how difficult these times can be. There is a sad and tragic side to living out here that is generally not talked about enough: suicide.

The old-school mentality of the hard bushman was to not talk about your problems and to not share your hardships and dark times. We all go through them from time to time. In many areas this is still the case and desperately needs to be worked on. Organisations such as Beyond Blue and the Australian Men's Shed Association are making great advances, but too many people are still slipping through the cracks.

I have written about working with our Aboriginal neighbours to agist cattle on their properties and helping them muster and improve their properties in return (see 'Working with Our Indigenous Neighbours', page 172). The main driver for this idea was Doodie Lawford from Bohemia Downs Station, who are next door to us at Bulka Station. Since those days we have expanded to include similar agreements with Louisa Downs Station and Lamboo Station. This was all through Doodie's hard work and perseverance, and a driving will to achieve a better life for his people. Along the way we became great friends and our families loved to spend time together.

In December last year Doodie committed suicide. My family and I are still battling to come to terms with this. The futility, the loss to his family and community, the hole it leaves in a tight-knit community and the vacuum of experience and worldly knowledge will be felt acutely for years to come. Mostly it's the loss of a friend.

Let me tell you a little about the man. Doodie was born on Christmas Creek Station, next door to us. His dad was the head stockman there for most of his life.

He was schooled in the hard lessons of cattle-station work from a very early age. He spent time away at a school in Perth but was soon drawn back to his beloved homeland. Bohemia Downs was taken over by his father and the community around twenty-five years ago. Doodie returned home with a passion to make a better life for his mob, and that's what he did. He worked tirelessly to improve and run the station to make it one of the best operating Aboriginal pastoral stations in the Kimberley.

Like all of us, things went very bad financially after the cattle ban to Indonesia and the subsequent quota restrictions. Together we worked to get through this grim period. Doodie has travelled extensively, was a member of the Pastoral Lands Board, a prestigious position in WA, ran training and education in stock and station work for his people, and generally put all his efforts into tirelessly and selflessly helping others. I believe he was one of the best people I have ever met.

The day of the funeral was truly amazing. Burying their loved ones is a very special event for Aboriginal people, and much time and planning goes into it. I knew this from past experience but nothing could prepare me for the scale of that day. Somewhere between 800 and 1000 people turned up to pay their respects. The car parade behind the hearse reached from the Bohemia Downs turnoff to the community, around fourteen kilometres. People from all walks of life spoke of their admiration for this incredible, selfless leader. Six horsemen leading the coffin and two helicopters flying at each side escorted Doodie from the community to his final resting place, next to his father in the cemetery on the station, followed by around 1000 mourners. What a tribute to a wonderful person. Bizarrely, I kept thinking, wouldn't it be wonderful if Doodie could see this.

Like all things that occur suddenly, I have to keep reminding myself that Doodie is not here. Sometimes I pick up the phone to dial his number to ask his advice, other times I am flying by and think I will drop in for a tea and a catch-up before reality hits. I think it is the wondering why, the 'could I have helped?' that haunts friends and especially family when these things happen. I have been told that once a person makes up their mind to commit suicide, there are very few signs that it will take place and you are generally too late. These questions can never be answered and to heal we must all move on as a community and remember Doodie as the great and influential man he was.

The Kimberley has the highest Aboriginal suicide rate in Australia. We owe it to Doodie and all the others who have fallen to do something about this and do what we can to prevent further tragedies.

Goodbye, my friend.

Where's the Deli?: A City Girl in the Middle of Nowhere

Jane Orchard, Yougawalla Station

'This is the life,' I thought as I walked onto the tarmac at Broome Airport to my 'private' plane with pilot and good friend Haydn Sale from Yougawalla Station. I was thrilled to discover I would be collected from Broome after initially thinking I might have to drive solo for seven hours. (Having seen *Wolf Creek*, I was not too keen on the idea.)

After excitedly jumping into the plane, I realised with some concern that the chestnut dashboard, wood panelling down the side – is that a choke? – reminded me of my grandmother's old 1965 Rover.

'OMG. I've got to get out of here!'

As the plane taxied for take-off, I shut my eyes, practised yoga breathing and held onto the seat for dear life. Then, all of a sudden we hit cruising altitude and I could start to unlock my hands, look out the window and take in the beauty below.

The expanse of the Kimberley is mind-blowing. It's hard to get your head around a station that stretches as far as the eye can see in every direction. Its beauty is awe-inspiringly magnificent. Yougawalla is lush and green after good rains; piled red rocks scatter the landscape with caves and crevices, the same as it would have been thousands of years ago. At sunset the sky is purple, pink, yellow and orange while the land beneath turns blue.

Two-and-a-half hours later, we were greeted at the Yougawalla landing strip by one of my oldest and dearest friends, Jane Sale, and her gorgeous children, Gus and Tilly.

After excited hugs and hellos, we jump into the four-wheel drive and set off down a red dirt track to the house. Ten minutes later the homestead emerged, tucked into the broad landscape and surrounded by several rocky outcrops. It consisted of a few cubic timber modules clustered together, linked with timber walkways and edged by a huge deck.

Three dogs greet us when we arrive, barking, licking and jumping with excitement at their new guest. (Or maybe it's because the whole family are home again?)

'I've never seen such friendly work dogs before!'

Jane and Haydn laugh. 'They work at catching dragonflies around the pool.'

Unlike other farms I've been to, the dogs are the 'lushes' of the household. Due to the massive expanse of these stations, it's the people on motorbikes, in cars and helicopters who do the real work when it comes to mustering.

That's what I can't get my head around. It's no big deal to travel three hours before you start work for the day. Would you ever think of travelling from Perth to Dunsborough and back in one day after working in 35-degree heat for eight hours? You'd be crazy! Here, it's just part of it. Jane shared with me that it took her over a year to come to terms with the scale, and some days it still surprises her.

Because I arrived on Easter Saturday, the staff had already started celebrating two days off after a hard week cleaning bores to ensure fresh, clean water for the cattle. The team are young and from all over – Canada, UK, Victoria and Tasmania. The men, although young, are rugged and handsome with red dirt constantly covering their clothes and faces, and the girls glow with tanned natural beauty after days spent outside. I loved that even after cleaning up before dinner, there were always remnants of red dirt in everyone's nails, mine included by the end of the trip.

Every meal is an occasion up at the house. Delicious roasts cooked by Jane for the staff every night, fresh from their land, with vegetables flown in on the mail plane every Wednesday. (How they coped without a mail-plane delivery for the first twelve months after moving to Yougawalla, I will never know! Now, that's planning.) Over dinner we laugh and share what brought us to Yougawalla. All had an interesting and different story to tell. It's clear that no matter what their background, they all love it here and want to stay. They are passionate about the lifestyle and the quality of stock they are producing here.

It was invigorating waking up the next day with the morning light as my alarm clock. Tilly knocked on my door, like she could sense my eyes were open. I realised it was only 5.45 am. Tilly and I agreed to make Jane a cup of tea in bed given it's sooooooooo early – there's no way anyone would be awake. We snuck quietly to the kitchen, and lo and behold, the whole household is up and about. It's action stations. Coffee is brewing. Lunch has been made and wrapped up for the team to get them through the day ahead. I'm at least an hour behind. Before I know it, they're off to work, getting the truck ready to go to Bulka Station.

As everyone leaves, a strange feeling comes over me. Was it guilt? How else could I feel as I stroll back to my room and put my bathers on for a morning by the pool? Quietly staring out onto the escarpment, down the hill I saw the fattest, shiniest, happiest cows I've ever seen, meandering to waterholes with calves suckling their mothers. It's clear they have a good life here. And it's not just the lush environment that makes them so clearly happy and content. When you talk to Jane, Haydn or anyone who works on the station, the cattle's quality of life is everyone's top priority. Why wouldn't it be? It's their passion and their livelihood. Only in the last week Jane and Haydn had invested in a course for low-stress stock-handling for all their staff to ensure the best handling of their stock.

While at Yougawalla, I was lucky enough to experience a muster. Haydn and I took off at dawn and headed for Bulka Station, which was twenty minutes by chopper. Bulka is very different from Yougawalla. It has natural springs and rivers everywhere so it is lush and green with much taller trees surrounding a more traditional farmhouse. As we land, a second pilot, Rex, arrives. He will assist in the muster of over 1000 cows spread across 150,000 acres. I am smiling from ear to ear as I meet him.

'Hi, I'm Jane. It's the first time I've been in a helicopter.'

'Me, too,' he said with a wry smile.

The skills of these pilots are incredible. The precision with which they fly these machines and move cattle with the help of bike riders and cars on the ground is awesome to watch. To me, they could have been stunt pilots in a *Mission: Impossible* movie. After nearly seven hours, the cattle were finally in the yards ready for drafting the following day. I'd like to think I helped Hadyn somewhat by spotting a few strays hiding in the trees and scrub that day.

On my last day at the station, I watched as Jane, Haydn and the team drafted the cattle. It requires a team of six people to split the cattle off into male, female and strangers. What I imagined would be a relatively simple process is quite the opposite. Concentration is high as they focus on getting all the cattle through the raceway as seamlessly as possible. It was here that I saw the LSS course at work.

After encouraging a group of cattle to move into one of the holding pens before entry into the raceway they settled down and stared at us. Well, all except for two ENORMOUS untagged bulls known as cleanskins, who tried to climb a fence! One needed Gazza to extract a hoof stuck in the railings – my heart rate definitely jumped at the thought of a bull jumping into the pen I was in.

Being on the ground and lucky enough to see the way a station functions has opened my eyes to a lifestyle most of us take for granted. What I take with me as I leave Yougawalla, and my wonderful old and new friends, is an understanding and appreciation of where my food comes from and the back-breaking work that is required to deliver it to my supermarket shelf. I hope everyone who has the opportunity to visit a station or farm of any kind takes that opportunity.

When You Can't Wait for the Flying Doctors

Haydn Sale, Yougawalla Station

All of us who live and work at the local pastoral stations are immensely proud that we produce food to help feed people all around the world. Some of the destinations for our beef include Indonesia, the Philippines, Malaysia, Brunei, China, Vietnam, Israel and other Middle East countries. The work on the station is often hot and hard with, at times, ridiculous challenges thrown at you – markets, weather and the isolation. But we love it and could not imagine doing anything else. When you weigh up the rewards of working in a beautiful place with great committed people – and animals – I feel privileged to be able to do it.

Part of living in such a remote area is the angst and worry for your family and workmates if there's an accident. We are four hours from the nearest hospital by road which, at times, is impassable due to wet weather. This worry became a terrifying reality two years ago when my wife, Jane, was seriously injured on the station.

Jane works extremely hard outside with our staff during the mustering season, often coordinating musters from the ground and controlling the yard work and drafting of cattle. I fly a helicopter we use for mustering the cattle and I am often away from the yards on another muster or at our neighbouring property, organising operations over there. The cattle are only handled once a year and are out of the yards within twenty-four hours to reduce the stress on them and returned to their natural environment. To achieve this with large numbers of cattle, the days are long and the work does not stop until it's done. Daylight starts and home in the dark are the norm.

From time to time, animals that have never been yarded come in with the mob. These have escaped musters in the past and are basically wild animals that have never been in contact with humans – 'cleanskins'. Cleanskin bulls are especially dangerous due to their size, sharp horns and generally aggressive attitude. On one muster in July 2011, a large cleanskin bull came in with a mob of cattle. We usually try to separate the bulls and feed them hay over a few days to let them calm down. We are careful in the first contact not to get in the pen with them and take care handling them.

On this day I was on my way to Bulka in the helicopter to do other jobs. Jane and the crew were taking care of the cattle in the yards and drafting. I realised not long into the journey that I had forgotten my satellite phone which I always carry for safety or breakdowns. I turned back to the yards to pick it up. This turned out to be very lucky indeed.

When flying in to land I noticed the boys jumping around trying to signal me and knew straight away something was wrong. When I landed and got out I saw Jane sitting on the ground with a large bandage around her head and blood all over her face and clothes. The boys were severely shaken and told me she had been attacked by a cleanskin bull. The bull had smashed a gate off its hinges right where Jane had been standing on the other side. It had attacked her, smashing her against the fence, continually throwing her in the air and partially scalping her right across the forehead and all the way to the back of her head. I did not know the extent of her injury until we got to the hospital and removed the bandages, but I knew from the boys' state it was serious. In hindsight, I am glad I did not know as it helped me to keep calm and think of a solution. It would have been harder if I'd known the true state of my wife's injuries.

Jane is the most courageous person I have met; to move out here from a city background and make a go of it shows that in spades. Once again, she was amazing. She was able to answer questions about herself, her injuries and seemed, in the main, quite calm. She had even given the boys instructions on how to bandage her up before I arrived!

The first thing to do was call the Royal Flying Doctor Service (RFDS) for assistance. I did that from my satellite phone and went through some basic checks of Jane's condition with a doctor over the phone. She needed help and she needed it fast as we did not know if she had internal injuries. The problem was, the RFDS plane had just left on another job and would be at least two hours getting to us. I knew this was going to be too long. I decided I had to fly her to the hospital myself in the helicopter. The risk was if she passed out on the way I could do little to help her, as you need two full-time hands to fly and it is only a two-seater machine.

I talked to Jane and she said she felt strong enough so we loaded her into the chopper and set off for Fitzroy Crossing Hospital, a trip of around ninety minutes. I think that was the longest ninety minutes of my life and I am sure it was for Jane. She had no painkillers and as the adrenaline wore off and shock set in, she was in horrible pain and started to look weak. I just tried to talk to her and keep her conscious but there was little I could do. She told me afterwards she was just trying to keep her bearings on our position to give herself something to concentrate on and not pass out. To watch her suffer was the most horrible experience of my life. She did not complain and was brave beyond words. Finally we reached the airstrip where an ambulance was waiting. They gave her morphine and the relief was palpable for both of us.

The RFDS offer a brilliant service to remote areas of Australia and they were fantastic in our time of need. The Fitzroy Crossing Hospital checked Jane over and stabilised her condition, but she still needed more scans and immediate plastic surgery for her head. The RFDS transferred us to Broome by air and had a jet on standby to transfer Jane to Perth for surgery. As luck would have it, there was a visiting surgeon in Broome and the procedure was performed there. Three hundred-plus stitches later, Jane's scalp was put back together. She also had broken ribs and severe bruising all over her body. Her recovery has been remarkable in both body and mind. Mentally, an accident of that scale takes its toll, but once again her courage has shone through and she was back to work in no time.

The accident brought in focus for us the daily dangers of working out here and the multiplication of that danger by isolation. We do everything we can to be safe, but sometimes accidents happen.

It's the final outcome that counts. I consider myself and my children very lucky to still have Jane and I have seen a side to her character that makes me swell with pride.

Whether it be patching up scratches and administering basic painkillers or antibiotics from the medical chests provided to stations, or sending a jet to an accident site, the RFDS does an amazing job for remote Australia. We couldn't live this life without the reassuring knowledge that they are there when we need them.

The Glass is Half-full

Jane Sale, Yougawalla Station

Agriculture is a glass half-full industry. An industry of optimists. There is always at least one uncertainty to deter you taking a risk with your money, but for the love of what we do, we put it all on the line anyway.

The weather is the largest gamble we take. Our friends in Queensland are suffering from the drought at the moment, made much worse for them financially because of another unpredictable element that affects our management – government decisions. Because of that one snap government decision to put an immediate halt to the supply of cattle to our closest neighbours back in 2011, our industry had ongoing effects that influenced our relationship with Indonesia and the small amount of cattle they were importing from us right through to 2013. Even with good seasons here in the Kimberley, we have struggled to find feed and water for the cattle meant for markets no longer available to us. This is the reason why Queensland properties in the drought areas have been hit extra hard, as they have to deal with extra cattle and less feed. This is also the reason why those involved in the industry until now have felt uncertainty at the lack of government support.

However, on the last day of February 2014, something pretty special happened in Broome. Farmers, industry stakeholders and representatives travelled from all over Australia to attend the Northern Beef Forum. A different venue was organised as the number of attendees was much higher than anticipated. These industry get-togethers are a great chance to catch up with friends that isolated lives keep us from doing regularly, but they have been unusually necessary in the last few years to sort out industry problems.

This time there was a feeling of confidence for our future, both short term and long term. The meeting was attended by many industry leaders, Indonesian government and business representatives, and an unprecedented attendance by ministers for the industry from right across the north of Australia, federal Minister for Agriculture Barnaby Joyce and state agriculture ministers Ken Baston (WA), Willem Westra van Holthe (NT) and John McVeigh (Qld). These ministers expressed their commitment to work together to support our industry. The gathering gave the producers and industry stakeholders a direct line to decision-makers. Haydn and I felt a huge sense of relief.

Barnaby Joyce referred to the way the industry had been treated in the past and how he wanted to move forward: 'We have to always be on the front foot and say, no matter what you have, if you find something on the road where something is wrong, you deal with that issue. You don't close down the highway, and that has been my approach to this industry and what I intend to do.'

After a long while, we finally felt like the industry representatives had our back, so we could concentrate on doing what we do. This does not mean we will bury our heads in work and become complacent, rather that we will keep working hard to manage our cattle and land. We will keep talking to and pushing government and industry representatives to invest in and research the industry and its markets. We will market our cattle to those who do the best job of looking after them, using transparent systems so we know they are being treated to the best standards. We will keep telling our story and help people not involved understand what it is that we do.

The strengthening of the cattle live export trade with record cattle export numbers predicted for 2014 due to rising demand in Indonesia and other new markets such as Vietnam and China means we are beginning the year with a positive vibe. That optimism resonated through the crowd in Broome.

It's time for us to get on with the year ahead. We have new crew arriving, and it's always exciting to meet them and to welcome old friends home. We have some exciting additions too. The kids have a very sweet new friend arriving in April. We met Beau, Gus and Tilly's new Welsh pony in Capel, WA, and it was love at first sight, especially since he shares his name with my first pony. (There was a bit of nostalgia involved in that decision.)

I have had my day with two-wheeler motorbikes. I would go down as the most uncoordinated rider in history, having spent many a day mustering and face-planting. The last fall I had, I left a sand angel behind on the ground. I finished the muster running behind the mob and was much happier for it.

I decided I needed a significant vehicle that I can take off-track on those long days mustering cattle when the distance is too far for a horse, a vehicle I can use in the scrub when I need to pull up a runaway from the mob, but can also putt along behind at a steady pace without stalling. So Lochy from Lochon Contracting is converting an old short-wheel-base LandCruiser to make me a bull buggy. The only issue we have had in the past with buggies is staff, male especially, jumping in and driving them too hard and wrecking them. I'm looking forward to when 'Pink Lady' (yes, I am a *Grease* fan) arrives at Yougawalla and has all her bar work complete. Lochy has even left the back seats in for me to pop the kids' booster seats in so they can spend a day out with me. Haydn shoudn't have too much trouble spotting us from the air either. I'm counting on these cosmetic touches to deter young males from going near it.

After my 2011 accident, the Live Export Ban and its aftermath, the year ahead is looking up. Our holding paddocks, our cattle, our staff and family are all well rested. I know the wet has expanded my waistline just like our cattle, so it won't hurt me to do some running around in the yards or hopping back on my horse. It's going to hurt physically, but I have confidence that it won't be too tough emotionally this year.

But hey, I am in agriculture and a glass half-full girl!

The Jillaroo: Not a Rachael Treasure Story

Andrea Cragie, Yougawalla Station

'So, what are you doing after graduation?'

'Um … err … I think I might go chase some cows.'

He looks at me in disbelief. I can see his brain ticking over. This girl has just spent four years at uni, written a thesis and graduated with honours. She's had an awesome scholarship and travelled around both the country and the world during her degree. As my fellow graduates packed their bags this summer and moved across Australia to pursue big-time careers or PhDs, I rolled up my swag, cleaned my boots and moved 4000 kilometres from home to get my hands dirty, collect bruises and run around in some crazy hot weather with lots and lots of cattle.

I now call the remote confines of Yougawalla Station home. Before moving to the Kimberley a little more than a month ago, I lived in Tasmania. My family have a farm near Devonport where we produce a range of vegetables, crops, livestock and cut flowers. But really, that sort of farm cannot be compared to cattle stations in northern Australia.

Like all young people finishing Year Twelve, I was faced with the choice of 'what do I do now?' I was lined up to study medicine in Melbourne, but thankfully realised that wouldn't make me happy in the long run. I took a leap of faith and enrolled in a Bachelor of Agricultural Science at the University of Tasmania instead.

Hindsight is a fabulous thing; looking back, the decision to do agricultural science was a natural progression and over the past four years I have really grown my passion for agriculture, particularly with the support of the Horizon Scholarship. (If you know of any young person pursuing further education in a primary industry–related field then encourage them to look it up, as it is truly a fantastic opportunity.)

Coming to work on a cattle station has been my dream since I left school. By the time I finished my second year of uni I was itching to get out of the classroom and have a 'gap year' jillarooing. But instead my parents said (quite loudly) NO, and looking back, I have to admit, however grudgingly, that they may have been right. I love it out here, and going back to uni would have been pretty difficult, and I would not have finished my degree. So I spent the last year at uni reading and dreaming and thinking about 'one day'. For all the posts I read on the Central Station blog, I never thought that I would be writing one of my own. In the cosy confines of ugg boots, track pants and a Tasmanian winter perhaps I did romanticise the idea of being a jillaroo, but come on, I was writing my thesis and like any normal uni student procrastination in any form was a welcome distraction. My head was, at times, filled with dreams of becoming an excellent motorbike and horse rider overnight, instantly shedding the ten kilos I had acquired through uni, gaining a perfect tan, handling cattle which were as quiet and used to human contact as the cows back at Mum and Dad's place, and having a close-by neighbouring station with plenty of attractive and gentlemanly cowboys.

That didn't happen.

I still struggle to trot on the horses and don't even ask me to start the bike by myself. Yes, my jeans are getting a bit looser, but I am far from fitting back into my old size ten. My tan is AWESOME – as long as you only look at my forearms and the V on my neck where work shirts don't cover; the rest of me is pretty damn white. And it's going to be a long time before the cattle here would let me pat them.

As for a nice boy living next door, well, let me go for a two-hour drive and I'll let you know if I come across anyone.

My city-soft hands have had a big shock as I handle barbed wire, climb through metal yards that have baked in the sun all day and bash my knuckles on things. I thought, and many of my girlfriends agreed, that I wasn't really a city chick and that my bomby old Holden ute and cowgirl boots were sort of cool, but never something they'd be caught dead in. Yet in spite of that, while living in Hobart I have, without realising, become quite accustomed to the weekly coffee dates with girlfriends, shopping, clubbing on the Salamanca waterfront and enjoying life in town.

Even though I have grown to enjoy, and at times crave, the comforts of city living, it is a passion for agriculture that drives what I want to do with my life. The best thing I love about agriculture is the diversity; not only are there so many products that are grown, there are many more positions related to the production of each. There is so much you can do within agriculture and despite the busy four years I've had, I haven't seen very much yet at all. Coming to work on a station is allowing me to experience another section of agriculture in Australia.

I love what I am doing right now, working for Haydn and Jane and learning so many new things, both practical skills for work and other things like living in such a remote location. I still have plenty to learn and my motorbike skills certainly leave something to be desired. But one day soon I will be able to keep up with the boys well enough to be allowed on a bike when we go mustering.

From fixing fences and working in the yards, checking bores and running lick, I really do have a good job. From the short time I have been here I think working on a station is a fantastic thing to do, and I would recommend it to anyone who is considering it. I would also encourage any young person to consider a career in ag. There are so many opportunities for everyone, and not all involve ending the day covered in dust and sweat, although I wouldn't have it any other way.

A Life of Luxury

Jane Sale, Yougawalla Station

The basics out here are the luxuries, because too often we are without them. A house pump breaks or the solar electricity generator hasn't got enough stored in the batteries to power the homestead, and all of a sudden you are reminded of what's important. So you have to plan on what you can do without, and surprisingly, that's quite a lot.

When your water, power, telephone or internet sources are compromised (this is not an uncommon occurrence), you are also reminded of what life was like for the pioneers, who had none of these luxuries. You feel grateful. This is a totally different attitude to when I lived in Melbourne and it was all managed by someone else. The power went out, so you picked up the phone, waited on hold for half an hour, got annoyed and, mostly, the power was up and running again before you spoke to anyone from the power company. It wasn't a huge price to pay for having the luxury of power.

Out here, even if you do waste your time being annoyed with the situation, you still have to, as we say, 'suck it up and get on with it', because you are essentially the power company, water board and IT technician, to name a few of the hats cowboys and girls wear. My father has always said since we started developing Yougawalla that the cattle stations and small businesses we run and work for are essentially small shire districts, and all services need to be maintained. This includes roads, utilities, housing, health and communication services and, most importantly, water and food for our population, human and bovine. You live out here because you love it (most of the time), and you are up for a bit of adventure and unexpected hurdles in your everyday life. It's tough, it's beautiful, it's unique and the land we live and work on covers a huge part of this country we all call home.

I wanted to give you a couple of examples of these breakdowns to demonstrate the urgency of some of the problems, such as cattle or people being without water. A huge part of these 'shires' we run sound extravagant, but are small businesses with large expenses that, if not managed correctly, can quickly outweigh your usually once-a-year income from cattle sales. If you call in the serviceman to fix the breakdowns all the time, you pay around a $2000 travel fee to get them out here, without their hourly rate when they are here. There have been so many of these problems over the years that I have lost track.

So I opened a can of worms. I sent a Facebook message to thirty of our station crew from over the years to ask them to jot down any breakdown or stuff-up stories they remember from their time at Yougawalla. The thread from this message has been inundated with yarns about all sorts of things going wrong. It got stuck for a while on just taking the mickey out of me and has been an absolute laugh to read through. I have been in stitches. It has reminded me how resourceful people can be, and I don't think this is something you can learn in a classroom. It's common sense and logic that some just have in their nature. You don't have to grow up on the land to have it either.

One of the stories was about a bore that broke down. It was providing water to four dams, which supplied around 1200 head of cattle. Haydn and a small crew set about pulling the bore. This involves pulling up metal rod casings that are screwed together and sit about sixty metres down the bore shaft to carry the water up. On this set-up, called a mono pump, it holds a pump at the bottom that sucks the water up. The crew pulled all the rods up and, on the last one, realised that the pump had rattled and come apart from the rod. So it was back to the workshop where one of our clever staff made a rod they called the 'Didj' due to its long hollow shape, that was designed to drop down and catch what was left down there. It didn't work.

A day later the crew came up with the 'Didj Mark II'. Finally, they had a result and started to pull up the mess at the bottom. But the wire snapped and we were pretty much stuffed. In a last-ditch effort they made a long hook to 'go fishing'. It was never expected to work, but worth a go. When they finally realised it wasn't going to work, they pulled up the fishing hook, only to find it was tangled in the end of the Didj Mark II and the original Didj, which had caught the rest of what we needed. Had the bore not been attached and all the gear still stuck down the shaft, we would have had to drill a completely new hole and replace the bore. The victory this day saved us around $50,000, so the cattle and the crew got a drink that night.

I became a solar repairer in our early days here. The solar power unit had just been put in and during the night the electricity had shut off. The next day I was here on my own with the kids. When the power is out here, unlike in the city, it means the phones go down (there's no mobile service) and, most importantly, there is no running water. So down at the solar inverter I found a couple of very thick manuals and between feeding kids (they were six months old and two-and-a-half years at the time) and keeping them occupied, I managed to read it. After a couple of false starts I got the power up and running. This once-city girl was very proud of herself that day. Writing this reminds me to mention that not only does the problem need to get fixed, but life has to go on, as do all the other jobs of looking after kids, pets, horses, cattle (and the husband) who can't look after themselves.

There are so many other stories about our resourceful staff. They used whatever they had in the back of the ute for a bit of bush mechanics, worked through the night to turn around a road train that had gone down the wrong dirt track, or used graders to pull out loaders or trucks from a bog. There have been breakdowns and weather trapping us, and the stories go on. It reminds us how tough some days can be. Add the hot weather to the equation, and they are really sent to test you.

We were recently down south of Perth on holidays and caught up with some other station friends who were holidaying nearby. I asked them what their holiday apartment was like and they said, 'Are you kidding? It's fabulous! The air-conditioning wasn't working so I called someone and they came and fixed it. If something goes wrong, it's not my problem.' A luxury holiday!

People surprise Haydn and me all the time and they surprise themselves as well. It seems that these tricky situations are the most remembered, talked about and laughed about events on a station. They are also the biggest lessons in station life and life in general. Of all the personality traits that are called upon or that you dig down deep for in our hour (or two) of need, the one that shines through the most is our sense of humour. If you can't laugh about these things, life out here would be pretty grim. A sense of humour is the most important luxury item to pack on a trip outback.

Wherever I Lay My Hat

Eric De Van Denshueren, Yougawalla Station

How do you know when to take the right risk? In some cases you don't have a choice. In others, you have to ask, what's the worst that can happen? When the risk pays off you feel amazing, and when it doesn't, well, we all know how that feels. Sometimes we take a big risk with a large pay-off. Other times it's just a matter of trying something for the first time to learn if we like or dislike it.

This is my story about how a small risk turned into the best opportunity of my life. I had been travelling and working in Australia for more than a year. At the time, I was living and working in Melbourne. Being the typical backpacker in Australia you tend to get a bit shaky when you stay in one place too long. Don't get me wrong, I love Melbourne, but I was tired of the old struggle of trying to save money, staying out late and waking up early, and the hustle and bustle of the big city. I was looking for something more. Something out of the city, something that felt a bit more authentic.

I never dreamt that I would land on Yougawalla Station, all 220,000 hectares (850,000 acres) of it, in the Kimberley. When I first got the phone call from Haydn I didn't even know what or where the Kimberley was. After working out some details with Haydn and talking to his wife, Jane, I decided that moving up to the station was a good opportunity. Somewhere to save money, work hard and probably learn a bit while I was at it. I left Melbourne pretty much on a whim, in the hope that Aussies are, as their stereotype suggests, friendly and honest. I hardly knew where I was going, what I was getting myself into and the love that I would find when I moved up to this place. And no, it wasn't a girl. It was the work, the lifestyle, the people, the adventure of it all.

I flew into Broome and landed at 6 pm. Haydn picked me up at 6 am to take me to a place a four-hour drive from town. Most people would think I was mad. I just figured, at the worst, I would work for a few weeks, hope they pay me, and my flights were covered in and out. No loss of time and a few weeks of something different. When we left Broome I couldn't believe how red the dirt and sand was. It felt like a true Australian experience, going out into the desert. I had been on a few farms before but nothing like an Australian station.

It's an odd place at a quick glance. You live in the middle of nowhere and your mail and food are delivered by plane once a week. Not only do you work with the people you live with, but you live with the people you work with. They send you out to the middle of nowhere and tell you to fix a bore, fence or gate.

They give you directions based on a few trees, a road, a gate, maybe a sign if you're lucky. You float between asking yourself whatever got you out to a place so vast. At the same time you thank yourself for whatever decision you made that got you to a place that really shows you it's not all about people and cities. It instils in you a sense of awe to know that the closest person is a two-hour drive away at the homestead. Sometimes you don't even see a cow or bird for the day.

But it's the cattle work that captured me. Most people think cows are dumb. Sometimes I'm still not sure whether they are smarter than they are stupid, or if it's that blind stupidity that leads them into looking smart. Either way, there is something about seeing cows look up at you as you drive by with their big floppy ears and senses at the ready. They take off at the sound of a car, motorbike, person or helicopter. Yet a person on a horse can practically walk up and scratch a cow on the back.

Seeing a calf or cow panic at the sight of a truck is pretty funny, but there is something quite majestic and powerful about watching a full-grown bull lumber around without a care in the world. It's the patience with which they walk off into the bush or up the race. They seem to know that no matter how much force other cows use or we put on them, they're still bigger and will get there when they are ready. It's great, too, coming home at the end of a hard day and sharing the stories of everything that happened. The cattle you saw freaking out, the way the old girls at the back didn't want to walk any more and would just keep eating grass, when the tough cleanskins finally made it into the yards, when you thought everything was going wrong and, for some reason, the cattle just stopped and decided, yes, they should walk calmly to the yards.

The yards are where a lot of the best action happens. Imagine taking a wild animal that sees people once a year. It just roams and does what it wants. Now confine it to an area smaller than the size of a soccer field. Multiply that animal by anywhere from a few hundred to a few thousand and imagine the chaos.

Generally most cows will move with the herd to try to get away from people. But not all are so easily moved. Sometimes they decide they don't want to move to the next pen. Sometimes they jump right out of the pen. Other times they make you jump out of the pen. It's all in a day's work, but you will find a way to get it done.

As with any farm there is a lot of hard work. The busy times are busy and the down time is needed. Often I am up before the sun and get home as the sun is setting. But tomorrow I don't have to get back on the same public transport to the same office to work with people I don't like, in a job that I don't like. I just look around at the flare of the sunset with its reds, oranges, yellows and the odd wisps of cloud, and think how glad I am that the job is done, and wonder what we are up to tomorrow.

I don't think there are too many places with amazing sunsets every single night like there are in the outback. They simply do light up the sky. It amazes me that a place with so little can hold so much life. There are no traffic jams, no sirens, no neon billboards, pubs, stoplights or pedestrians. Just a few people working a large space with great satisfaction. Whether it's working with animals on your own, in a team or with a machine, every day holds something different.

Living it Loud

Lauren White, Yougawalla Station

When I first left Canada for New Zealand in 2011 I never could have guessed the path my life would take. I absolutely loved my time in New Zealand and would go back in a heartbeat. I wouldn't live there, though. Australia, on the other hand, that's a different story.

While I was in NZ people would ask me if I intended to travel to Australia. My answer was very noncommittal. I didn't like the idea of Australia: I'm not a beach person and I was never a big fan of the heat. I can think of a hundred things I would prefer to do over lying on a gritty bed and baking myself like a pizza. I didn't know much else about Australia apart from the fact that it was a country with a lot of beaches, the Great Barrier Reef and Uluru, which I had only known as Ayers Rock. My response to people's queries about my future travels was that I may spend a couple of weeks across the ditch to do a bit of diving on the reef, but that was all I was interested in. It's funny how things change.

As my year in New Zealand came to an end I realised I was not ready to head back to Canada. My life was just starting. Also, I couldn't afford the flight back, and Australia was the cheapest place to get to with the potential of finding work. So off I went, to a place I had little interest in visiting, which is now the only place I want to be.

A few months in Sydney went by where I made some great friends but life was pretty average. Time spent in Cairns and Airlie Beach was beautiful but didn't quite tickle my fancy. Then I got a phone call. A job interview. A job. Then I caught a bus. I was driven inland. Dropped off. Picked up by my new boss. Driven another couple of hours inland. It was dark out and I had no idea where I was or what my surroundings were.

The sun came up the next day and my breath was taken away. I had gone from a city on Australia's east coast to a cattle property in Australia's outback. The dirt was red, the trees sparse, the kangaroos plentiful. There wasn't another house to be seen in any direction. The air was sweet and the water sweeter. There were frogs living in my toilet and a snake under my house. Cows grazed below my window and twelve dogs ran around and played. This wasn't an Australia I had seen on a postcard. It wasn't the Australia I had heard of from other travellers or seen in movies or read about in books. This was the outback and it was even better than I had imagined.

Day after day, I was amazed by the life I was living. Rounding up cattle while sitting atop a horse, collecting eggs each day from the chook-pen near the house, hopping on the four-wheeler and taking the dogs for a run, taking my camera out and driving around the 70,000 acres that I had to myself. In time I realised that I was where I wanted to be.

After a year of property work in Queensland I was offered a job across at the Kimberley. I packed my bags, tucked in my shirt, buckled my belt, pulled on my hat and boarded a plane to Broome. I wasn't certain what to expect. I had worked on a number of different properties around Clermont, but this was very far away and very isolated. Luckily, the owners were amazing, their little kids hilarious and the crew were all brilliant to work with. I was flown to the property by chopper when I arrived as the roads were too wet to drive. I knew straightaway it was going to be yet another experience to add to the books, and it was.

Nine-hour drives to town, regular helicopter flights, bull catching on the Canning Stock Route, learning to speak the native tongue of an Aboriginal group from the Fitzroy Crossing area, camel hunting with the contract fencer – all adventures I had never dreamt I would go on, all now treasured memories and favourite tales to tell.

Through all my time in Australia I worked different jobs in the outback in different areas of the country. I met folk from all over and tried many things. I fell in love in more ways than I imagined possible. I fell in love with the work. I fell in love with the town. I fell in love with rodeos and XXXX Gold. I fell in love with the people and the friends I'll never forget. I fell in love with a cowboy and every one of his dogs. The dirt roads, the landscape, swimming in mucky dams. The rain when it came and the sun when it didn't. I even fell in love with 45-degree days. I fell in love with it all, in love with a lifestyle. I fell in love over and over again every single day.

My heart broke when I had to return to Canada. I had never expected to feel so at home in a place so far away, in a place I hadn't had much interest in to begin with. It just goes to show that it's worth giving everything a shot because life can surprise you in ways you would never have guessed. Someday I'll return to Australia, back to the place that stole my heart and my breath away each and every day. For now, I'll have to make the best of what I've got and maybe, just maybe, I will fall in love with the country beneath my feet.

Greener Pastures

Kayleigh Gulliford, Yougawalla Station

After eighteen months of life out on Yougawalla Station it was time to relocate back to Perth. We were heading back to a life we once knew, trading in the 'Big Red' for the 'Big Blue'. Other than the dreaded thought of packing up a house and saying goodbye to people who have been the closest thing to family since I've been in Australia, I was excited.

I was excited for change. Not only was I trading the desert for the ocean, I was trading an eight-hour round trip to the nearest supermarket for a potential ten minutes. I was trading a monster trip into Broome to hit the piss to a simple taxi ride into town. I was trading in some serious hard yakka for a cruisy little city number.

Above all else, I was looking forward to the social scene.

A year-and-a-half later, my thoughts are so different. When you're ready for change, it's so easy to romanticise and think the grass is going to be greener. Since moving back to Perth it has become very apparent that we live in a society that focuses on the things we don't have, as opposed to the things we do. We have a constant need for instant gratification. All this just creates 'first-world problems'.

I once lived in an environment that faced daily battles over the welfare of livestock and was strongly dependent on weather and a mail plane to deliver your weekly groceries, never mind the nearest hospital being four hours away. Yet everyone got on with it and did whatever had to be done. I now live in an environment where if the queue for a coffee is too long, the commute to work takes an extra ten minutes or fast food just simply isn't fast enough, then the toys come out of the pram and teddy goes into orbit!

Although the decision to relocate was the right one and I can meet my friends with a short taxi ride into town and have a 38-hour working week, I don't have a sky so free of pollution that you can see the Milky Way. I don't get to see the moon rise looking like the biggest jaffa cake I have ever seen. I don't get to hear the blissful sound of nothing. And although I have thousands of people around me I don't have that feeling of community and support. People always ask me 'wasn't it lonely up there?' and yes, at times it was, but it's also amazing how you can feel more isolated in a big city with thousands of people around you than in a small remote community.

I'm thankful for my time and experience at Yougawalla and for all it's done to educate me about life beyond the city. I realise the huge effort by our farmers that has gone into my evening meal, which I now drive ten minutes to buy at the supermarket. Above all else it's taught me to appreciate 'the little things in life'. All I hope is that this stays with me and I remain grounded in the consuming hustle and bustle of city life.

Stories from the Top End, Katherine and Barkly Tableland regions in the Northern Territory

Life's a Bore

Stephanie Coombes, Newcastle Waters Station

What comes to mind when you think of cattle stations? Jackeroos and jillaroos covered in sweat and dust, mustering thousands of cattle on horseback? The crackle of a two-way radio as the helicopter buzzes in the sky? The sizzle of a branding iron and the noise of cattle moving through the yards?

Amongst all the campfire stories of wild beasts that broke from the mob, machinery that first-year jackeroos returned to the mechanic in various states of disrepair, and the skill (or lack) of the camp cook, there is a member of the station crew who often goes unmentioned – the faithful old bore runner.

If you travel beyond the homestead gates and past the cattle yards, the station may appear to be peaceful, quiet and uninhabited. If you travel further down the track, eventually you will hear the gentle humming of a motor.

Day after day, all year round, these motors work to pump water, the lifeblood of all cattle stations, from below ground to tanks, turkey nests (an above-ground dam made from rammed earth) and watering troughs across the station. It is the primary job of the bore runner to ensure these motors keep a constant supply of fresh, clean water to the cattle.

There are two bore runners on Newcastle Waters because of the sheer size of the property and the number of cattle: about 66,000 head of cattle spread over a million hectares. Twenty-two-year-old Jimmy looks after the western side of the station, maintaining the twenty-two motors that pump water to sixty-one watering points. These watering points are divided into three areas or 'runs,' as it would be physically impossible for Jimmy to cover that much ground in one day, let alone undertake any maintenance or repairs.

Jimmy is up before daylight with the rest of the station staff, and his first job is to fuel up his vehicle, which has been fitted with a 450-litre diesel tank and metered pump. On just the southern 'run' Jimmy will make a 300-kilometre round trip and transfer the majority of the diesel on board into the motors.

Each motor pumps water to more than one watering point. Each watering point has a trough for the cattle to drink from and either a large tank or a 'turkey's nest' to store the water that has been pumped. As he arrives at each point Jimmy's first job is to check the level of the tank or nest. Depending on the water level, Jimmy then decides how much fuel to put into the motor. The tank/nest is also checked to ensure the water is clean and that no big branches or leaves have built up, which can cause a problem in the pipes and contaminate the water.

Once the motor has been refuelled, it must be given a pre-start check before being started to ensure the oil and water levels are correct. Then the motor is turned on and left to pump water until it runs out of fuel. The motor is given enough fuel to increase the water level to the point where it can comfortably supply all the cattle that rely upon it until Jimmy returns in a couple of days.

Before driving off to the next watering point, Jimmy fills in a record sheet of each bore run, noting the amount of fuel he used, the level of the tank/nest when he arrived, if any cattle were at the trough when he arrived and if so how many, if any dead cattle were found (if so they are to be dragged far away from the watering point) and any general notes and observations.

Each motor is serviced around every 200 hours, when the old, dirty oil is drained and replaced with new clean oil, and the fuel, oil and air filters are cleaned. Because of the number of kilometres he travels, the bore runner's car is also serviced every two weeks.

On the odd occasion, though, there are repairs that need to be made too.

Like a car, the bores also have a belt that eventually becomes worn and needs replacing. Another job that may need doing is 'repacking' the bore. The shaft that moves up and down a cylinder to pump water is sealed at the top to stop water from spilling out. Occasionally the seal will need to be replaced with a clay-like material to stop water from leaking.

As Jimmy can only do one bore run at a time, often the station pilot will do a 'flying' bore run to check and record the water levels of the tanks and nests that are not being checked by the bore runner that day.

According to Jimmy there are a few things that are important to have on any bore run:

- A good playlist, and a long playlist. When most of your day is spent driving you want to make sure you're not listening to the same songs over and over again.
- Your phone or a camera as you never know what you might see out there – wild dogs and cats, snakes, swans and, of course, cattle. It's also handy in case you see something that you want to show someone back at the station, which may be hard to explain, such as a damaged fence, a busted pipe or something broken on the bore.
- Lunch. Once you leave those homestead gates in the dark of the morning, more often than not, you won't be going back through them until it's close to dinner time.
- Plenty of rags to wipe your hands on – you're bound to get covered in dirt, diesel and oil throughout the day.
- Tools and spare parts to fix motors, bores, water troughs, fences and just about anything you will pass on a bore run.
- A passenger, otherwise known as a gate opener!

The job of a bore runner is much more than just turning on motors and checking water levels. They are the eyes and ears of the station, the unofficial 'overseer'. Managers rely on bore runners to keep an eye on the condition of not only the watering points, but the fences, roads, supplement and most importantly the cattle, as they are often in the cattle yards or the office.

Life as a bore runner is anything but a bore.

PMT: Pre-mustering Tension

Jo Bloomfield, Hodgson River Station

PMT (pre-mustering tension) is a common affliction of all people involved with herding animals across Australia. It can occur in sporadic, intense doses or slowly, and affects both males and females. It is definitely more intense amongst those who are in charge and required to organise, delegate or simply pay for the requirements of a muster. It affects some people more acutely than others, but is directly proportional to long-term outlooks and issues relating to animal health, weather, staff, input costs and marketing.

PMT is highly contagious. Few are immune, although there is the occasional 'special' person who remains unaffected. These people are viewed with much admiration, suspicion or outright jealousy by others. Symptoms include feelings of dread, excitement or worry, mainly in the lead-up to the first muster of the year. The sufferer will be nervous, stressed, short-tempered and constantly attempt to multi-task to alleviate the condition. Sleep will be affected, mostly badly. Symptoms only minimally subside during mustering and stock-handling, but may only completely disappear when the last healthy animal is released and/or a healthy pay cheque is received for the work involved, or preferably both.

Instant treatment is yet to be found that doesn't involve having healthy animals and being paid for those animals. My husband likes to talk with similarly afflicted people on the phone for hours. These people carry out musters on several properties in all circumstances, while rebuilding machinery and visualising new and wonderful improvements. It seems after a number of hours, this talk is so exhausting the actual muster will seem like child's play and easily dealt with, thus the symptoms of PMT are temporarily relieved.

Some who have tried alternative treatments consume copious amounts of alcohol during the muster, preferably with others who are also affected and can offer companionship, sympathy or simply a chat. Unfortunately, the aftermath includes side effects of blurred vision, headaches and sensitivity to loud noise. Others tend to alleviate the constant pressure of PMT by having temper tantrums or targeting anyone within hearing distance, including on UHF radio channels. Again, the effort is of little use except as comic relief for one's partner.

The cure is to get out there and muster, get the job done and take each day as it comes. But relief is only temporary and PMT will rear its ugly presence the next time mustering comes around.

We are in PMT stage; we are getting ready to muster. While we do general maintenance such as fencing and repairs, getting ready to muster is different in that it often involves checking the equipment to be used such as trucks, trailers, bikes and yards or ordering materials which will be required through the year when working with cattle.

For my husband, who gives orders outside the house yard, pre-muster is going over the truck and trailers that we use for station cartage of animals or for general goods freight. He will repair any metal fatigue areas or generally service machines like the four-wheeler motorbikes to ensure a trouble-free operation.

As 'minister' of finance, I organise the materials or goods we need while mustering. This may be obtaining quotes, placing orders and organising items like ear tags, vaccinations and treatments, and ensuring we have what we need to carry out branding, castration and dehorning.

With our son, our only worker, we will all spend time going over the stock yard. If we require major repairs or modifications to anything we will do this before muster. A few days before putting cattle in the yard we will grease hinges or points of movement, ensure all water points are clean and the sprinkler system is working for dust suppression. We'll clean the areas around the dip and crush, tidy up any fallen tree branches that may affect movement and make sure everything opens, shuts, slides, swings and latches as it should.

Pre-muster involves making a basic plan of attack over which much debate occurs as to which paddock will be mustered, in what order, how, where and, most importantly, when the activities are likely to occur.

Once this plan has been devised, a helicopter is booked and last-minute preparations finalised. This may involve making sure all radios are working, safety equipment like helmets are available and, for me, cooking biscuits that are anywhere up to 40 per cent sugar.

For larger properties, organisation of staff before mustering is a major issue. I tend to concentrate only on finding a home tutor for our daughter. If we are able, we will employ one or two other people for short periods to assist.

Mustering and Mexican Stand-offs

Jo Bloomfield, Hodgson River Station

Our property is relatively small compared to the average property up north, with most of our activities governed by the weather, the wet and dry seasons. What makes mustering difficult is the ruggedness, scrub and volume of natural surface water still available through springs and soaks even through much of the dry season.

Our usual way to muster is to use a combination of yard traps at a water point and a hired helicopter, with us on motorbikes taking up the tail. Cattle are creatures of habit and while cunning in that they know exactly what the bumblebee in the sky is, they tend to follow their well-worn and usual routes to and from water and other areas.

Traps are like swinging gates in a small holding paddock at a water point. There is usually an 'in' and an 'out' trap. The animals walk through the 'in' to get a drink and when they like they can walk back 'out'. When we muster we close the 'out' trap so that the animal is actually captured. This method of capture relies heavily on the animal not having other water sources available so it must use the bore site to get a drink. It also depends on the animals having respect for a fence, because, should the animals decide they wish to vacate, it doesn't require any great effort for them to go through a fence and escape. This is very common with cleanskin bulls and old steers.

Mustering generally means sending the chopper up early in the morning. We use an extremely experienced chopper pilot who has worked this area for many years and knows the country well.

What makes a good pilot besides the obvious of cattle-handling skills and flying ability?

A standout requirement is a very controlled temperament, to be able to stay calm and focused when everything on the ground is going to absolute hell. Being the eye in the sky, they can see and anticipate things happening long before the person on the ground is even aware. This includes seeing people hurt because they hit things, bikes and people. It is for this reason that the chopper is the main mustering tool and most of the time actually work on their own.

They sweep the paddocks, working in sections, moving back and forth to steadily move the animals to a muster point. Skilled chopper work is an art, a highly dangerous one at that, but is absolutely vital to the economical gathering of cattle over large areas.

Normally the chopper will go up for several hours before we even start to assist on bikes. The pilot will start in the furthest sections of the paddock to begin moving the animals they see towards the waters. The four-wheelers that we use are meant to only come up the rear of any mob, keep up stragglers, make sure lazy bulls or small calves don't lie down and generally keep a mob moving as the chopper may fly off to gather more cattle in their constant movement of sweeping the paddock.

We do have some rogue cattle, generally old cleanskin bulls. If they are particularly difficult or dangerous to deal with and refuse to cooperate or stay with the mob, they are shot. Being on the receiving end of a cantankerous animal while on a bike or in a heavy rock area is not a pleasant feeling and as our kids are our main workers we simply don't bother with these mongrel animals. Even if we could sell them at $600 a beast they are of little value if they hurt people, machinery or other animals.

A muster of an area to get the cattle together usually happens over a full day. Cattle tend to work well for three to four hours, require a break and are then cooperative, ready to be worked again. So we muster for several hours and if the paddock is large or the water point a long way away we will put together a 'tailing mob' (literally a group of cattle).

By midday we aim for a cleared or open space and hold the cattle within an area that they can have a rest, sit down, allow calves to rest and drink and generally have a break from walking. Many will snooze. People need this break too; bouncing around over rocks and gullies can be tiring and a drink of tea and lunch is usually had by a small campfire. The chopper will land and refuel, and the animals and machines will take a few hours' break. Should any animals attempt to walk away someone on watch will gently ride around at a distance and put the animal back in the mob. Tailing is one of the oldest methods of holding cattle since cattlework began. It is also the best way to teach a herd that quietness and calmness are the order of the day and that galloping or not staying with the mob is hard work and not accepted.

We tend to muster towards areas that have fence-lines or, even better, laneways. Fence-lines have roads along them while the laneways have two fences very close together to act as a long paddock. Animals will follow these structures as the fences and roads act as guides for the cattle to follow.

We'll move the animals off the camp at lunch and, if required, the chopper will continue to scour for more cattle as we proceed to a water point or stockyard. After the initial excitement of capturing animals and keeping them in hand, by midday most animals are placid and cooperative.

Yarding up is the term used to get the cattle in behind closed gates, normally strong steel yards, not just a barb-wired paddock. It can be completely uneventful with every single animal entering the yard and the gates closing without anyone so much as raising a sweat. At other times, it can be a comedy of errors.

Bulls, herd bulls at that, are usually the worst to yard up and instigators of most problems. They suddenly become territorial in gates and will block a gate by simply standing side on in it and picking fights with any other bull trying to move past. This stops the flow of animals coming in and confuses the tail-enders as they have bikes pushing them forward but nowhere to go. The animals in the yard become flustered with all the activity and may start to come out of the yard, confusing the herd even more as the nice 'flow' that may have been occurring a moment before is suddenly altered and the forward momentum lost.

Sometimes it is simply a Mexican stand-off, a couple of hundred animals facing the wrong way looking back at several bikes. Lucky cattle aren't good at maths and most don't realise they outnumber us 200 to 1 but when they do realise, and it only takes one to test their nerve, then all hell breaks loose as they try to go in either a massive surge as one or split in several directions. If the mob rush back at you there really is not much you can do but stay on your bike, get around the lead, block them up and start yarding up again.

If we have some cattle in the yard a person must rush forward to close and capture what we do have while others on bikes go back and hold the 'breakers'. The person in the yard will move the captured animals into other yards to lock them in, leaving a vacant yard for the breakers to come back into. This usually works well and given room there's not normally another escape. Should the yard space not be available, a person has to hide at the gate and keep the ones in the yard getting out with the gate open while others are brought in.

It looks quite ridiculous, actually. I've never been called small or dainty but I can hide behind a six-inch-wide railway-iron post and attempt to be very still to not spook incoming cattle in the hope that after the last one enters I can close the gates. If the last ones coming in are cranky and looking for a fight you're always ready to shoot up the top rail to get out of their way and close the gate at the same time. I have absolutely no agility or pace when moving, but even I can find wings when something's blowing snot all over me.

On occasion you'll get a few ferals (misbehaving cattle) when yarding up who have become flustered, hot or simply cracked the shits. They refuse to follow the other cattle and won't look for the gate. They see their only escape as past you and into the scrub, or they become fixated on attacking the bikes. There are times when we literally shoulder these animals around: we will have two or three bikes around the animal and push the animal into a yard. One person will be up the side steering at the shoulder while the others push at the rear, nudging if required to keep moving the animal forward. Should the animal move away from the steering person, then the person at the rear takes the other shoulder and steers the animal back. Generally by reasonable persuasion we can walk an animal back to the yard and capture them. It sounds very rough, and it can get rough for a larger animal, but a weaner or cow mostly walks back in – once they see their herd, they are happy enough to join them. Most times we win; sometimes, the animals escape.

Yard up is only finished once those gates are locked and the chains are tied down. It is surprising how many animals have figured out how to lick gate latches and let a whole mob out. We can return to a yard the next morning, only to find it empty, with a full day's muster and chopper expense wasted.

Our Landing at Gallipoli

Jacki Bishop, Gallipoli Station

I am Jacki Bishop, wife and mother of three children, native to Victoria. Yes, I can hear you say 'Oh, a Mexican', and you would be right. My maiden name was Hodge, and my ancestors had a fairly good foothold farming Hereford cattle in Snowy Mountains country. So I guess you could say this life was in my blood. I had a passion for horses from a young age, driving my parents mad by galloping around our small farm.

When I ventured north, I thought I could ride. The reality was, I knew how to sit on a horse but had no idea of how to work with cattle and horses. Now with three beautiful children aged six, four and two and the most wonderful husband, Brolga, my cattle work is on hold but my passion is very much alive. My husband and I share a love of station life, and we are lucky to be where we are.

Gallipoli Station, owned by North Australian Pastoral Company (NAPCO), is an outstation of Alexandria Station, which, with the Soudan outstation, were named after military conflicts in Egypt in the 1880s. Additional land was purchased in 1918, so the owners continued with the military theme, naming it Gallipoli after the campaign. We are an outstation to Alexandria Station in the Northern Territory, ninety-six kilometres north of Camooweal, just a pinch over the Queensland border, or about three-and-a-half hours' drive north-west of Mount Isa.

We transferred here from one of their channel country properties during the April school holidays and have not stopped learning since.

Lesson 1: Moving house with three small children is at the top of my list of things to not do again anytime soon.

We arrived at Gallipoli like gypsies, our caravan and poor Nissan Patrol loaded to the hilt: me, my husband, Chloe (our governess), our three kids and two dogs.

Lesson 2: Do not let the husband and stock-camp workers unload boxes and furniture unsupervised.

In hubby's defence he had an almost impossible time limit and had to fit in a brief tour of the large property, so I had to wear the aftermath. Unpacking started the next day. Chloe set up the classroom while I tried to find the bunk beds in the mountain of things I thought were useful at our previous, bigger home.

* * *

One of the many advantages of our lifestyle is we get to live alongside animal families, which has given us a deeper insight to the complexities of animal family groups and intelligence. I can't help but think how lucky we are to be a part of it.

By our second year on the property we had added to our furry family four horses in addition to our two dogs. Except for the pony, they have watched my three children grow from babies.

While helping Miss 6 pamper and fuss over our horses, Master 4 was on the fence 'talking' to one of our horses who was tied up while drying off. Next minute, there was a squeal, followed by a very upset boy at my feet, dobbing on the horse. After a bit of a cuddle and an injury evaluation, which was nothing more than a graze, I got the full story.

He had been very quietly pinching the horse the whole time he had been over there and she had had quite enough! I had failed to notice him then, but had seen him doing so before and had had stern words about what was likely to happen if he kept doing it. There is nothing like a life lesson courtesy of our wisest horse, who was also a mother, to push the point home. I had known retaliation would occur at some time and as much as I had warned him, as the biggest stirrer in our family, he is always looking for a rise from someone.

A few years ago, when my daughter was about two, we were washing cars over in the shed, as the bore water combined with direct sunlight tends to leave an annoying mineral sheen all over the freshly washed vehicle. The horses had seen what we were doing and had come over in hope of getting a hose-down. We were not hard to convince and obligingly gave them a bit of a bath. They had settled down not far from the shed, a little way over but not in front of our house yard. The time limit for shed jobs for Miss 2 had reached its peak and she set off towards the house. I was still busy packing things away but called out to her to wait. She was not going to have a bar of it! She was halfway across the compound before I finally set off after her. I had taken little notice but our younger mare had headed out from the mob to stand herself directly between my daughter and the house gate she was heading for. At that moment I didn't take much notice but as I took Miss 2 back, our little mare turned back around and walked back to her mob to stand with them again. I thought, 'Well, that was peculiar' since she had no reason to do that – no grass to chew on or other horses to talk to. Then I realised she had walked away from the others to block our little one up! I'll be buggered – she just blocked my daughter up!

This shouldn't have been difficult to understand as our horses had an annoying habit of hanging around the house like bad smells and an uncanny knack of always knowing when one of the gates had been left open by accident and they could come in and eat the lawn, which they knew they were not allowed to. I'm sure they knew every word I was yelling at them too but they had to do that victory lap every time before they exited the crime scene, their tails elevated and nostrils flared!

All the time the animals have been around us, they have observed us as much as we observed them, at least for the last two years of Miss 2's life. I guess they had seen that the rules for this little human were probably not much different from theirs. This mare had a foal around her too, so I should not have been surprised by her actions. Although she had the tendency to pretend to be sour towards adults, she was always the first to say hi to the kids over the fence.

* * *

One of the things I really enjoy about where I live is the people we meet and work with.

Every year we generally get some new faces around the place, whether they are new to the industry, transfers within the company or maybe even an old hand trying out a new place. All have a story to tell about where they came from and how or why they ended up 'out here'. I can't help but relate because it doesn't seem all that long ago (it was) that I was in the same boat. Some become sick of the city or their home town and want to get away to experience something completely new. They come from all walks of life and all ages and even from other countries.

Towards the end of the year, when the heat really starts sucking the life out of everything, us included, I love looking back to the start of the year at what our crew was like, who has come and gone, and how we have all changed and developed from our experiences. We become a little, no, a lot like proud parents when there's a well-balanced crew that has learnt to work together and things just work. With animals that can be unpredictable, that takes time. When you invest time in staff, you hope something will come back.

It's nice to see fresh-faced jackeroos arrive, work the season and leave on holidays/ transfer or to go back home, well on their way to becoming men. It's even better when they come back to stay another year. I can only put it down to confidence in themselves and what they have achieved. The jillys (jillaroos or female station hands) leave the year with the same feeling, with confidence they can change a tyre, service their car, ride and shoe a horse and ride a motorbike, things they may never have learnt or been exposed to if they had not ventured out to try station life.

Then there are our quiet achievers, those who don't live the exciting life of the stock camp but whose jobs are equally important, our pumpers. On Gallipoli, we have two pumpers or bore runners, who have the essential job of keeping water up to our stock. They cover hundreds of kilometres every week. They are the eyes for my partner Brolga, keeping him informed of any changes that have occurred, where cattle have moved and broken bores.

Then there is the cook. If you get a good one they are equal to gold; if not, it sours everyone. It's most important to the boss's wife, because if there is no cook, guess who gets the job, nine times out of ten? And that is generally not a good scenario for anyone. In all, a happy, harmonious and hardworking crew is the ultimate goal. In our time out bush we have made some lifelong friendships and continue to meet wonderful personalities. I can't help but wonder who we'll meet next year?

Living in Dirt

Raine Pugh, Farrcombe Contracting

Living in a temporary camp for most of the year can be a challenge. We have no internet, phone service, television and, for several hours of the day, no power.

Our staff members simply live in swags, tents or the back of their cars. My partner, Potter, and I think that we have served our time living like this and now spoil ourselves with a gooseneck, complete with a queen-sized mattress!

Depending on location and the job we are attending to, our kitchen will vary from being an outdoor set-up under the awning of the gooseneck or in our camp kitchen van. This does not allow for a very sterile environment as the dust storms, ants, birds and wind all test us.

We use a barbeque as our oven, cooking everything on it, from cakes to roasts.

Mother Nature often tests our wits. Last year our crew returned to camp after a weekend away for Easter. Our camp was set up on a black soil flat at Police Hole Yards on Auvergne Station. Potter sent me ahead with the crew to check the road and ensure it was suitable for the truck. On inspection I radioed Potter to tell him the situation was probably not ideal as some light showers had made the dirt track slippery.

Potter, Ben (a friend turned crew member) and the truck stayed the night at the homestead in the hope that the road would dry out. The rain really settled in; the crew dragged their swags and bags into a small shed erected at the campsite and had to share their space with the generator, bikes, dogs, dog feed and horse feed.

Boredom was our greatest challenge. We had one book between the six of us and not a single magazine or deck of cards. We sat around in our raincoats under the awning with water swirling around our feet. Each day we would go for short walks to assess the road in the hope there had been less rain elsewhere.

After about six days we were running low on generator fuel and meat. It was often raining too heavily to send a helicopter in with supplies. Luckily for us, the manager managed to winch himself in with the Toyota and dropped off supplies. It was a relief to see another human being. A day or so later it was dry enough to tail the horses in while leaving the truck at the main homestead. Weeks like that make you wish you lived in a house!

But rain isn't the only element to descend upon us. In September last year, we were based at Mt Doreen Station in the Tanami Desert, probably one of the most remote places I have been. We moved our camp from bore to bore as we would spend a week at each set of yards (located at each bore) to trap and process Herefords. At the end of the day we would often return to our campsite to find a sandstorm had completely covered our belongings in fine red sand. We would shake it out and dust everything off and try again for another day.

* * *

In any job there are days when things don't go according to plan. Not every job promises the possibility of rolling into your swag at 8.30 pm, but when things don't go according to plan outback, you can end up walking cows and calves at 9 pm in the moonlight, then still need to travel back to camp, wash and feed horses, cook a feed for the camp, shower and then maybe think about hitting the pillow, only to wake again at 5 am. In this line of work one has to be adaptable as plans change every minute. Sometimes lack of information may lead to a change in circumstances.

Earlier this year we were walking a mob of cattle on Newcastle Waters Station. The fixed-wing pilot had told us there was a good spot along the fence-line we were following where we would be able to water the cattle. So off we went. Crew member Bronte and I were in the lead on our horses. We reached some mud, thinking we must be getting close to this watering point. Potter was growing impatient, wanting to know when the lead would get to the water. We had to keep telling him there was no water in sight but the mud was getting boggy and the horses were struggling. We persevered but when there was still no water in sight we decided it would be madness trying to walk the large mob we had through the middle of what appeared to be a half-dried swamp.

Bronte and I were trying to turn the cattle around when we well and truly bogged our horses. The mud was up to the horses' hocks and they refused to move. We spurred them, we towed them, we hit them with sticks but they just stood there. The rest of the crew were on bikes and unable to come to our rescue. They had to gather the mob and walk them around the swamp while we continued our mission. We pulled our boots off and did all we could to get the horses to move. Eventually Bronte was able to get her horse to some slightly drier ground and out of her sticky situation. Unfortunately, wherever I attempted to go, the mud only seemed to get worse.

I unsaddled my horse, Harmony, and tried to tow her barefoot through the mud. She was so exhausted that I had to let her rest for twenty minutes before I got her to try another five steps. She is usually a very flighty horse but was so exhausted that she let me rub her head, legs and belly without flinching. After about four hours we were close enough for me to walk back to the truck that Potter and Bronte had brought closer and cart some water to her. After giving her a drink and washing the dried mud from her legs she was able to move better. Finally, after five hours of being stuck in a swamp, we were free. The horses were loaded onto a truck and taken back to camp while the bikes continued with the mob. They didn't reach the holding paddock until after dark and no water was ever found on the fence-line.

Often the principle of 'if you want something done right, do it yourself' applies. Another incident happened after one of our crew members was asked to hook the dog trailer to one of our vehicles so we could leave for our next job. But when we left the station, Potter received a radio call in the truck that the vehicle and trailer behind him had somehow separated. On returning to the scene about two kilometres from our departure point, Potter found his trailer upside down and back to front, with all the dogs in a jumble. After a few words, he and the crew managed to open most of the cage doors to release the dogs.

A couple of the crew had to wait until we were able to get there to help to tip the trailer back onto its wheels. We were fortunate that none of the dogs was hurt, just a little shaken up. We concluded that when a certain individual had hooked the trailer up, the catch had not been locked down. After hitting a bumpy patch on the road the trailer detached, did a full 180-degree turn and flipped. After a day of very costly repairs, we were able to leave for our destination the next day.

Horns, Tail Hair and Second Bum Holes

Trisha Cowley, Katherine Research Station

I've got a pretty cool job. I work as a Beef Cattle Extension officer for DPIF based at the Katherine Research Station. I work with producers, taking the results from research projects and applying them practically in the paddock. I'm fortunate. For a start I live in the NT, secondly I get to work with cows and thirdly, I get to work with leading cattle producers who never fail to inspire and motivate me.

I grew up on a sheep and cattle farm in south-west Queensland and am living proof that 'you can take the girl out of the bush but you can't take the bush out of the girl'. I went to university in Brisbane and studied psychology after my parents urged me to do anything BUT agriculture, but then decided to head to the NT for a year of fun jillarooing. Eleven years later I am still here, with no desire to head back south just yet! My husband and I have recently gone into the cattle game, which allows me to put my money where my mouth is.

I can vividly remember being told about the ringer who was horned by a scrub bull that gave him a 'second bum hole', or so the storyteller said. Horns on cattle are definitely dangerous, particularly with the increasing proportion of station hands who have zero to one year's experience under their belt and aren't as savvy around cattle. While I like to think that I am not too bad on my feet around cattle, my braveness in the yards evaporates pretty quickly when a big set of horns turns up! Horns are also dangerous for other cattle, especially during transport and yard work, when they are in confined spaces and can't escape from bullies.

Traditionally the beef industry has worked to protect people and cattle from the danger of horns through dehorning, the process of physically removing the horn at a young age. However, some producers have instead taken the option of breeding polled (i.e., naturally hornless) cattle, eliminating the need to dehorn.

This isn't as easy as it sounds. The proportion of polled to horned cattle is low in many breeds, including Brahmans, which are the predominant cattle breed in the northern NT due to their hardiness and tropical adaption to heat, humidity and parasites. Further, just because an animal is polled doesn't mean that it only passes on polled genetics to its offspring.

At the moment I am working with a couple of producers in the Katherine region who have been introducing polled genetics into their herds for the past five to ten years. Both Garry and Michelle Riggs from Lakefield Station and Keith and Roxie Holzwart from Avago Station are breeding the horns off their cattle as they believe it results in better welfare for the animals, better production by minimising the post-weaning growth setback, and meets the animal–welfare expectations of the broader community. Both families have been breeding polled bulls for their own use for a number of years, chiefly due to the difficulty in sourcing good polled genetics.

Unfortunately, polled Brahman stud breeders are few and far between, and while this is certainly changing, both families have found it difficult to source bulls that tick all the boxes – polledness, fertility, structural soundness and temperament. It was particularly frustrating buying a bull that the vendors claimed was 'true polled', but in fact a carrier of horns.

Let me give you a quick Polled Genetics 101 lesson. The polled gene has two forms: polled (P) or horned (H). Every animal has two copies of the polled gene, so potentially they could be PP, PH or HH. The polled form is dominant over the horned form. This means that only HH animals are horned. It is slightly more complicated than that, as there is an interaction from another gene that controls scurs, which are loose horny growths that are not attached to the skull. PP animals are polled, but PH animals are either polled or scurred, but some are also horned. Are you confused yet?

An animal gets one copy of the polled gene from its mother and one copy from its father, and consequently randomly passes on one of its copies to its progeny. PP animals are considered 'true polled' as they pass on the polled copy to 100 per cent of their progeny. However, PH animals are carriers of horn, and will only pass on a polled copy to half of their progeny. Therefore, using PP sires in preference to PH sires will speed up the time taken to breed a polled herd. Since PP and PH animals can both be visually polled, it is desirable to be able to distinguish between them. Typically it can take thirty years to change a horned herd into a polled herd through visual selection. Now, thanks to CSIRO, the Beef CRC and Meat and Livestock Australia (MLA), there is a DNA test available that takes the guesswork out by determining whether an animal is PP, PH or HH, all through a tail hair sample. Using the test to select PP cattle can reduce the time taken to breed a polled herd by twenty years.

Keith and Roxie and Garry and Michelle now use the Polled DNA test to source PP bulls and to make selection decisions in their own stud herds. They are part of an MLA-funded project that is demonstrating the practical use of the Polled DNA test in breeding polled bulls. As part of the project, we are testing progeny of PP bulls in their stud herd. From visual assessments at branding at Lakefield Station, 66 per cent of progeny were polled and 34 per cent were scurred, thus no calves needed dehorning – an excellent result. DNA testing revealed that 75 per cent were heterozygous polled (PH) and 17 per cent were homozygous polled (PP). While it will take some years before Garry and Michelle reach a pure polled herd, using a PP bull had immediate effect through removing the need to dehorn.

We are doing a similar demonstration at Avago, including comparing the proportion of polled, horned and scurred progeny from using PP versus PH bulls, which will demonstrate the ultimate power of using the Polled DNA test. Keith and Roxie are weaning the progeny soon and holding a field day to provide the results later in the year.

This project is yet another example of the beef industry adopting new technology and management practices as they strive to improve the welfare of animals under their care, while improving productivity and profitability. Hats off to them. Their ingenuity and commitment never fails to inspire me, and my job allows me to learn from and work with families like the Riggses and the Holzwarts every day.

You're Mad!

Sue Witham, Mt Bundy Station

If you have ever had to sell the family farm and move, you will understand the stress our Mt Bundy family went through to make a new start in the Northern Territory. This included arranging a clearing sale, packing up fifteen years of house and farm equipment, relocating all the livestock, two sulking teenagers, a six-year-old, five horses, four mad kelpies and the family ginger cat and then driving six days and 4500 kilometres.

You are probably asking 'Why?'

Well, that was eight years ago and the cattle industry was prosperous, our family had outgrown our family-owned, mixed-farming partnership in southern WA and we were keen for a new challenge. Both my fairly young parents had died suddenly, which made us realise life is, as they say, short. After much deliberation, hair-pulling, door-slamming and tears (and that was just me), we eagerly headed north to take up a small historical cattle station with a fledgling tourism venture, just 110 kilometres south of Darwin.

We had stud cattle and feedlot sheep and cattle in WA and looked forward to the challenge of having Brahman cattle and the northern export market.

As you may imagine, we all had a fairly steep learning curve on dealing with tourists, cleaning guesthouses and living in a tropical environment. As a good old farmer's wife, I was used to feeding shearers and contractors of all sorts, but taking over bed-and-breakfast accommodation and serving meals at all hours of the day to non-English speaking French, Italian and German strangers was a humorous occupation. The sulking teenagers were the main source of exasperation. Because we had dragged them kicking and screaming from their boarding-school friends, their beloved farm and all they knew, and demanded that they enjoy the new enterprise their wise mother and father had arranged for them, they rebelled.

Our thirteen-year-old son, Ben, and fifteen-year-old daughter, Bec, timed the rebellions well – they happened just as I was serving the overseas guests. I look back now and wonder how on earth we survived. We had arrived like a travelling circus, in the middle of the peak tourist season, to live in our camper trailer for four weeks while the ex-owners slowly moved their belongings from our new house (which also contained four bed-and-breakfast rooms).

Our four kelpies, straight off the farm and used to chasing sheep for a living, had been trapped in the horse float with the ginger cat, two motorbikes, lounge chairs and the TV for the six-day journey. They spent the first week barking at every vehicle that came down the driveway, and after about 100 tourists, decided they were having no effect at scaring the strangers. So they moved on to chasing the wallaby population and having 'bark-offs' with the local barking-owl population.

While we were learning the hospitality business, we were also busy schooling the two sulking teenagers via the School of Isolated and Distance Education (SIDE). Our youngest daughter, Kasey, was happily enjoying time away from all this chaos at the local primary school nearby, in Adelaide River. Unfortunately, the nearest high school was 110 kilometres away. It was hard to keep Ben concentrating on schoolwork when he had been released from boarding-school prison and thrown into a teenage boy's paradise of barramundi fishing, pig hunting, crocodile dodging, buffalo chasing and cleanskin (unbranded) cattle. As you can guess, his life wasn't too bad now.

Scott, my husband, was working out on his new domain and sourcing a cattle supply to start our herd and get back to doing something familiar. Repairing dilapidated fencing and water points were the first priorities. The nine houses on the property were all screaming for attention too and being the all-round, can-fix-anything farmer, Scott also transformed the 1960s American-built homesteads into a marketable accommodation product.

On a Serious Note

Sue Witham, Mt Bundy Station

Almost four years have passed since we tragically lost our son, Ben. When people say they have 'lost' someone, I often think, 'What? Down the back of the couch or in the supermarket?' Not us. We lost him in such a way that he is never coming back. He would've been twenty-one this year.

We could not speak to each other the day Ben got sick, because the fear of opening our mouths and speaking would only make it real. How can it be that our son, our brother, is lying in the emergency room fighting for his life? He is strong, he is fit, he is young, and he is Ben.

To tell the full story of Ben's death is daunting and I am used to sanitising it so much it seems trivial. It is still hard to comprehend that a teenager so full of life, so kind, so gentle, so funny and so great can be struck down suddenly with what doctors diagnosed as Acute Lymphoblastic Leukaemia (ALL).

Ben spent his seventeenth birthday in ICU and passed away a few weeks later. That is the short version. It would take weeks and too many puddles on the keyboard to explain much more. While we were arranging the funeral the Live Export Ban was announced. I cannot thank enough our family, friends, staff and total strangers who took control of Mt Bundy while we attempted to understand what had just happened to our world.

It was coming into peak season and with 200-plus people in the caravan park all accommodation was full. We had spent five weeks in Adelaide fighting for Ben's life. We had been flown down to Adelaide via the 'care flight' jet from Darwin, and we were grateful for the assistance of the Ronald McDonald House for somewhere to live. The trade-off of living in a remote part of Australia is that some health services are just not available, and if in need you have to uproot and go to where the treatment is. This was the case with Ben. He was too sick and Darwin could not treat him.

The events that unfolded after Ben's death could not be written even in a novel. Some final tests were taken just before he died. The doctors were baffled and still could not agree on why Ben was so sick. A result of one of these tests was high arsenic levels, which sparked a criminal investigation. The national news had a field day, the coroner was alerted and Mt Bundy was closed to the public, with all staff and guests evacuated in the middle of the night.

The following debacle was a comedy of errors. All residents and employees were tested and supposed high levels of arsenic were found, yet no evidence at all was found at Mt Bundy. A week later the powers-that-be declared they had a false positive result and had misread all the tests: Mt Bundy, its residents and Ben did not have arsenic poisoning and never did. As you can imagine, this was a disaster for the business, but it was too little too late. The damage was done. Not only had we lost our son, we had no income, no tourists and couldn't sell any cattle either.

A coronial enquiry eighteen months later proved negligence on the part of the doctor at the Adelaide hospital.

In moments like this, something intangible kept us going. Our two daughters were mourning too. Bec had started a science degree at uni and gave that up to be home with us for a while. Kasey was eleven, and it was tough. My husband, Scott, was inconsolable.

The cattle wandered, the girls kept an eye on them, calves needed tagging and desexing. We struggled on numbly, going through the motions. Things were tight financially, tourist numbers were slowly returning but we were fairly quiet as the rumour mill worked overtime via the tourist network. The cattle trade looked promising but we had nothing ready to sell.

Scott eventually got a short-term job on an iron ore mine in the Pilbara as a driller's assistant, a fly-in, fly-out role. He needed to get away from some painful reminders and work out his grief. We all battled on, trying to regain some normality. Thank god for friends and family and, at times, perfect strangers.

The next couple of years were a blur as we determined to pick the business up again after major losses from cancelled bookings. We worked hard, and probably hid ourselves in the work: developing new markets and renovating accommodation.

We developed a four-wheel-drive tour of the property and its wildlife, checking cattle, water, World War II history and chatting with guests about the industry and the export debacle. The tour finished with a beer on the hill overlooking the flood plains at sunset.

We are now back on the tourist map and busier than ever. Our horse treks had to give way for viability reasons – insurance was a big cause – so we replaced them with more weddings, conferences and catering events. We are the home of the Adelaide River Music Muster hosting singer–songwriter Beccy Cole this year. We had a huge amount of interest from film crews wanting to capture the dust, sunsets, cattle and horses.

We have had some great fun and adventures over the years: taking celebrities on horseback across the flood plains, wobbling around, trying to look the part of a ringer. Some could ride well and others needed velcro. We have had the likes of Daniel MacPherson, the *Biggest Loser* cast including The Commando, *McLeod's Daughters* stars and most recently UK chef Jimmy Doherty and *Masterchef* runner-up Lynton Tapp on an outback food and TV shoot. I am hopeless with celebrities as most of the time I don't even recognise them. Once we had well-known author Di Morrissey at our dinner table for three nights before I realised she was *the* Di Morrissey!

The cattle are still important to our business, but we only run a few hundred now, a nice little red Brahman mob, with a few ferals thrown in and a few water buffalo. We now have a following for school groups wanting to explore the cattle industry and often have groups on a mini muster, involved in tagging, branding and learning why we do what we do to our cattle. We get tears, screams of delight and fear, kids who don't want to leave and parents who want to thank us for showing their precious city-born child a glimpse into food production. We also explain the care of the country with fire and flood, our friend and enemy. With a 1.5–2 metre rainfall, we experience some serious flooding (a curse) and pasture growth (a blessing).

Kasey, our youngest daughter, has been home-schooled for the last two years, doing grades eight and nine through the School of Isolated and Distance Education

(SIDE). We all needed to regroup after Ben's death and this has worked well for us. It also means she is our right-hand when it comes to horses and all-round help.

Bec returned to university to study an agricultural science degree, leaning towards cattle genetics. She also works in a large West Australian winery. She comes home as often as she can, mostly to tell her dad which bulls to keep. We left her in charge one year, which resulted in the most bulls we've ever had; only a handful were castrated because she liked the look of all of them.

Bec and Kasey are deviously planning to run a cattle station together one day. And Kasey still cracks the whip for tourists when she needs phone credit.

'I haven't been anywhere for a month!'

'Miss Chardy', www.misschardy.com

I am starting to turn into captain psycho cranky pants. It is nearly a month since we returned to the station from holidays and I haven't been anywhere since. Unless you count a trip out into the paddock to meet the neighbour.

I am finally able to notice the signs of my imminent hermit attack. I now know when it is time to go somewhere, to visit someone, to get the hell off the station and out into the big wide world. There is only so much #getsortedwithchards, cleaning and officework a girl can handle.

What is the telltale sign, I hear you ask? Well, it is when I start to dress up of a night-time. I have a shower and pop on some 'town clothes' so I can feel human. It even involves a necklace and sometimes even make-up. Surely I am not the only one who does this? On Saturday night, for our anniversary, I even put heels on …. So this weekend I am heading up to a friend's place, a station to our north-west. They are moving and I am going to give her a hand to pack and there will be plenty of time for a chardy on the verandah; well, a G&T in her case. I may also have the blender, Midori and Cointreau packed – you never know when you might need to put your (Japanese) slippers on.

This morning my son Clancy and I will hit the road. A trip away from the station is not like your average just jump in the car and drive a few blocks to your friend's house. You need to clean the car, fuel the car up, make sure you have done all of your station jobs, that is, vegetable order, bread order, food order, get the satellite phone and make sure it is charged, pack a lunch/snacks, fill up the water cooler, fill up water bottles and pack your bags. I have also learnt that it is important to pack your wallet and mobile phone, even if you don't need either. A few years ago when we were at said friend's house my son Tom fell and broke his arm. Long story short, we ended up in Townsville Hospital (yes, in another state and by the sea) and had to borrow friend's mobile phone to take with me. Lucky I had packed a decent suitcase too.

So, once you have yourself sorted it is time to crank up the music and start driving. Today's drive is a three-gate drive that even involves a little bit of bitumen and will take about three-and-a-half hours, perhaps longer because I am not sure how good the road will be.

I am quite excited about this outing even if there isn't a town involved. I always feel quite refreshed and motivated after visiting friends.

* * *

Mrs Savvy B and Co have come over to visit this weekend. I have been missing her after our fabulous holiday on Magnetic Island over two weeks ago.

Mr Savvy B and Mr Chardy are going for fathers of the year and have taken the four boys fishing, while Mrs SB has come here to hang out with Clancy and me. Because both our wagons are still in Camooweal (after we had to fly back in from holidays), I had to drive out and meet her and bring her back here to the house. Just a quick trip to meet them, only took a couple of hours out and back, but my goodness, the road was bumpy, I thought the ute was going to rattle to pieces.

There is certainly no popping over the garden fence for a visit. Oh no, that would be far too easy. Instead I packed a snack for Clancy and we all met halfway at one of our major intersections along the Eastern Freeway, also known as the Wine Road – don't worry, not a toll booth in sight.

This is about a sixty-kilometre drive for both of us. It involved three utes. The boys all then headed north to a waterhole and Mrs SB jumped in the ute with Clancy and me and we hit the road back home to Chardy HQ. Bump, bump, bumpity bump!

Mrs SB and I have made a pact: when we get together we are not going to just sit around and drink wine and waste time. We are going to help each other with something that needs doing, a little project. That is the definition of a good friend, isn't it, invite them over so they can help you out with your crappy jobs. I love it.

Today we are getting my verandah sorted. It always seems to be in such a mess so we are onto it. And you should see Mrs SB go. While I sit in the cool air-conditioning tap-tap-tapping away she is out there working up a sweat, moving things and chucking crap out. I have a verandah around the whole house, and it always seems to be in such a state, but we are getting it sorted once and for all. Isn't it great to have a fresh set of eyes and a different perspective? It is going to be so great once she is – we are – done. What a champ.

Later this afternoon (much later hopefully, ha ha ha) Mr SB, Mr Chardy and the children will come back here for the night. I am sure I will be sad in the morning when I have to say goodbye to them. I am always in denial when they have to go and try so hard to convince them to stay for just a little bit longer.

How Barry the Bike Helped Me

'Miss Jodie'

When the 2014 FutureNTCA crew (young members of the Northern Territory Cattlemen's Association) were given a bike as part of a professional development program, the team decided that it would be used to promote mental health awareness. I went along with the idea, saying I knew a few people close to me who had been affected by anxiety and depression and it was something great we could do for our rural community. But truth be told, the person I knew who had been affected by these illnesses was me.

This is one of the hardest things I've ever written. I'm laying it all on the line, leaving myself completely vulnerable. For the visual readers amongst us, I feel like I'm walking down the main street of my home town completely naked, waiting for the rotten tomatoes to be hurled at me. That's how vulnerable I feel writing this.

The reason I'm sharing so much information with the world and hoping to come out relatively unscathed is because I'm hoping that by sharing my story, someone else is encouraged to seek help, or even deeply consider their own experiences and current mental stability. If just one person does that, then I consider this experience a win. I'm not here to whinge to the world (I have had a pretty awesome life), and I'm not here to seek sympathy – you'll know it when I do. I am just hoping that I'll be able to help someone in some small way.

The first time I went to a GP and said I'm not feeling so crash hot even though I have nothing to be miserable about, she said (and I quote, word for word), 'But that's not you, look at you – you're smiling.' I had never seen this GP before. She didn't know me from a bar of soap. She had to look up her book version of medical Wikipedia to search the symptoms of depression and anxiety. So I walked out of there and paid my $75 fee for absolutely no help whatsoever. As a 22-two-year-old, I took that to mean that I was being ridiculous – 'toughen the heck up, you weak and worthless waste of space'. This didn't help the negative shark-infested tank of thoughts swirling in my head.

One thing you may not realise about people struggling in this way is that they probably don't show it. They may have developed an invisible mask that acts like a shield to protect themselves from showing others how desperate and confused they really are. For the scientists out there, depression can be like a fast-paced feedback mechanism; one negative thought feeds another negative thought, which feeds another, which feeds on the first, and the cycle continues. It becomes difficult to see anything other than this walled-in roundabout that just keeps on happening, even (or perhaps especially) when you 'know' there is no reason for it.

'You have a roof over your head, incoming wages, friends, family and good health, yet you still can't be happy? What's wrong with you? You are so pathetic' – at least that's how the cycle was going in my headspace. You know when you're in a stock camp without a phone, TV or internet and all of a sudden your entire world is what's happening right in front of you? The smallest things are the biggest dramas because that's all you can see, there's nothing to keep it in perspective? That's what it can be like with depression, or at least it was for me.

The second time I went three years later, I got a great GP. She was amazing. Her name was Robyn. I walked into her office and cried. I couldn't speak, I just cried. I didn't even know what I was crying about. I had nothing to cry for, but I could not help or stop myself. She cancelled her next appointment, sat me down and told me what was going on. She prescribed me some medication and made a referral for me to see a counsellor.

That went well for the first week, until I decided I was feeling better so I didn't need the medication. When the counsellor bought all the bull I was feeding her, in some warped way, I considered it a victory. It's not that I didn't want to get better, it's just that I was insecure and a strong part of my personality is that I am a people pleaser. Even though I didn't know this counsellor, I wanted to make her happy, so whenever she frowned at whatever I was saying, I made sure I didn't say it again. In fact, next time I'd say the opposite.

Three appointments later she had me 'cured'. It was a miracle! Not really, I'd just lied a lot and now I didn't have to go to appointments in the middle of the work day while avoiding the question of why I wanted to skip out on work, yet again.

The next time I had a run-in with the black dog was three months ago when my dad passed away. Without a particular reason why, I couldn't pick myself up off the couch, even though I had an important event to organise and jobs that needed doing with ever increasing urgency. Despite this, I couldn't make myself move. The fear of the event/life not going well had me glued to the couch, without even the TV on for background noise. I was afraid of the future. I called my good friend and said this is where I'm at. She said, 'Book yourself in. You can't do this any longer.' So I did, and I went.

I said to the GP, 'I know me, I know how I work, and although I've never been in this particular boat, I am familiar with this ocean. I need help. I can't continue like this.'

He listened. He gave me a script for medication, and lastly he sat back and heard me talk about this online facility that provides lessons to help people affected by depression and anxiety beat their thought patterns and non-helpful behaviours – the website I had learnt about when FutureNTCA chose to promote mental health awareness using Barry the Bike.

MindSpot.org.au is a website that provides lessons online to help people overcome their illness while helping them to recognise and change their thought and behaviour patterns. When a person registers to participate in a course, they are automatically assigned a mental-health professional to check up on each participant each week and see how they are progressing.

My GP was blown away. He had never heard of it.

'Why don't more people know about it?' he asked.

'I don't know,' I said, 'but they should!'

I think this is an invaluable resource, since someone who lives remotely can gain help or assistance without having to go through the rigmarole of coming to town.

For those who are unfamiliar with station life, 'going to town' can be difficult. Just getting there can take hours, and by hours I'm talking up to eight hours just to get to town. Not only that, but unless you have friends you can stay with, there is the significant cost of accommodation as well. On top of that you will be given a list by everyone else on the station of things they would like brought back, not to mention the stores (collection of groceries, parts and supplies) from every business in town. The thing that stops people most, though, is having to justify why they want time off to head to town in the first place.

Let's face it. Some people just aren't good at lying and would prefer to self-medicate in whatever form works for them than admit to someone they work with and possibly admire that they want to book in for a free mental-health check.

I am happy to say that I am still on medication and I am thinking I might be here for a while. The relief the medication is offering is overwhelming (although the start was quite rough – I have never vomited so much in my life). I recognise that short periods of anxiety are normal, stress can really improve performance and everyone feels sad at times, but to have my imbalances corrected so that I am not constantly burdened to the point of collapsing is such a relief.

So if you recognise some of the things I have experienced, or think someone else you know might be feeling the same way, show them the Mindspot website. It's confidential, it's helpful and can be done in the privacy of your own home and it's free. More harm will be done by not mentioning it.

The Head Stockwoman

Stacey Haucke, Alexandria Station

What's it like being a female head stockperson on Australia's second largest cattle station? For me it's a challenge that I enjoy. To begin with, the size and the number of people here were a bit overwhelming. I have a camp of six people; most of them are girls, which I think is great, and I'd like to think we could give the boys a fair run for their money.

The people in my camp come from all over Australia. One's from South Australia, a few are from New South Wales, there's a Queenslander and a couple from New South Wales. There have also been a couple of West Australians.

We have spent a lot of time out at 'camp' this year. We have a truck that carries a water tank, lighting plant, diesel, avgas (for the aircraft), horse feed, fencing gear and saddles. The truck also tows a kitchen van. Once we have a couple of truckloads of horses, motorbikes and our stock-camp poddy calf (who thinks she's a dog!), we're away. Some of the yards we stay at have a shower and toilet block, while others have only a hole in the ground for a toilet and we've taken the 'shower trailer' out. There's also a shed at each camp for everyone to camp in. There have been some lovely cold mornings while we've been out. When it's one degree Celsius out, plus the wind-chill factor, it makes it pretty hard to crawl out of your swag.

We generally go out to camp for two- to three-week stints. This usually gets us to finishing the paddock or paddocks at that particular set of yards. Our job while out is to draft the weaners off the cows. The weaners are then trucked back to the yards at Alex house for the weaner camp. We also pull off cull cows in some paddocks and castrate any bull calves that come through. At one particular set of yards we had to scruff the calves (catch them by hand), which was pretty funny to start with until everyone got the hang of it.

We've finished mustering the cows and are now doing stud heifers. There's a mob of meatworkers going soon too, so we are back in at the house for the rest of the year. There's lick runs, fencing, bore mechanic offsiding and all the general bits and pieces to go on with, as well as a couple of campdrafts coming up.

The bit I really enjoy about my job is helping people pick up new skills and seeing their confidence grow. This year I taught most of my camp how to shoe a horse, and a couple have learnt to ride a motorbike as well. The Barkly holey ground sorted us all out pretty quickly, while shoeing was met with a few grumbles until everyone got the hang of it.

What made me become a head stockperson? I guess it was a natural progression. I've made a career in the cattle industry and I'm not quitting it anytime soon. To be able to say that I've run the stock camp on Alexandria is to me an achievement in itself, as I've come in straight up this year as a head stockperson. I think there is still a lot of the 'oh but you're a girl' attitude around this industry, and we have to work that much harder sometimes to get recognition. For me to say I've done this might convince another girl somewhere along the way to stick with it.

This year at Alex has been a challenging and interesting one so far. There have been ups and downs, but I wouldn't trade the opportunity I've been given. I wasn't overly excited about going to work on the Barkly. There are holes and cracks in the ground everywhere that are rough-going on a horse and motorbike, and the wind in winter is downright rude, but you'll fall in love with the sky pretty damn quickly. The sunsets and sunrises, as well as the stars at night in this part of the world, are in a league of their own.

* * *

I have fronted up for another year of big sunrises and sunsets, but my job title has changed. This year I'm the stud coordinator, the 'stud chick' for Alex's composite stud. This has seen me trade the stock camp of around six people for a camp of me, myself and I – mostly. In saying that, all the work with the top stud cows, heifers and bulls is mostly done with the help of the weaner camp, while the stock camp helps out with the commercial bull breeder herd.

While I was happy with my job last year, the opportunity to learn and expand my knowledge was not something to pass up. I've always had an interest in the stud side of things, but it's also taken a long time for me to 'settle down', as my parents would put it, from that 'cow-chasing bug'. There is more fine detail to my work this year and it definitely has been a fair learning curve. Learning to read hundreds of tag numbers, weights, flight-time results and scan result numbers without getting them all mixed up has been a challenge at times. Learning to step back from yard work hasn't been easy either. Boss man said to me the other day, 'Even though you feel like a bludger, you have to just sit there and do your numbers only.' Meanwhile I'm champing at the bit to help yard up or something.

We've been busy since Easter with all the stud cattle, doing weaning, preg-testing, scanning heifers and doing 600-day weights on the number four heifers and bulls, as well as bull selection.

We had Sam Harburg and David Johnston come up for the bull selection. I think we scored the two coldest, windiest days the Barkly could deliver. Trying to keep all our paperwork together was a bit of a struggle. More paperclips, an extra coat or two and a beanie did the trick. Even the poor bulls were pretty cold and had all their gear well and truly tucked up, making some of the selecting a little difficult.

We've pretty much finished the cattle work for the stud now; there are only two top stud groups left to preg-test. My next job will be pasture monitoring, which involves going to about thirty-odd locations over the whole of Alexandria and recording what plant species and percentage of grass cover are at each particular site. This is all put together at the end and sent to head office.

I also keep an eye on our broodmares here too. At the moment there are twelve foals to be weaned later in the year. These foals are our future workhorses here and at Soudan and Gallipoli.

Many people ask me how I cope living with so many people. It's true, it is like living in a small town here and we do have a street called East Street. This, I think, is the best bit for me because I live in East Street, so I'm just a little bit apart from everybody. I can easily spend a weekend doing my own thing and hardly see anyone at all. In saying that, I reckon some of the kids in the quarters do a hell of a job putting up with each other. There are people from all kinds of backgrounds here and to get along in a small area for a season is a good effort. People just have to learn to be more accepting and respectful of others; some cope with this and others don't. That said, we are not the only station on the Barkly or anywhere with large numbers of people working together.

I'm a lucky girl to be able to have some of my own horses here with me. It has been very enjoyable so far this year having the time to ride more after work. I'll admit that, at times, I missed having that opportunity last year. I'm pretty sure that my horses are feeling happier about getting a little more 'relaxed' attention now too. We've been to two camp drafts so far this year and there are a few more to go.

My dogs also make my time here more enjoyable. Having this pair of clowns to come home to at the end of the day is pretty good. There's always a dog version of a hug – 'I'll just launch at you, mum, and you gotta catch me.' Even after a long day this makes me smile. I do a bit of fence-checking on my own now, so Dooley and Nipper are often my main offsiders. I just wish they'd learn to do a tie-off properly or bang a steel picket in for me every now and then.

We've got the Brunette camp draft/races/rodeo coming up and everybody is already keen for the next social do. You can't beat the enthusiasm. Then it's more fence-checking and riding horses for me, as well as whatever else needs doing. I am thoroughly enjoying my job and its challenges. I reckon I might be hanging around for a while yet.

Going Back Outback

Alexandria Rose, Birrindudu Station

In 2009, fresh out of high school in a NSW coastal city, I went to work for a season on Birrindudu, one of Australia's most remote cattle stations, located on the Northern Territory–Western Australian border. Our closest contact with civilisation was an Aboriginal community three hours north-east; we were a nine-hour drive from any town. It was an isolated and an alluring world.

The story of the city girl who goes country has been told many times so I'll spare the tales of how hard it was to give up my manicures and lattes; instead, I'll let the land do the talking. Let me take you back outback.

* * *

It's sunrise and the hot wind is already blowing in over the Tanami Desert. The Toyotas roll into the yards and break the constant rumble of the cattle. Eight of us jump out of the vehicles and scurry in all directions. With a strike of the match the branding furnace comes alive, spewing out heat in all directions. There is a heavy swish of the knife blades as they take to the sharpener. Dust rises and thickens as the holding yard stirs. The first lot are being pushed up the race and we settle in for a massive day. The crush slams shut. Hides sizzle, blood drips, beasts limp. It's 6.30 am, sweat is pouring and you've just branded one of 500.

* * *

Birrindudu made it easy to fall in love with everything I saw around me. Here, on the station, the colour of the Australian sky that I'd grown up with took on a new and extreme beauty when contrasted with the redness of the desert dirt. The penetrating silence of the nights out in the middle of nowhere was surreal, topped only by the vastness of the outback sky. The natural lines of a beast began to mean something to me when I ran my hands over its hide. Even the wind took on a special quality because it was pregnant with the scent of cattle. At Birrindudu, nature made me privy to her intricacies and wonders. Nothing I had ever seen before had filled me with such lonesome contentment.

* * *

On stations, the physical demands and personal risk required to complete a task is unheard of in any other kind of job. But as a ringer you tend to find fun and enjoyment in being a shit-kicker. In the midst of mates the work doesn't seem so bad, and the range of jobs means you're always doing something different. The best of the best stockmen and women are all-time all-rounders. At Birrindudu everyone could weld, run bores, muster, draft, change oil, fix flat tyres, shoot, cook, load, unload, shoe … the list is never-ending. I never did manage to learn how to do everything, but I constantly tried to play catch-up and figure out exactly how to boldly master so many different skillsets. The boys in particular had a fearless capability which we relied on whenever something had gone to shit, and the girls — well, they kept everything else running smoothly the rest of the time.

* * *

James was a memorable character, a man of pride, integrity and strong work ethic. The photo featured on the front cover of this book is one of many that shows his crazy, fearless determination to be the fastest, most agile and best all-rounder ringer. How could any of us have known that it was fate knocking at his door?

Before the accident, station life possessed an uncanny gleam and glow about it. I found enjoyment in everything and the combination of the environment and the exhilaration, challenges, laughter and friendship made time evaporate faster than the steam off the troughs. I never let my mind become preoccupied with the possibility of the experience ending.

And then the accident happened.

For all the speculation, it was just a roo that made the ute roll. Nothing more, nothing less. The one animal we never thought twice about shooting had had its ultimate revenge.

Everyone else was fine. Heck, even the dogs walked out of the wreck. But Casey said as soon as she looked at him she knew without a doubt. She ran through the night for help, but there was no running from the nightmare that the clarity of day would affirm.

That night we all lost more than a mate; we lost a family member. I like to think that James left the realm of mere humans to settle somewhere with the likes of other bush legends. He's probably up there arguing with Clancy of The Overflow or Ned Kelly about the entry requirements to make it into the Stockman's Hall of Fame.

After the accident, work fell into a monotonous pattern of muster, draft, weigh, wean, repeat. But now there was no fun, and no longer enough beauty in the things I had learnt to love. Everyone had gone and I wanted out too, but my time in the Territory wasn't over yet.

* * *

From about 100 metres away, Tim picked out a fat heifer he wanted for dinner. She was grazing away peacefully on the edge of the scrub, without the slightest inkling that within the hour she'd be on our plates. It was a clean kill, as always.

We slit her throat to let the blood drain away from the meat and then began to butcher her as if the contents of a box were being slowly and carefully unpacked.

We worked away, slicing, carving and carrying as the sun busied itself with setting across the flat. When the hooves and hide were all that was left, we cleaned our knives and left nature to take care of the rest.

There is something significant and beautiful about being that close to your food source, about being connected to it enough to feel the blood drip onto your hands and to feel the warmth of the meat as you respectfully take it away from the bone. I wonder how many supermarket shoppers ever get to speculate what happened prior to the shrink-wrapped meat they toss in their trolleys.

* * *

We took refuge in the Toyota to escape the dust at lunchtime. It was then that I realised the state of my hands. I'd been gripping the bike handles for so long and hard that I had a handful of blisters. When I opened my fingers to take a closer look, the fragile creases of pooled blood broke apart, exposing the delicate skin below them. It was no longer possible to tell dried blood from dirt. God knows how many times I'd come off the bike that day.

That is what it looked like to live and breathe cattle. That is what it looked like to work a job that is unforgiving in a place that is remote and harsh. The rough, bloody hands were my membership card to the most exclusive club in Australia – the ringers from the Top End – and for that I didn't mind the searing pain.

* * *

After James's accident and by the ten-month mark, my thoughts and feelings about Birrindudu were tainted and my romantic notions of horses and land had been dispelled by the fifteen-hour days of shooting lame cattle in the thick of drought and dust storms.

One long day, after we'd finally yarded the cattle, I looked to the horizon. I saw the day turn to night on the edge of the Tanami Desert and I knew that my time was up. The next day I flew out on the mail plane, never to return again.

My time at Birrindudu indebted me to the NT outback. Not only is it the most imposing, majestic and beckoning place in the country, its people are the lifeblood of Australia.

It took me a while to believe it, but these days I accept that I won't have the chance to go back out there again. It seems that my inner cowgirl sold out in the battle against my city-slicker, latte-sipping traits. But every now and again the cowgirl makes a reappearance. Like when I pipe up over the Live Export Ban among my animal-activist friends, or when my answer to the question 'Strawberry cider or Indian Pale Ale?' is 'Ya got any XXXX Gold, mate?' I think it was even my inner ringer that revived the term 'bloody oath' among my feminist reading group.

Stories from Far North, Central, South-West and Channel Country regions in Queensland

Teaching an Old Dog New Tricks

Jenny Underwood, Eversleigh Station

'You're mad! Why do you want to go to live and work way out there?' This was the reaction from friends when I announced that I was heading west to take up a teaching position at Cameron Downs, a one-teacher school on a cattle and sheep property, sixty-five kilometres south of Hughenden in north-western Queensland. After twelve years of classroom teaching in a variety of schools I felt I was ready for a change.

The school was opened in 1967; this original school building was workers' quarters that had been converted into a schoolroom and accommodation for the teacher. When I first arrived, I taught six pupils from three families and I had up to sixteen pupils from pre-school to Year Seven. Some of the children travelled up to sixty kilometres one way to come to school.

My family, however, weren't at all surprised by my decision. I am a third-generation teacher and, although I wasn't from the land, my family had always lived in rural areas. I grew up in the Lockyer Valley, west of Brisbane, surrounded by farms, with the one-teacher school being the focal point of the community. My father was the school headmaster as well as my teacher throughout my seven years of primary education. I loved country life and the simple upbringing and values that came with it.

I have never once regretted my decision to move west. City life had become too fast and impersonal for my liking; I much prefer the simple things in life and here was a golden opportunity for me to enjoy two of the things I loved: teaching children and being a part of a close-knit community.

'You'll probably land yourself a grazier and end up living out there forever!' I was told. That was the furthest thing from my mind when I arrived at Cameron Downs in 1993.

But in September 1997, I *did* marry a grazier and my life headed in yet another direction. After six years at the little school I resigned from teaching in 1998 and became a 'farmer's wife'. No longer was I the teacher; I became the student and learnt to look at life from a totally different side of the fence.

My 'new' life revolves around the myriad responsibilities of running a property. I have a good and patient teacher in my husband, Roger. He has taught me a love of the land and a respect for the livestock we raise. Each day presents a new experience, some of which can often be challenging.

I no longer work a five-day week with circles on the calendar marking off the school holidays. Now two of the most important days are Tuesday and Friday – mail days. I have never been a keen shopper (much to my husband's delight) so I rarely go to town, let alone the big smoke. Just about anything we need is brought out of Hughenden (100 kilometres to our north) by our obliging mailman or a neighbour. My main wardrobe is very basic, consisting mostly of work shirts, jeans and a pair of work boots. I have a well-worn old paddock hat and a good hat for more 'social' occasions.

Instead of meeting friends for coffee and a chat, I love nothing more than going out into the paddock and having smoko with the cattle. Spending time and watching the cattle interact with their calves and each other brings me more pleasure than I ever thought possible. They are my time out, and the best therapy I know. We can learn so much from these gentle beasts. I am constantly amazed by them, particularly a young heifer when she gives birth to her first calf. Their innate mothering instinct is phenomenal.

I don't have a hobby as such. I will never profess to be a gardener and I am definitely not creative when it comes to the finer arts. But I do see the beauty in nature and I spend endless hours appreciating it all through observation and the lens of my camera.

I think everyone who lives in the bush has a story to tell. I find it easier to tell my story to family and friends through photographs. Nowadays there are endless opportunities to chronicle our daily lives with the range of media that we have readily available. It's true when they say a picture is worth a thousand words.

* * *

They say that life begins at forty. I still had a year to go to reach that milestone, but certainly my life changed completely, and for the better, in 1998 when I resigned from the Department of Education and became a full-time grazier. After eighteen years, I was suddenly back on 'L' plates and learning a new career from scratch. My classroom was the wide open spaces of Eversleigh, our home block, and Aireworth, an additional block about eighty kilometres north-west of home. My students were now four-legged creatures: Droughtmaster cattle and Merino sheep.

As soon as I walked out the door I was at my workplace, seven days a week. Unlike my city friends, I didn't have to battle traffic jams to and from work, I had no noisy or nosy neighbours and each morning I awoke to the beauty of nature in the form of a glorious sunrise and each day ended in a spectacular sunset. You can't get better than that.

I had a whole new daily routine and a totally different lingo to learn, especially when we were still running sheep as well as cattle. The only way I could tell the difference between a wether (a castrated male sheep) and a ewe was that they ran in separate paddocks and eventually a ewe, if the ram had done its job, would have a lamb with her. The sheep had to be jetted for flystrike and after shearing the sheep were drenched in a shower dip to prevent lice.

In spring the sheep were brought in to be crutched – the wool was cut away from around their backsides and eyes – and the wethers also were crutched around their pizzles to prevent flystrike and wool blindness and to get rid of any stained wool. Towards the end of the year the sheep were shorn and lambs were marked and mulesed. We sold the last of the sheep in 2003 and to be honest, I don't miss running sheep but I do miss having mutton to eat.

We went on weekly 'water runs' so that poly pipe lines and water troughs could be checked and cleaned out. Once I was confident enough to find my way around the property I did these runs on my own. When I do a water run, Roger is never sure when to expect me home; I take a lot longer than him because I spend most of my time chatting to the cattle and taking photographs. My sister, to this day, is still intrigued when I say that I am doing a lick run – putting out a dry supplementary urea-based mix that enables the livestock to use the pasture better, especially when the quality of the feed is poor.

Mustering is done on a four-wheel bike as I could never quite confidently master a two-wheel motorbike at my age. This is one of the few times that I decided that you can't teach an old dog new tricks. Apart from when the days are really hot, dry and dusty, mustering can be very enjoyable. It gives me time to take a good look around and I am able to switch off – no computers and no phones to distract me – and I can also forget about all the housework and paperwork waiting at home.

Moving to inland Queensland, I began to appreciate just how big rural Australia is. Geographically, we live close to the centre of Queensland, 100 kilometres south of Hughenden and 220 kilometres north of Longreach. Our nearest shopping town is Hughenden and the nearest major centre is Townsville, about five hours away. Eversleigh is about 18,000 hectares and Aireworth an additional 6000 hectares – a total of just over 59,000 acres for the pre-metric readers.

We breed Droughtmasters and have done so for more than forty years. The Droughtmaster is an Australian breed of beef cattle developed in the early 1960s and well suited to the conditions of northern Australia. Between the two properties, we generally run about 1700 breeders (cows) and their progeny (calves and weaners). Our stocking rate is one beast per twenty acres (1:8 ha) so when the seasons are in our favour that equates to about 3000 head.

Our country type is predominantly open, Mitchell grass downs with flood channels to our western side. Our creek and river systems flow south, joining the Cooper Creek catchment system that eventually ends up in Lake Eyre in the centre of Australia. Much of our country is flat – millions of years ago the area was part of the inland sea and dinosaurs reigned supreme. Our average rainfall is around 450 mm per year (18 inches in the 'old scale'). The seasons are totally unpredictable. Within a short period we experienced our highest and lowest annual rainfall figures. In 2000 we measured 950 mm, only to measure 161 mm two years later.

Most of our rain falls in summer during the wet season, generally with storms starting in December till about March. Well, that is what should happen, but the last two years have been very challenging as the rains haven't arrived and much of inland Queensland and NSW have been in drought. Last year we measured just under 200 mm for the year, and most of that fell in the first two months of 2013; so far this year we have had 180 mm in small falls.

In a proper big wet we can be isolated for many days and even weeks. We have a large cold room, which means we can store cold and perishable goods for a while and a large pantry enables me to buy a lot of groceries in bulk. I have learnt that just about any foodstuff can be put into a deep freezer even when the label says 'unsuitable for freezing'. Even after the rain has stopped it can be some time before we are able to move around in a vehicle and get to town. On occasions when it has been a prolonged wet, the local council has organised food and medical drops to be delivered by helicopter.

One of the toughest realities I have had to learn is to accept that our lives and livelihoods are totally controlled by the weather. While there is very little we can do to manipulate it, we do our best to prepare for unfavourable seasons and whatever nature wants to throw at us. A flood can tear down fences and wash away stock standing in its path. Locust plagues can devastate pasture within a matter of weeks or even days. Unseasonal showers and misty days can turn dry feed into black, mouldy stubble in the blink of an eye. Bushfires started by lightning can roar through your country, killing and maiming stock as well as destroying valuable grass. Drought is a slow and insidious beast gradually sorting out the weak from the strong.

We are now entering our second year of a poor wet season. Vital rains have once again failed to materialise. As all primary producers do, we take the good seasons with the bad. Careful planning, and at times, drastic measures, have to be taken to ensure that the stock are kept in good order until the rains come again.

* * *

As a teacher, my year was organised into four terms of ten to eleven weeks with school holidays in between. During the year there were various public holidays as a bonus.

As a grazier, I basically work seven days a week, fifty-two weeks a year. Weekends are no different. Of course it's not all work and no play. We do take breaks and even splurge and have a holiday from time to time – generally when we go to a bull sale! To be honest, our idea of a holiday is to sit at home and watch it rain, but that hasn't happened very often lately.

On the land you quickly learn that if a job needs to be done, regardless of what day it is, it gets done. By the same token, if we want to take a day or two off, we can, regardless of what day of the week it is.

The same applies to public holidays and weekends. While we don't necessarily get to take time off, we are always aware of these days. Murphy's Law states that if a machine is going to break down or you urgently need a part, it will happen on a public holiday or a weekend, when you can't ring anyone.

Although the year started off on a positive note with a good wet season, once the tap was turned off in February very little rain fell during the rest of the year. Generally around November, we start to look hopefully towards the north-west for signs of storms and the arrival of the monsoon.

We rarely make plans for Christmas. We figure it's either going to be too wet (still waiting on that dream to become a reality) or too dry, and we would be feeding cattle and watching out for dry storms and bushfires. The end of the year was hot and we were feeding molasses and cottonseed to our stock as well as dry lick. (Molasses is a byproduct of sugarcane, and a good source of energy for livestock in times of drought. Here the cattle are eating M8U, molasses mixed with 8 per cent urea. The urea is added to help the rumen to create 'bugs', which help convert the ordinary pasture into more usable protein.)

The demand for molasses throughout Queensland was so high that stocks eventually ran out. We were very fortunate to get our two 6000-gallon (27,000-litre) tanks filled at the beginning of November but once those tanks are empty and it still hasn't rained, it's going to be a long wait until the sugarcane-crushing season starts again mid-year.

Christmas Day was fairly subdued as the district was in drought. We spent a quiet day at home but didn't realise that Murphy was subcontracting for Santa

Claus and decided to pay us a visit. The following day I went to check the time clock on the bore and noticed that the bulls in that paddock had 'mud' up to their knees. I thought it was mud until I detected the familiar and distinctive smell of molasses. To my horror I discovered that one of the storage tanks had burst and the bulls had been having a lovely time paddling in the huge pool of molasses.

The temperatures had been relentless all week and the ground was very hot. That pool of molasses had absorbed every bit of heat. Roger tried to walk through it in bare feet but it was so hot he had to wear gumboots. Because the bulls had been paddling in the 'puddle', there was all sorts of debris and vegetation floating in the molasses, which caused the pump to keep jamming. It was sticky and frustrating work, made worse by the heat, flies and the pump constantly breaking down.

Unfortunately, the jamming pump was starting to get the upper hand in the battle to save the molasses. A lump of dirt ended up jamming the pump completely, which meant that Roger had to take it up to the shed and take the whole pump apart to clear the blockage. By the time the pump was back together it was nearly dark. We went home to have a quick bite to eat and couldn't believe it when we heard heavy rain on the roof! It was only a quick downpour of eight millimetres, but it had made the road down to the tanks so slippery that we had to wait for it to dry out.

We gave up that night and figured that the molasses wasn't going anywhere and we would attack it again early the following morning.

That was the plan, but now we had a new problem. We had managed to get a fair amount of molasses pumped back up into the tank the previous afternoon, but all of a sudden the pump couldn't force the molasses up the poly line any more. The rain had thinned the molasses out and for some reason the pump would no longer do its job.

That was the straw that broke the camel's back for Roger and he had to admit defeat. However, we still had to empty the area of the pooled molasses so that we could continue to fill the mobile mixer for future molasses runs. Eventually Roger dug a trench with the tractor to open up the sides of the 'pond' and we stood and watched in silence as 2000 gallons (9000 litres) of the 'black gold' gradually streamed away across the ground towards the creek. It was heartbreaking to see all that molasses going to waste especially when we knew we couldn't access any more.

As it turned out the gods did smile upon us a few days later when we had fifty millimetres of rain over two days – a belated but very welcome Christmas present. However, the smell that lingered along the creek served as a bittersweet reminder that it was no use crying over spilt molasses.

Poddies

Jenny Underwood, Eversleigh Station

A poddy is a baby animal that is reared by hand. Most cattle and sheep stations rear poddies from time to time. While it is always best for a calf or lamb to be reared by its mother there are circumstances that necessitate hand-feeding the baby animal. Sometimes the mother dies, leaving the calf orphaned, and if it isn't found quickly it will probably die, especially if it is young. Sometimes a cow develops 'bottle teats', which the calf is unable to suck properly. At other times the calf can become separated from its mother or mismothered, or the cow may become too sick to rear the calf on her own. To save both their lives the calf will be bottle-fed or raised by a milker cow.

We have had a number of poddies over the years, each with its own name and special character. Some can be easy to rear and cause you no heartache whatsoever; others refuse to suck a bottle and alternative methods of keeping them alive have to be found. Some will be powering along and just as suddenly become sick and die for no reason.

The important thing for any newborn mammal is to get colostrum. Colostrum is present in the mother's milk for the first few days of lactation. It contains proteins and many of the vital vitamins and minerals needed to fight diseases and guard against viruses and infections. Fortunately, colostrum is available commercially and many a calf's life has been saved by giving it colostrum when it is first brought home.

Our current poddy is a heifer calf called Lydia. As far as I know Lydia was one of twin heifers born to a young cow in a paddock near our house. I am certain that Lydia was the elder of the twins and she managed to get her initial feed of colostrum after she was born. Why the young mum didn't take both her calves we will never know but at the tender age of twenty-four hours old Lydia came home to live with us.

Apart from a bad case of colic, which was worrying at the time, Lydia has been a delight and no trouble at all. She loves her bottle and comes running when called; that's if she isn't waiting already. She likes nothing better than to come with my dog and me on our daily walks. Most of her days are spent lying around and exploring around the house yard or outside in the paddock just beyond the fence.

Lydia has one funny habit and one very annoying habit. The first is a love of vehicles – she spends a lot of her time sitting right beside the door of the work ute or between the four-wheeler bikes or under the truck or whatever machine is handy and has wheels.

Her annoying habit is the need to do her business on the cement right outside our back door. Believe me, it is not easy to housetrain a poddy calf!

Generally we allow three bags of calf milk per poddy before they are weaned from a bottle, usually at around four months. Before weaning, the calf is generally given calf crumbles and/or pellets to help with the transition. By this age the calf will have started to eat grass or hay (or electrical cords, the washing or anything lying around that looks so-o-o interesting and good to chew).

The hardest time for owner and calf is often when the poddy is fully weaned and banished from the house yard and joins other weaners in the paddock. Some poddies are grateful that you have reared them and given them the love and attention that they missed from their mother. They will greet you in the paddock and let you give them a scratch and a cuddle. Others are just plain obnoxious and pretend that they have been highly offended by the separation and totally ignore you.

Some poddies become mothers and go on to have and rear their own calves; others which are steers may grow to become bullocks and spend most of their lives on the property. No matter what happens to the poddy calf, each has a special place in its owner's heart and exemplifies the devotion that livestock breeders and their families have for their animals. Children who grow up rearing at least one poddy in their life learn the importance of love and respect for the animal, and that each is an individual in its own right.

The Story of Goliath

Jenny Underwood, Eversleigh Station

Nothing gives me more pleasure than to see a newborn calf with its mother, especially if it's a first-calf heifer, a first-time mum. Her innate mothering skills kick in not long after the birth and she rapidly transforms from a carefree 'teenager' into a cow with responsibilities.

However, not all calvings are straightforward. Some heifers and even cows, like humans, can have difficulty, and where possible we will help a cow deliver her calf.

A cow's pregnancy lasts about 283 days, more than nine months. In March 2012 we undertook our first-ever artificial insemination (AI) program. Because we knew exactly which day the heifer fell pregnant, we could determine fairly accurately when she would calve. To be on the safe side, we brought the heifers home to a holding paddock near the yards. This enabled us to check on them regularly and walk a heifer to the yards if she needed monitoring or assistance.

The summer of 2012–13 was a shocker – we had dreadful heatwaves and week after week of mid-to-high 40-degree days. The heifers started to calve a couple of days before Christmas; that was all well and good if they calved early in the morning or late in the afternoon when it was (supposedly) cooler. Each heifer had an identification tag in its ear, so we knew which animal to check on, which made things easier for monitoring purposes.

At the end of December we had to go to town for most of the day, so I rode the paddock before we left and found a heifer that had calved early that morning. Late that afternoon we checked on it and she and her new calf were going great guns. For some reason, I decided we should check the rest of the paddock before it got dark. Often a cow will stand away from the main mob when she is getting ready to have her calf. We noticed one heifer wasn't grazing contentedly like the rest. When I saw her tag number I realised that she still had a couple of weeks to go before she was meant to calve. But there, at her feet, curled up into a tight ball, was the tiniest little calf that we had ever seen. At first we thought it might have been dead as it wasn't moving and it was obviously premature.

We were surprised when it gave a muted little bellow. It was far too weak to stand by itself so we knew that it wouldn't have had a drink. It was almost dark and it would have been futile to walk the heifer to the yards so we rushed home and mixed up a solution of electrolytes to feed the calf, a tiny bull. We hoped the electrolytes would be enough to rehydrate it and keep it alive until morning.

With trepidation we went back to the paddock early the following morning. The heifer was still standing where we'd left her and her tiny baby was still alive but weak. I put the calf in the front of the ute with the air-conditioning on and the heifer followed me to the yards about a kilometre away while Roger coaxed her along with the bike. Roger put the mother into the crush so that he could milk her as her udder was full. The calf needed to get the all-important first drink of colostrum if he was to have any chance of survival. We fed him using a bottle but as he was too weak to stand, it wasn't an easy task to ensure the milk went into the right stomach and didn't choke him.

We repeated this process three or four times a day and each time the heifer would patiently walk into the crush and be milked out. She was so quiet we didn't even need to use a leg rope to prevent her from kicking out. The little calf could only drink a small amount of milk at a time. During the day it was unbearably hot and he was panting so much that at times he couldn't drink at all. He was still weak and unable to stand unassisted. He really felt the heat.

It would have been easy to give up and let the calf die but we were determined to give him the best chance at life that we could. His mother made it so much easier for us too, allowing us to milk her with a minimum of fuss. I avoided taking many photos and we didn't name him in case the worst happened and he didn't live.

Then, on the third day, a miracle happened. The little calf stood on his own – not for very long, and it was a wobbly old effort, but he did stand. We brought him over to his mum and encouraged him to suck. He was so tiny that he could only just reach up to the heifer's teats. Fortunately, she wasn't an overly tall cow or the little calf would never have been able to reach her udder on his own.

We were overjoyed and so it was time to give the little man a name. Because of the mighty effort he had put in and due to his 'enormous' size he was christened Goliath. When Goliath was born he reminded us of one of those sharpei dogs, the ones with all the wrinkles and excess skin.

The heatwave continued and we brought more heifers into the yards so that we could set up a shade shelter for them and their calves. Goliath now had some mates and once he became a little more confident on his wobbly legs he would try to play like they did when the sun had gone down and it was cooler. Gradually Goliath began to fill out and wasn't quite so wrinkly, but he was still much tinier than the rest of the calves, even the newborns.

He continued to thrive and amaze us with his determination to live. Full credit also has to go to his young mother, Eversleigh Ember. She was incredibly patient and the most attentive heifer imaginable. When the time came to let the heifers back out into the holding paddock to eat some green pick that had come up after a shower of rain, little Goliath found it hard to negotiate the rough ground.

Six weeks after he was born, Goliath and his mum were returned to the heifer paddock. Just before going through the gate Goliath's mum, Ember, turned to look at me. I am sure she was saying, 'Thank you for looking after my little boy so well; I will take over from here'.

Goliath is still with us today – he is sixteen months old and, for now, we have kept him a bull. He's never going to be a tall animal but we figure that if his grit and determination can be passed on to his calves he deserves to be given a chance and live out his days on Eversleigh.

Schooling and Socialising
in the Outback

Jodie Grant, Manners Creek Station

One common topic when talking with people unfamiliar with outback living is about having children 'in the middle of nowhere'. Common comments include 'but it's not fair on the children', 'they can't go to school', 'they will be disadvantaged with home-schooling', 'they can't have a social life', 'children need to socialise with children their own age' and more. Trust me, I have heard them all when it comes to what we are doing wrong by raising our children 300 kilometres from town. Socialisation and education are just the start of how our family are supposedly suffering; health and welfare are other favourite topics.

What gets me is that we aren't even talking about people with an understanding of how everything works out here, and of the systems and programs in place. City people who don't live the way we do often conclude we are in the 'wrong'. Recently, while not directed at remote families as such, there was a book on how home-schooling your child is detrimental to them.

What I noticed after spending my life in the city and then moving to a cattle station is the social side. Families may be hundreds of kilometres apart, but the effort is made from time to time to have a really good catch-up. Maybe it's not every week, but it does happen. When I lived in the city it was an effort for good friends to drive *ten* kilometres to say g'day. People are either too busy, too tired or it's too far to travel. There is always a reason they can't. You may see hundreds of people in a day, but how many of them do you really talk to? Everyone just rushes past and they don't stop to get to know each other. Out here you have staff on your station who become part of your family, you live together, work together, eat together – beyond that, your neighbouring stations become your mates and regardless, you always help each other out.

On a visit to Melbourne once we came across a lady with a flat battery who needed jumper leads. I didn't have any in my car, nor did any of the thirty-odd cars she pulled over and asked before asking us. Five kilometres down the road was a servo where we could buy some. We jumped in the car, bought her some leads and jump-started the car. This poor lady had been stranded with young children for over an hour and no one thought to buy a set. She was gobsmacked by our generosity but we thought nothing of it. Out here people travel hundreds of kilometres to help someone out, so a five-minute trip to grab a pair of jumper leads was nothing. These are the values we are instilling in our kids. They go beyond how many kids they played with each day and how they were schooled.

There are brilliant services that help bring station children together, including outback playgroups. We are lucky enough to have two services like this. We are on the border of Queensland and the Northern Territory, so we have access to both services. They fly or drive out to the stations and every month or so a station hosts the playgroup. Nearby station families travel out and while the kids are occupied the parents can have a bit of a catch-up too. These playgroups may be a 400-kilometre–plus drive, but if you put in the effort you get the rewards.

School of the Air is a great set-up. The children honestly don't miss a thing. Emily attends Mount Isa School of the Air, which is a combination of phone and computer. They have their classes over the phone, and slide shows and information come up on the computer. There are chat boxes to enable them to talk in a group, individually to students or to the teacher. If you sit through a class, they have their own fair share of general chatting between classmates when they should be concentrating on their schoolwork!

They have school days or multi-school for secondary students, where they go away for school. They live on the school campus with normal classes and social activities at night. They also have school camp and other school events where everyone gets together.

I don't think how your children are educated or where they live is the issue. You pick what best suits your family's needs. It is the values you instil in your children, the attitude they have in life and the respect they have for others that's important.

Swimming to the Pub

Jodie Grant, Manners Creek Station

Living where we do, we don't see rain much at all. I think my two-and-a-half-year-old daughter has seen rain (*proper* rain) perhaps three times in her life. She doesn't know what this stuff falling from the sky is and is rather afraid of it. However, living on dirt roads with creeks and rivers nearby, if we do get a big rain it can make access in and out of the station pretty much impossible by road.

This year we were caught out thinking we had all we needed and did not expect to be flooded in. We managed to get 120 mm of rain in one week on the station and all around the region. This was a great saving grace for many stations around, including us, giving some much needed green pick.

We weren't too worried once the road dried up; if the rain was just around the station we would be able to get into town before too long. That was before we got a phone call that the Georgina River had gone up and was still rising. Even after the rain stopped, the river kept rising for a couple of weeks. After about a week and we were still stranded, my husband, Dusty, was getting worried. He rang the local pub, seventy kilometres up the road towards town, to find out if he could get past the river, which was up by 2.5 metres and flowing strongly.

There was no way we could get through, so we told Dusty he'd just have to sit tight and wait it out. It's easy to say, but try living with a smoker on his last dregs of tobacco. I was a bit over hearing every night how he'd better get some smokes soon. I was thinking of ways I could get some, but there weren't any. I sent messages to friends down the highway in the other direction to Alice Springs, only to hear they couldn't get through, so I called stations towards Boulia, but to no avail. The river was up at their end too.

Once the water around the station dried up a little, Dusty thought he would go for a short drive just to see how far he could get. At least that's where I thought he was going. I might have been a little suspicious if I had known he had packed a backpack and garbage bags. Clearly he had a plan: he was on a mission to get smokes.

While Dusty was out, I got a phone call from our neighbour. He was going to fly the chopper into town and offered to pick up cigarettes for us. I was excited and said that would be great, thinking how proud Dusty would be to come home to me holding a carton of smokes for him.

Dusty was still out – he'd been gone a long time – when our neighbour arrived to drop off the smokes. In passing conversation I mentioned that he should be back by now. My neighbour said there was a ute parked at the river when he flew over. I'm like, 'Nah couldn't be him, he knows he can't get past the river.' As the chopper left, I eagerly waited for Dusty's arrival to see his reaction when I handed him the smokes he had been craving for the last three weeks. The river at this point was still high and flowing strongly, and there were five deep-flowing water crossings to get through before he could even get to the pub, the nearest place to pick up smokes. There was no way he was going to get smokes any other way in the next two weeks or so.

Finally I heard the dogs barking. I knew Dusty was home. I raced outside with a grin on my face, showing a sense of accomplishment, to see him equally pleased with himself, a grin on his face and backpack in hand.

'You were gone a while,' I said. 'How far did you get?'

He handed the backpack to me.

'What's that?' I asked.

Dusty's response was, 'Take a look. I got smokes.'

My face dropped. 'You what? I just bought you a carton of smokes. It was brought out in next door's chopper'.

I opened his backpack to find smokes, beer, Coke, chocolate, lollies and spare powdered milk for the girls in case we needed it.

Clearly he had put thought into this. He bought something for everyone: smokes and beer for him, Coke and chocolate for me (my weakness) and lollies for the girls.

'But how on earth did you get to the pub?'

He replied as if the answer was obvious, 'I swam!'

'Across all five crossings?' I asked.

'Yep, then walked to the pub, put everything in garbage bags, tied them up, put them in the backpack and swam back with the backpack on my back with all the stuff,' he said with a cheeky smile.

Next time I see him leave the house with a backpack and garbage bags I'll know he is up to something.

Man Up

Sarah Streeter, White Kangaroo Station

I prefer not to define myself as a single parent. There are countless women raising their child/children on their own, whether it is due to the end of a relationship, their partner spending weeks or even months away working, or a plethora of other circumstances. I'm no different. We are the good and bad parent. For most of the time we are the sole provider of love, comfort, sustenance, discipline and learning for our children. Although, for this time at least, I do find myself defined by the experience of raising a child on my own while running a cattle property.

The acres here do not span the magnitude of millions of the properties I have had the fortune of experiencing in the Northern Territory, and I am grateful that a trip to town is less than an hour's drive. As well as one small child, I am the guardian of close to 1000 cows, a mustering plant of horses, three kelpie working dogs, thirteen chooks, one cat and a milking cow. Those numbers have experienced natural fluctuations, sometimes with a brief tear shed. Regardless of whether I've been up four times a night feeding a baby, comforting him when he is teething or just survived a bout of household gastro, each and every one of these souls requires me to get out of bed in the morning and have them at the forefront of my thoughts for the day.

I've had to be creative to fit in what needs to be done around the limitations at each stage of my child's infancy and early years. A portacot in the yard filled with toys while loading cattle trucks and a spare infant seat for going in the front of a work ute have been indispensable. Only on one desperate occasion has a portable DVD player come with us to bide me some time while setting up a pump on a dam, when I knew I was pushing the boundaries with what we had already fit in the day. With some pride I can say that I can count on one hand the number of times we've only had toast for tea.

At the forefront of my thoughts is when things go wrong, there is no one on the end of a UHF radio to answer my calls. It has required me to think on my feet, think ahead, think creatively and think of the consequences for every action that I take. And it has made me think more of myself as a woman.

With 14,000 acres and not a man in sight, I've had to 'man up'. There were times that have called for more strength, resilience and pure grit than I thought I had. Like finding a 200-kilogram calf stuck in a water trough at the back of the property, jammed in under the rails that were intended for stopping such situations from happening. Unable to get traction with its feet on the bottom of a slippery trough, it had obviously been there for a couple of days or so. He was weak from the struggle, but still had enough fire in his belly to make the situation physically more difficult than it already was.

I thought the situation was beyond me, but what other option was there? An hour or so of cutting away posts, trying to provide some strength to the calf by pulling, pushing and lifting, filling the bottom of the trough with rocks, sticks and dirt finally allowed him to get the traction he required to get his feet under himself and leap out. Bloody ungrateful sod immediately turned to me and snorted his nose before blowing past to run in the direction of the mob. I sat there in the dirt for a moment, physically spent, grateful that my little boy seems able to spend hours entertaining himself when need be so I can get a job done.

Unwanted visitors of the scaly kind are another I really would prefer someone else to deal with. Seeing a six-foot brown snake sliding past the front steps of the house with the neighbours' daughters playing within metres and my own child starting to test his legs and walk is the catalyst for a chemical reaction in our brains and bodies that most mothers faced with a situation endangering their child would be familiar with.

I stop dead still and quietly, almost calmly, say, 'Girls, don't move, there is a snake. Go back inside with Reid and close the doors.'

Letting the snake go is not an option; it's likely he's been watering at the garden tap and will be back. Next time it may be a child who is not watching where he is stepping. In those seconds, thoughts are running through my head: 'Gun? I've never used the 410 shotgun. Why didn't I get Dad to show me how to shoot it?

Where's the key to the gun safe again? By the time I sort all that out this bastard will be nowhere to be seen.'

I start walking to the shed. 'Seriously, Sarah, what do you think you're going to do? Use a shovel?' It seems that there are two voices in my head now. 'Well that's the only option here, isn't it? What do they say, approach a snake from behind and it can't get you? Or was that from the side? Why didn't I take more notice?'

I pick up the post-hole shovel for fencing and take the short walk back to the house. Long handle, great. Small shovel head, doesn't give me great chances. He's still there, making his way slowly into the garden bed now, unaware that he has been detected. Both voices in my head are now muttering 'Jesus Christ, Jesus Christ, Jesus Christ' (my inner dialogue resorts to blasphemy in a crisis). One pipes up with 'If you're going to take a hit, better make it a good one, girl'.

I approach from behind and when I'm within about three feet of his tail he gets suspicious. I lift the shovel high above my head and bring it down, aiming about a foot back from his head, wanting to give myself the best chance of making contact. I use the side of the shovel, which gives me an extra ten centimetres or so of 'blade' to work with. I know the first hit isn't a good one; I just grazed him. I go to town, making half a dozen or so full-swing hacks at him, not realising all the time I was yelling like a mad woman with the effort and adrenaline behind each swing.

Picture one of those horror movies where in the final scenes the terrorised woman stabs the evil killer over and over again in a blind, desperate rage. I'm glad the girls had shut the door of the house, hopefully muffling the sounds. I stop when the snake was a bloody pulp, my chest heaving, hands shaking. A voice pipes up from some corner of my mind where it was hiding for cover and says, 'Well, Sarah, if that wasn't the most stupid thing you have ever done …'

Multi-tasking

Sarah Streeter, White Kangaroo Station

They say women are better than men at multi-tasking. Mothers tend to have a skill that allows them to attend to several tasks as if they were working from a body with more than two sides of a brain and certainly more than two hands.

Dinner, bath and bedtime is a hectic span of an hour or so in any household with small children. Working in rural industry also means that this is peak business time. Those who have been outside using the daylight hours for physical labour have now come into the office to do business. And those who tend to pick up the phone during the 'witching hour', 'terror time' and 'momentary madness' are men. Men who either have children so far flown from the nest that they can't recall this reality, or those who are escaping that exact reality in their own house by burying themselves in the quiet reprieve of the office.

'Have I caught you at a bad time?'

'Oh no, of course not,' I reply as I wrangle a child back into his chair to eat his spaghetti, intervene before that spaghetti can be propelled at the walls, or throw an object at the mongrel moggie who has found the pot of spaghetti on the stove and will soon make his meal.

'I'm calling about some red polled Brahman semen …'

A considerable part of our cattle business is the Brahman Stud, which my grandfather founded almost fifty years ago. Our breeding program focuses on heritable traits that are profitable and desirable for northern Australia cattle herds – fertility, growth, polledness (meaning lack of horns), temperament, meat quality, etc. – made all the more relevant as our breeding herd is located in the north, where the animals must face the same environmental challenges and constraints as the herds within which the genetics are extending. For many years we have been selling semen in elite sires domestically as well as overseas. We are seeing a trend towards greater use of semen in artificial insemination (AI) in northern herds in recent years, where more value is placed on genetic improvement. The use of semen allows for careful matching of a sire's traits to the individual herd, right down to an individual cow level. I very much enjoy the interaction with clients that often comes along with this. Our industry is a very passionate one, and the sharing of knowledge and experience in cattle production and breeding is rewarding.

Multi-tasking. Semen sales and client relations. Where am I going with this? Enter a two-year-old. The time? Witching hour, of course.

Why I answer the phone, I don't know. I should let the cool, calm Sarah on the voicemail recording take the call, but I settle in to talk details of sires with a client looking to do quite a large-scale AI program. The small child seems happy enough to play contently with his armful of tractors until I am free for bathtime. Some clients know exactly what they are after when they pick up the phone. Others are looking for our experience and knowledge of individual bulls to guide their choice, going into great depth as to their type of cow (body size, breed content etc.), problems they would like to correct and the direction they would like to take their herd. I enjoy this way of doing business, as we explore different options, build an understanding and often learn from each other's experiences with cattle breeding.

My concentration is broken by the high-pitch 'Yip yip, yippety yip' from the boy in the next room. Then a chant of 'Mum, Mum, Mum'.

I ignore it for a moment, still talking. 'We have found that Red Dollar's daughters have great longevity in the herd and good udders.'

Then I look over my shoulder to the little hands being shown to me by a very proud child. What is that? Is that what I think it is? Oh my, that is what I think it is (no pants in sight). It is up to his wrists. Breathe, Sarah.

'Jacob Rio is a bigger framed bull, more suited to a moderate size cow.'

What the hell has gone on? Child skips away in delight, with each skip leaving a footprint of mess on the kitchen floor. Thankfully I have a cordless phone and quietly follow the child, not making eye contact. I pounce and we head to the bathroom with soap and water, the phone still to my ear.

'Have you seen the young polled sires towards the bottom of the webpage? Rio Grand is a son of Jacob Rio and is from an exceptionally fertile cow line.'

Soap, water, towel and the child is clean.

It was no mean feat to get the task done quietly. Not cute, not adorable, not tonight.

'Are you familiar with the poll gene test, as we have three young sires that are homozygous for the poll gene.'

I follow the messy footprints around the house with a handful of wet wipes. The discussion on the phone shifts to the latest stud-sale auction results. I pounce on another sticky mess on the floor, almost in triumph. Wipe, wipe. Oh dear, it is on the couch. Wipe, wipe. How did it get there? Wipe, wipe. Only once did I casually say, 'Sorry about the background noise, I have a chattering toddler.'

We wrap up the conversation with the client planning to email through photos of his cows for me to look over and advise further the package of bulls that would be suited to his herd.

There is nothing quite like having a client on the phone to force a sense of calm on a mother who might have otherwise either blown her top or burst into tears. Both mother and child survived the memorable episode and I built a good relationship with a new client which led to a considerable sale. I did have to call him back the next day though – I had given him the wrong email address. Where was my head at!

When it Rains

Kylie Savidge, Southampton Station

What will happen when it rains? Who knows how far away we are from drought-breaking rain? What will be left of our lifetime's hard work? It's a multimillion-dollar question.

When it rains, dams will fill, creeks and rivers and watercourses will flow again. It will take a few months for the grass to grow and months more after that before cattle are in a saleable condition. Cattle will have to come home from agistment, calves will need marking, a bang-tail muster will be needed to count what's left. (Bang-tailing involves cutting off part of the hair on the end of a beast's tail so when you see them in the paddock, you know that they have been processed and counted. It doesn't hurt them and is just like getting a haircut.) It will be months before any income is made, months and years before the debt is paid off for the 2013 drought.

I worry now about my father and his health. I worry I am not doing enough. I worry about my kids and what we will do at Christmas as money is tight and, yes, though they understand that we can't afford much in the way of presents, it is still a worry.

I worry how we are going to make ends meet and pay the bills that come in. To bring in a few extra dollars we sell feral goats if we happen to catch a few, and Brian shoots kangaroos on a professional basis one night a fortnight, which is all we can fit in time-wise.

I worry about Jack away at school who rings or texts me every day to see how I am and to hear about what is happening on Southampton. This is a kid who dragged a cow out of a dam and shot her so I didn't have to do it. I told him he didn't need to do it as I could. His reply, 'But, Mum, it makes you cry and I don't like to see you cry.'

I worry about Ben and Meghan because I have no time to spend with them on weekends or on holidays. I have no time to go riding with Meg for fun. I can't take Ben pig-chasing. I can barely keep my eyes open long enough to read them bedtime stories. During the week we have time together, mostly doing homework or cooking and now that swimming has started, we spend time at the pool. But none of that is really fun stuff.

I have a husband who worries like hell about me.

So for now we will keep on keeping on and praying that this drought will break soon.

Will we be OK? Yes, I believe we will but it is a tough road to travel. I am lucky to have a house in town with green grass and no water worries; I am sure that it helps keep you sane. We are also lucky in having the friends that we do and the support that they give.

All we need is rain.

Ties to the Heart

Kylie Savidge, Southampton Station

After reading our story you may wonder why we continue to do this, to stay in a place that often brings heartache, challenges our very soul and quite regularly rips away at our emotional borders.

Why? Because it is a beautiful land, it captures you with its space and freedom, with vast areas of open country that are so very beautiful and yet, at the same time, so harsh and unforgiving.

I love the changes of the seasons when it goes from the bright, dry harshness of the summer to the gentler shades of winter, stark and cold as it sometimes is. But this land captures you, heart and soul. The colours of our country are a sight to behold, from the bluest of blue skies, to the harsh bright reds of the ground, the deep greens of the gum's grey-box leaves, the blue-grey colours of the mulga and the diamond stars in the blackest of nights – they grab hold of you and never let go.

Smells abound: flowering sandalwood, the damp scent of wet earth after rain, the dusty smells of cattle yards that linger on your clothes, the smell of branding smoke in your hair, the scent of spinifex and gidgee that come on the southerly wind after a change in the weather. Then there's smoke from the lunchtime campfire or the stump fire where we all sit around in the winter and tell tall tales. This is what feeds your soul. For those of us who live out 'bush' they are all part of what keeps us going. This is why we get out of bed before dawn when it's already thirty degrees and climbing, or minus two from a bed that feels so warm.

The summer of 2013–14 with weeks of more than forty-degree days, the hottest day being forty-nine, that was harsh. Winter has been mild until now; our first really cold week was during the first week of the school holidays, down to minus two with ice and frost all over things. It certainly hasn't been that cold and has been colder in past years, but we take it as it comes and appreciate the beauty.

Summer is a busy season, with early starts to beat the heat, and if we are really lucky we can have a midday siesta (but only if the power supply keeps up to the demands of the air conditioners). Late afternoon brings little relief from the heat when the blazing sun is beginning to slide and work can be completed, or jobs for tomorrow can be planned or prepared for. Quite often the temperature is still in the high thirties at 9 pm. It certainly makes you appreciate the hardiness of the pioneers.

As we work by the sun, regardless of the time, daylight saving has no benefit or meaning to us. There are no hours we can save, what needs doing is done, whatever the time, and getting in at 9 pm and having to then prepare an evening meal, tidy the house, do washing, prepare lunches, answer emails, return phone calls or bake cakes and biscuits for smokos the next day leaves us little time to rest and relax.

Stock work is kept to a bare minimum in the hot months, as it's too stressful on both animals and humans. When we have been forced to work stock in the heat, careful planning is required. Water drums and dishes (troughs) are positioned at strategic points along the route, where cattle may be walked to allow for drinks or wet-downs. A support vehicle with additional water, plus a tucker box and shaded cages often tails the cattle, providing an 'interchange bench' for the dogs, and a lift for young calves who tire quickly in the heat. Very hot ground can blister the pads on dogs' feet.

Winter is the perfect season for all the maintenance jobs that are required to keep a working property operational, including fencing, cattle yard repairs/ improvements, scrub clearing or even dam de-silting. The days are shorter, mornings are later and afternoons earlier. It is time to recharge your batteries and prepare for the summer ahead.

There are also the rewards when you see contented, happy cattle camped under shady trees around dams, chewing their cuds and watching their calves at play.

Native wildlife abound and birds and mammals become your friends on your daily trips around the property.

The swan dubbed Mr Lonely Swan turned up on the house dam one year, stayed for two years, left and came home with his mate. When we go to start the pump on the house dam to fill the tanks, he would cooee out and swim over quite close and watch with keen eyes as we got the pump started. But once Mrs Lonely Swan turned up she would scold him, telling him how dodgy humans were and to come away right now. They hatched a brood of cygnets and once they were grown, left us, and were not seen again.

There are two pairs of resident brolgas that live along the watercourse and each hatch out two young every year. They stalk regally along, keeping a close eye on us when we are mustering or doing lick runs, never coming overly close but always just there.

A pair of sea eagles come in good seasons and nest in the same tree every time.

We have whistler ducks, black ducks and grey teals that arrive in hundreds on the watercourse, literally the day after the rain stops falling.

How do they know? Where do they come from? How do they know to come here? They just do. It leaves you in awe of nature.

The little wallaroos that live near the bore pump watch closely when we start it up late in the evening. They are never afraid but still cautious.

All of this and so much more is why we keep going, day in, day out. If you don't love what you do then you cannot be happy doing it. We love it.

Dealing with the Black Dog

Kylie Savidge, Southampton Station

In August last year I went to the local GP and told her I was feeling like I was in a glass cage. I could see what was happening outside and around me but I couldn't feel anything; I could understand what was going on, but did not feel anything. And by feel I mean experience emotions: I didn't feel sad or happy, I just did not feel. I was diagnosed with emotional burnout and reactive depression due to the seasons (drought), and what was happening in my personal world.

I did not want to acknowledge I had depression. Depression was for those not as strong and capable as me. Emotional burnout I could accept, but depression? And talk to a counsellor and go on antidepressants? Hell, no.

I came home in shock. This couldn't be happening to me. I was just tired, that was all, and being tired was understandable as I was juggling children, schooling, the property, Brian working away and life in general.

After talking to Brian and a couple of very close friends, I went back to my doctor and was put on an antidepressant and given an appointment with the counsellor. This I felt was a waste of time as what the heck was I supposed to talk about? I wasn't going through anything that anyone else wasn't and it was to be expected that I would feel like I wasn't doing enough. I couldn't make it rain and I couldn't be everywhere all the time. I felt like I was failing – failing my kids, my family, the cattle who depended on me, failing my husband – and I was spiralling down into a darkness that I wasn't sure I could get out of. I would get very wound up and anxious trying to make everything perfect for every occasion. I got out of bed every day, first because of my children Jack, Ben and Meghan, and secondly for my horses. I was surviving and I knew that when it rained properly I would be OK. I just wasn't sure when that was going to be.

I reluctantly went to see the counsellor (who is just the loveliest person), and told her how I felt and why I thought I was feeling this way. She shook her head at me and told me that what I was feeling was normal and not to be so alarmed about things I could not control. You cannot worry about the weather or what people do and or think. These things are beyond your control. Worry about what you can change. I am sitting here now, shaking my head, wondering what more I can write. What can I say? I don't want this to sound like a 'poor me' story. I have kept this battle very private; only a select few friends have been privy to it.

I have learnt that depression can hit anyone in numerous ways and it is still a 'one day at a time' journey for me. Most days are better, some are not and I don't really have a strategy for dealing with this – more a 'just get on with it' attitude.

If this touches a chord with you or you think, 'Hey, that sounds like so and so', please don't be too stubborn or proud to tell somebody you trust that you need help, or to ask that person if they are OK and if you can help. A simple gesture like dropping off a warm meal because they have been late getting back to town for the school week, a phone call, an invite for coffee or having the kids for the afternoon can mean so much to someone.

Depression can hit anyone at any time and be disastrous. My world didn't quite collapse, but it very nearly did and, as a result of this, coupled with a few tough years, my marriage did not survive.

I am slowly moving forward, taking my time. Some wonderful people who are the best of friends and who have been there for me all the way, before I even plucked up the courage to talk about this, need to know how much I appreciate their love and friendship. I want to say thank you to them.

Last but not least, my kids, who are my world, I love you to the moon and back!

Mustering at Harry's Camp

Anita Ganzer, Abingdon Downs Station

Our staff are currently at one of our mustering camps (Harry's) which is about twenty kilometres from the homestead. Harry's Camp lasts for four to five weeks, most times without a break in between. Harry's Camp is on the bank of a huge lagoon that provides water for the camp and the occasional swim (never mind the crocs, they're only freshies). The camp is powered by a generator. There are three tin shacks. The first has two showers heated by a donkey (donkey being water heated in a 44-gallon drum with a fire pit underneath), two flushing toilets (very modern) and a washing machine. The second is the kitchen and dining, and the third is the sleeping quarters (with a wall in the middle for women on one side and men the other). Some bring tents and some sleep in the back of their utes.

It's a long time to work straight with barely a day off but the paddocks are just too big to stop once we start. But once we finish the staff generally can get anywhere between seven and ten days off to recharge their batteries, visit family and have a holiday. Given our location, two days off on weekends makes it impossible to travel to family and friends so a week or so off is well received.

Harry's Camp is the one everyone looks forward to as it is the first camp of the season. Long-term staff love it and new staff get excited about it. I thought I would share with you some of their opinions about their experience at Harry's so far.

What do you enjoy most about mustering camp?

Clay, our resident five-year-old 'mad fella' (been with us all of his little life): 'I like camping and going swimming. I like helping Dad at the yards, and I like riding my motorbike and Courtney.' (Courtney is a horse.)

How do you manage your two boys (aged two and five) at camp and is it harder to get them to bed on time?

Toni, our head stockman's partner and jillaroo who has been with us for eight years: 'The boys are very happy when you finish work so they just want to play with you which makes it harder to get them showered and into bed on time. It's the only time they are allowed to be dirty all day because otherwise they would need to bathed three times a day! But it's good having the boys at camp and they keep everyone entertained.'

What do you like most about camp cooking?

Harley, current cook/station hand on his first season with us: 'I get to be outdoors cooking with great scenery. I like getting the fires ready in the morning and in the afternoon. I love camping out. I also get to drive the poddy wagon on mustering days.' (A poddy wagon is a ute with a cage on the back that follows the mob and picks up baby calves that can't walk great distances.)

What do you least like about camp cooking?

'Nothing, really. Sometimes the early starts. I wish I had a bigger stovetop. Sometimes the mosquitoes are bad at night on a hot night.'

What's a typical day on a muster day?

Squeak, head stockman who has been with us for thirteen years: 'After a quick coffee, we work out who is riding horses and who is on motorbikes. Then horses are saddled, bikes are fuelled, chopper fuel is loaded onto the truck that takes the horses out to wherever we start mustering. We head out to a spot and wait for the chopper to bring in the first mob. The horses will tail the mob generally in a direction towards the yards as bikes are collecting mobs being brought in by choppers on the way.

'I spend all day on the two-way guiding people and getting instructions from the chopper pilot and generally communicating with everyone – it's pretty easy to wear a radio battery out in a day. Most muster days we pull up around lunchtime, usually timed to be around waterholes for cattle and horses to have a drink and have a spell and calves a chance to suck on mum. We all have a quick break and a corned beef sandwich (menu doesn't change on muster days) while keeping an eye on our mob.

'Then we head off towards the yards again. Once we reach the yards, the choppers are usually still with us, and we proceed to "yard up" the cattle for the night. Choppers are on standby at this point as it can get a bit tricky getting them all in. Not every day is the same; sometimes it's smooth sailing and other times it's like a bomb's gone off. Never a dull moment.'

What's a typical day on a yard day?

Hudson, the second in charge, who has been with us for two years: 'After breakfast, we feed weaners from the previous day's muster while someone puts the sprinklers on to keep the dust down and someone else is getting branding gear ready. We then yard them up from the big yards they were put into the night before to smaller holding yards to start processing.

'We get our orders off Squeak on who is doing what jobs for the day, for instance cattle counter, drafting, branding, spaying, spaying offsider, penning up etc. We break for smoko around 9.30, have lunch at about 12.30 then generally keep going until the processing is done. If there is enough time we will turn them out to their designated paddock.'

Fire-fighting, Ringer Style

Renee Kohler, Abingdon Downs Station

As the end of the year approaches, so does fire season. We aim to burn some of our country before the first storms to get good grass growth through the wet season, but we generally get beaten by human error through machinery or by lightning.

At the first sign of smoke our boss Campbell has the chopper fired up and in the air determining whether or not we need to jump into the role of firemen and women. Once we get word from Campbell that we need to fight we are in a frenzy: loading the fire-fighting unit onto a Toyota and filling it up with water, the spray tank on a four-wheeler, the burning unit on a four-wheeler and filling it with a mix of petrol and diesel. We have another vehicle with a pump and pipes and extra fuel and some tucker for us. Plus the old grader gets a rude wake-up call, gets greased and oiled, ready to go. Then it's just a matter of everyone getting in or on something and heading out to the fire.

Once we get to where we need to be the grader takes the lead to widen existing roads or make a new road or firebreak. Once the grader has a big enough lead ahead the burning bike follows, lighting up the roadside on the same side as the existing fire. The aim of back-burning is to send the new fire towards the existing fire so they eventually meet and burn themselves out.

A little further behind the burning bike is the water bike, which sprays any flames still burning at the edge of the road where it was lit up once it's headed away from the road a little to stop any chances of wind carrying fire across the road and also to wet any trees close to the road that could cause trouble. Behind the water bike is the vehicle with the big water tank and pressure hose to tackle the big stuff: putting out trees, logs, cow poo and anything that could make an escape across the firebreak. The vehicle behind has already been to set up the water pump in a dam to refill the water tank on the vehicle and goes about patrolling the burnt area.

Fighting fires is generally not an overnight ordeal; sometimes we can be out for four or five days or more. There's no shower, flushing toilet, cooked meals or toothbrushes. If there's a chance someone might have the opportunity to run back to the homestead to get a loaf of bread and a container of old frozen runny stew from six months ago, we appreciate it! Or someone like me might make a really quick curry of all things that turns out to be hotter than the fire itself – sorry, guys!

As far as sleep is concerned you are lucky to have a power nap here or there. Scrunched-up newspaper makes a pretty good makeshift pillow, or your boots. I can remember it got pretty cool one night and Campbell and Anita were curled up in one of the deep tyre tracks in the river crossing, trying to stay warm at 3 am and get a few minutes' shut-eye.

It is never smooth sailing; there's always something that goes a little pear-shaped. One year we had two water bikes going and Campbell came over the radio from the chopper for the first bike to get back to the other bike as quickly as possible as it was on fire. Another time, we thought we had the fire pretty well under control until the wind changed direction. My husband, Jason, tried to grade a quick track in front of the flame but the flames were over the top of the grader and he got a little bit hot. But he did manage to control it. About an hour or so passed and we were getting near the river when over the radio comes 'IT'S JUMPED'. This time Campbell got in the grader, did about two swipes and was singing out to Jason to get back on. Jason and that old grader have a special connection (apparently the way you talk/yell at it determines how well she'll work for you!). There was also another time when the fire got too hot for the bike that was back-burning (it had the firestarter on board) and the fuel drum on the back caught on fire.

I must say I never look forward to fire-fighting, but I do have many memories of that terrible loud crackling noise of fire coming your way, of fireballs jumping through the treetops, of being so tired you think you can't go on but you do, of your eyes being so sore and puffy from the smoke that you can hardly open them and they constantly water, of your teeth being so furry because you haven't seen a toothbrush in a week, of being so dirty and smelling like smoke for the next month, of times when you look back and think, geez, that was way too close and how lucky we were.

I've seen the total devastation an early fire can cause, where everywhere you look is black and bare. You just cling to the hope that it will rain soon.

From the Editor

For the Love of Cattle

Stephanie Coombes, Central Station website manager

I love cattle, I really do. I love all cattle, but unlike a politically correct and diplomatic parent, I do have favourites, and that is anything with big floppy ears and a hump – Brahmans.

A few months ago I swapped my cowboy boots for ballet flats and an office job. I'm absolutely loving the challenge and the opportunity to use my ag science degree, but so far these are projects that don't require me to be in the cattle yards. So, when given the opportunity to take a week off and go work for another company in their yards, you can probably guess what my answer was …

This week has been good. Hot, tough, tiring, but good. It's good to remind my muscles and the skin on my hands what it's like to be swinging off a shovel, to wake up and not have to fuss over hair, make-up and clothes, and to finally master the bobcat.

On the first night, the moment I got out of my car to open the gates I was hit by that smell you only get at feedlots or on live export boats, the smell of lots and lots of cattle in one place. I love it.

I turned on the outside light of the donga I was staying in to see hundreds of Brahman steers staring back at me from their bunk (feed trough), chewing away on their dinner. I was happy. Just happy to be back with cattle.

The next morning I was the first one out to work, having arranged to check the cattle with the boss before feeding out. Aside from the occasional moo and the sounds of passing traffic, the yards were so quiet. No clanging of gates, humming of engines, or crunch of wheels on gravel. Not another person in sight. I made my way through each pen slowly and quietly, taking it all in – not just the cattle, but everything. I checked the bunks to see if there was any feed remaining, the hay feeders for hay, the troughs for water and to see how clean they were, all the while keeping an eye on the gates, fences, shelter and bedding.

Checking the cattle is my favourite part, and I was really excited to recognise a couple of brands and realise that most of these cattle were from a station one of my friends lives on that I had visited before. Most of all I like to see how the cattle react to me; generally if you are quiet enough, they will be too. Then the fun really begins!

Once the cattle feel comfortable (relatively speaking) their personalities start to come out. Some will follow you as you walk about (but freeze the second you stop and look over your shoulder, pretending like they weren't stalking you), others will snort and stare you down before darting back into the mob, and then there are the ones that stand their ground and bat their eyelashes at you, fooling you into thinking that you might just be able to pat them, only to back away as you reach out your hand. Sometimes if you just sit really, really still they'll come quite close for a look, sniff and slobber.

I am always trying to find my next bovine bestie, because where's the fun in working with cattle if you can't enjoy their company? I love a cow cuddle – I feel like it is some sort of prize to be won with cattle that aren't pets. Good handling will train cattle to be quiet, but you can't just walk up to any old cow for a pat. When I find one that will let me get up close and personal I feel like some sort of 'cow whisperer'. I know how ridiculous that sounds, but I feel that that moment is really special because it means there is a level of trust between that animal and me – it trusts me enough to override its innate fight-or-flight response.

Sometimes it's not trust that leads to a cow cuddle, it's a hunger that overrides any fear, or even greed. You could never say I'm not opportunistic, because if I see some greedy buggers totally involved in their feed, I will try to sneak a pat, whether it's a poddy calf gutsing itself on the milk feeder or a full-grown cow on mineral lick or pellet.

Another good opportunity to attempt cow cuddles is when cleaning troughs. This is when curiosity overrides that flight response, plus cattle love drinking fresh running water. As the trough is emptying and filling up again, a number of cattle will wander over to inspect your work. If you stay still enough and leave the trough broom or scrubbing brush nearby they often come to sniff it before working their way over to check you out. This is when I've been sniffed, had my hands, face and even my jeans licked (who knew denim was so tasty?) and water bottles pulled out of my back pocket. This usually does end in the cow deciding they've had enough and walking away after a moment, but that's OK!

Then there is the last group of cattle who give good cuddles – calves! Actually, there is one more group I am forgetting – the odd cow who freezes in the raceway or chute as you're trying to encourage it to move along and it just won't budge. While our default plan is to give it a smack on the bum and try to push it forward, I have had the odd success from patting them on the face and threatening them with kisses and cuddles if they don't move. #Winnerwinnerchickendinner #totalfluke #noonewantsaStephcuddle

Back to the cutest type of bovine bestie – calves! There's not much explanation needed here. They're ridiculously cute (most of the time) and because they're so little, even if they don't want to be patted, you can more or less pat them anyway.

Sometimes when you're being pushed to push cattle through the yards faster and faster and every other cow is rubbing someone up the rails you can temporarily lose your perspective and your passion for the job and the industry. Spending the week up in these yards, as hard as I worked, was like a retreat. I really got to immerse myself in the company of the cattle and remembered why I love working with them.

PS: It wouldn't be right to write about bovine besties and not mention Snooki. On a boat of several thousand heifers headed to China, somehow I found Snooki, or perhaps Snooki found me. Snooki was always up for a cuddle, selfies and even exfoliated my face with her sandpaper-like tongue on the odd occasion. If I could have shipped her back to my house I would have, she is a one-in-a-million cow and I hope the babies she's making in China are mini versions of herself!

Glossary

Disclaimer: Like all languages, terms and phrases used in the pastoral industry are constantly evolving. Below are a few of the more common terms in use today. There are regional differences with some terms, so some definitions below may differ depending on where you are located. A special thank you to Anne Marie Huey of Dampier Downs Station for helping put this glossary together.

Avgas Aviation gasoline.

Bang-tail To 'bang-tail' is to cut off the hair at the end of a cattle's tail, so cattle that have been processed can be identified out on the station and the following year.

B&S Ball Bachelor and Spinsters Ball. Originally they were a way for people living in the country to meet potential spouses, but these days they're a chance to let loose and catch up with mates.

Breaker Young horse that has been recently broken in and is still in the early stages of its education.

Bullock Castrated adult male.

Bull buggy/catcher/wagon Mustering vehicle.

Bush (v.) To 'bush' cattle is to let them go from the cattle yards, back into the bush.

Campdraft A horse sport involving cattle.

Cleanskin A mature animal that has not been branded, earmarked or carries any other identifying marks.

Coacher muster A method of mustering where cattle are brought into a mob with other animals then walked to the yards using horse, bikes or vehicles.

Cradle A restraint box designed to hold calves and weaners for management procedures such as branding, castrating, ear marking and dehorning. Similar in concept to a crush, but has the added ability to lay an animal on its side.

Crush A restraint box used to hold large animals in order for management procedures such as vaccinations, pregnancy-testing and ear-tagging to be conducted.

Draft To sort cattle into different groups – this may be based on age, gender, breed etc.

ESCAS Export Supply Chain Assurance Scheme – government regulations that ensure Australian animals can be traced throughout the entire live-export chain, from property of origin to point of slaughter.

Head bale Part of the crush designed to hold an animal's head during management procedures such as ear-tagging and tipping. It usually consists of two sliding panels that catch the animal behind the ears.

Heifer Young female cattle.

Jackaroo Traditionally a young station hand destined for management. Today, the term is commonly used to describe any relatively inexperienced male station hand.

Jillaroo Female version of a jackaroo.

Killer A beast designated to be killed and consumed on the station.

Lick Mineral supplement fed to animals to improve diet quality.

Mickey A young, uncastrated male animal.

Mob Herd.

Pads Cattle tracks.

Poddy An orphaned or abandoned calf usually being hand-reared.

Portable panels Fencing that can be easily assembled, disassembled and moved as necessary (similar to the fencing put up at music festivals).

Race A narrow 'laneway' within the yards, usually leading to the crush or calf cradle, that only allows the passage of one animal at a time.

Ringer A skilled and experienced male or female station hand. These days it's considered an old-fashioned term.

Sale cattle Cattle that are sold throughout the mustering season.

Scrubber Similar to a cleanskin, usually with a bad attitude.

Steer Castrated young male animal.

Tail (n.) The 'tail' of the mob is the back end of the mob.

Tail (v.) To 'tail' cattle is to sit behind the mob, either on horseback, on a bike or in a buggy, and keep the mob moving forwards, usually at a slow and steady pace.

Turkey nest An earthen tank used to store water.

Water point General term for a place where the cattle drink. This could be a trough, turkey nest, natural spring, dam, river or creek.

Weaner A young animal that has been removed from its mother (weaned).

Wing Two funnel-shaped fence-lines strung with shade cloth that guide cattle into the yard.

Acknowledgements

Jane Sale, Central Station website founder

Many have supported me in the labour of love that is the Central Station website and, over the last months, accumulating permissions and choosing the blogs for this book. I cannot possibly list everyone who has been involved and would like to say a general thank you to my friends both in the Kimberley and Australia wide who are always lending me an ear, giving advice, a shoulder to whine on or a glass to wine in.

A few I must mention by name. Thank you to Haydn Sale, my husband, who has led me into so many adventures (sometimes unknowingly) and is my inspiration and greatest strength. My children, Angus and Matilda, who are so adaptable and adventurous – you make our lifestyle possible and fill it with joy. Thanks to my father Russell Peterson and mother Jenny Bowman for being great business role-models and showing me the benefits of hard work, but mostly for all your selfless support and encouragement.

Harold Mitchell, Doug Flynn and Lynne Flynn, thank you for supporting my time spent on the Central Station project and more importantly for the faith you have shown in Haydn and me in the development of Yougawalla Pastoral Company and our family, both financial and moral. You are great friends and partners.

Thank you, Gary Meally, my life saver.

Catherine Marriott, thank you for helping the women of the Cattle Industry realise their voice, especially on social media. To Helen Campion, Jane De Long, Barbara Camp, Lisa Wood, Anne-Marie Huey and Kirsty Foreshaw, thank you for brainstorming the idea of Central Station in the middle of traffic jams and cocktail hours in Jakarta and Lampung, Indonesia.

Grace Harrison picks up the ball and runs with it every time I drop it. Thank you, Gracie.

Thank you to Katie Stackhouse and the publishing team at ABC Books for realising the potential of the *Central Station* book.

To Stephanie Coombes, thank you for your passion, tireless hours and innovative management that makes Central Station what it is.

To Ann Pilmer, my generous and insightful friend who spent countless hours reading, offering advice and editing from a 'city slicker' point of view, thank you so much. Thank you to Rodney Lamplugh for his publishing contract and legal advice in an area in which I am extremely green and inexperienced.

Thank you to all the readers of our website, Facebook page and now this book, for reading about our very different lifestyle and being interested in the full story of how our lives and the supply chain works.

Our sponsors are so generous in supporting us. Thanks go to them for enabling us to promote our industry. Your financial support helps to advertise our website and also support its administration. Finally to all the people of the Northern Beef Industry who have given their time and incredible knowledge to share on the blog even if it has not appeared in this book. Each and every one of you is an inspiration and a true pioneer.

Stephanie Coombes, Central Station website manager

Managing Central Station is one of the best jobs I've ever had. Each time I receive someone's blog, I feel like I am the only person at a world premiere – I get to read all of these wonderful stories before anyone else.

I'd like to thank each and every person who has contributed to the website. Thank you for taking the time to be involved and putting your stories out there for the world to enjoy. Your stories have taken me on a roller-coaster ride of emotions, had me in fits of giggles, and brought me to tears on more than one occasion. Through communicating with you all so often over the past three years, I feel like I have been gifted a great big extended family. To those who I have met since Central Station began, it honestly felt like we'd known each other for years. For those who I have yet to meet 'in real life', as far as I'm concerned, we're already mates. Thank you for coming along on this ride with Jane and me – I appreciate all of the effort you put in, even though I think I've acquired a few grey hairs over the past three years.

Jane – the brains behind the original concept – thank you first and foremost for coming up with the idea and trusting me to manage the project with full autonomy. Thank you for your patience and support along the way, and – most importantly – for being my friend.

Finally, I would like to dedicate my contribution to this book to the Snell family of Wongawol Station in Western Australia. In 2008, the Snells took a chance on a city girl with zero cattle experience who viewed the industry through a (somewhat distorted) *McLeod's Daughters* lens. Wongawol was where I fell in love with working cattle and station life. With a few reality checks and steep learning curves along the way, Wongawol became my home away from home, and the place where many wonderful memories were made. For not only giving me a chance the first year, but allowing me to come back twice more, and hopefully many more times ... I thank you.

PHOTO CREDITS